Louis P. [from old catalog] Mercer

The World's Religions in a Nutshell

Louis P. [from old catalog] Mercer

The World's Religions in a Nutshell

ISBN/EAN: 9783743308190

Manufactured in Europe, USA, Canada, Australia, Japa

Cover: Foto ©Thomas Meinert / pixelio.de

Manufactured and distributed by brebook publishing software (www.brebook.com)

Louis P. [from old catalog] Mercer

The World's Religions in a Nutshell

THE WORLD'S RELIGIONS IN A NUTSHELL

BY
L. P. MERCER

GLOBE LIBRARY. Vol. II, No. 295, Aug. 29, 1898. Bi-Weekly. Year, $7.00.
Entered at Chicago Post Office as Second-Class Matter.

RAND, McNALLY & CO., PUBLISHERS, CHICAGO AND NEW YORK.

The World Believes in Ball Bearings

THE No. 9 WHEELER & WILSON

Is the only Sewing Machine made with

Ball Bearings

WHEELER & WILSON MFG. CO.,
82 and 80 Wabash Ave.
CHICAGO, ILL.

When answering this advertisement please mention Globe Library.

READ

Sons and Fathers

BY HARRY STILLWELL EDWARDS.

The Story that won the $10,000 Prize in The Chicago Record's Competition.

Bound in English Linen with Gold Back Stamps. Price $1.25.

RAND, McNALLY & CO., PUBLISHERS
CHICAGO AND NEW YORK.

… WORLD'S RELIGIOUS CONGRESSES.

REV. L. P. MERCER,
New-Church Temple, Chicago.

THE WORLD'S RELIGIONS

IN A NUTSHELL

A Religious Symposium Representing
Christianity, Hinduism, Buddhism,
Judaism, Mohammedanism,
The Brahmo-Somaj,
and Woman

BY
REV. L. P. MERCER.

Chicago:
RAND, McNALLY & COMPANY,
PUBLISHERS.

Copyright, 1893, by Rand, McNally & Co.
Copyright, 1898, by Rand, McNally & Co.

CONTENTS

CHAPTER.	PAGE.
I. INITIAMENT AND PREPARATION,	7
II. OPENING SPECTACLE AND SPEECHES.	17
President Bonney,	20
Rev. John Henry Barrows, D. D.,	24
Cardinal Gibbons,	30
Archbishop Latus,	31
P. C. Mozoomdar,	32
Pung Quang Yu,	35
Rt.-Rev. Reuchi Shibata,	36
H. Dharmapala,	37
Virchand Gandhi,	39
C. N. Chakravarti,	40
Swami Vivekananda,	44
Miss Jeanne Sorabji,	46
Prince Wolkonsky,	49
III. A RELIGIOUS SYMPOSIUM,	53
The Hindu,	54
Orthodox Christianity,	64
Liberal Christianity,	82
Buddhism,	86
Judaism,	104
Mohammedanism,	112
Roman Catholic Church,	117
The Greek Church,	125
Japanese Criticism and Appeal,	130
The Brahmo-Somaj,	137
The New Christianity,	147

CONTENTS.

CHAPTER.		PAGE.
IV.	A Religious Symposium — Continued,	156
	God,	156
	Incarnation,	187
	Sin and Reconciliation,	199
	Revelation and the Scriptures,	222
	Immortality,	246
	Sociology,	261
	Woman,	282
V.	The Denominational Congresses,	289
VI.	Farewell Meetings in Columbus and Washington Halls,	293
VII.	What Will Be the Result?	325

THE WORLD'S RELIGIOUS CONGRESSES OF 1893.

CHAPTER I.

INITIAMENT AND PREPARATION.

WHEN the record of the achievements of the World's Columbian Exposition shall have been fully written and considered by those far enough removed from the event to form impartial judgments, it will be found that the most remarkable and unique in kind and substantial in results are those of the Auxiliary Congresses, covering more than twenty departments of thought, and embracing over two hundred distinct congresses, participated in by distinguished specialists. As the accomplished and efficient secretary of the World's Congress Auxiliary said in summing up the work: "Never before in the history of the world has there been a programme of subjects and speakers prepared, the proper execution of which required the term of six months. Never has there been created an organization with 210 working committees, a local membership of 1,600, and a non-resident membership of 15,000. Never until the year 1893, which marks a new epoch in the intellectual progress of mankind, has any individual gone so far as to outline even the prospectus of a course of lectures that covered the great departments of thought, as outlined by the president of these congresses in his general programme. These congresses have held 1,245 sessions; we have had 5,974 speakers, and the total attendance at all the congresses is over three-quarters of a million. It was a gigantic undertaking, but it has been successfully accomplished."

The original idea of the world's congresses was first published by Hon. C. C. Bonney in the *Statesman* magazine for October, 1889, in these words:

"The crowning glory of the World's Fair of 1893 should not be the exhibit there to be made of the material triumphs, industrial achievements, and mechanical victories of man, however magnificent that display may be. Something higher and nobler is demanded by the progressive spirit of the present age. In connection with that important event of the world all government, jurisprudence, finance, science, literature, education, and religion should be represented in a congress of statesmen, jurists, financiers, scientists, literati, teachers, and theologians, greater in numbers and more widely representative of all peoples and nations and tongues than any assemblage which has ever yet been convened."

The idea was extensively discussed, and received with much public favor. Subsequently the matter was taken up by the Directory of the Columbian Exposition, and under its authority the World's Congress Auxiliary was organized, with C. C. Bonney as president, T. B. Bryan, vice-president, Lyman J. Gage as treasurer, and received the indorsement of the United States Government. The work of organization commenced in October, 1889, was completed and the first of the congresses opened in May, 1893. The last congress embraced in the great scheme was held during the last week in October; and the president in summing up results could say: "That these congresses have been successful far beyond anticipation, that they have transformed into enduring reality the hopes of those who organized and conducted them, and that they will exercise a benign and potent influence on the welfare of mankind through the coming centuries has been so often, so emphatically, and so eloquently declared by eminent representatives of the different countries and peoples that these statements may be accepted as established facts. That the material exhibit of the World's Columbian Exposition in Jackson Park is the most complete and magnificent ever presented to human view is generally agreed, but a multitude of eminent witnesses have declared, after attendance on both, that the intellectual and moral exposition of the progress of mankind presented in the world's congresses of 1893 is greater and more imposing still. Thus the work of the World's Congress Auxiliary takes its enduring place in human history, an imperishable part of the progress of mankind."

In the whole series of congresses the "Parliament of Religions" has taken preëminence, and justly so, not only because of the importance and universal interest of the subject, but because it was central in the original conception and its success the constant care of the president of the Auxiliary. In his closing address to the Parliament of Religions Mr. Bonney said: "The wonderful success of this first actual congress of the religions of the world is the realization of a conviction which has held my heart for many years. I became acquainted with the great religious systems of the world in my youth, and have enjoyed an intimate association with leaders of many churches during my maturer years. I was thus led to believe that if the great religious faiths could be brought into relations of friendly intercourse many points of sympathy and union would be found, and the coming unity of mankind in the love of God and the service of man be greatly facilitated and advanced. Hence, when the occasion arose it was gladly welcomed, and the effort more than willingly made."

It was in this faith, and in the hope of realizing this result, that the "fraternity of learning and virtue" was conceived, and the idea of the congresses proposed. In conversations with the writer, in the spiritual intimacy of years, the desirability and feasibility of such a universal conference was often dwelt upon, on the ground of our common faith, that a universal medium of salvation has been provided by the Lord with every nation that has a religion, and that to bring into friendly conference the representatives of all the great historic faiths and of the denominations of Christendom would develop the fact that to acknowledge the divine and live well is the supreme and universal condition of religion, and would lead to the recognition of a universal bond of brotherhood in *faithfulness to what one understands to be from the divine and to lead to the divine.*

When a meeting of ministers, representing all the denominations in Chicago, was called in September, 1889, to aid in the creation of an interest in the great Exposition and its location in Chicago, this idea of a great religious congress and of other international conventions was communicated by myself and others, to whom it had become familiar; and in a sub-committee, consisting of Bishop Fallows, Dr. George C. Lorimer, Dr. Hiram W. Thomas, Rev. Jenkin L. Jones, and the writer of this review, the subject was fully discussed, adopted, and embodied in an address, which was signed by the whole committee of ministers, and given to the press October 1, 1889. In these meetings of the representatives of the Chicago churches, while the general plan of "international conventions composed of the scholars and thinkers and workers of all countries" was adopted, the dream of a friendly conference of all religions was perhaps by most regarded as utopian, and except for the earnest and sanguine advocacy of a few bold spirits would scarcely have received the indorsement of that body. It was said that religions had never met but in conflict, and that a different result could not be expected now. It may be assuredly said that but for the high faith, catholicity of spirit, great tact and patience, and the sublime persistence of the president of the Auxiliary, who dreamed only of success, under the guidance of Providence, the result which has now become history could never have been realized; and his "patient and titanic labors," as Doctor Barrows said at the opening of the parliament, "will one day be appreciated at their full value."

Immediately upon the organization of the Auxiliary the president appointed as General Committee on Religious Congresses Rev. John Henry Barrows, D. D., chairman; Rt.-Rev. Bishop William E. McLaren, D. D., D. C. L., Rev. Prof. David Swing, vice-chairmen; His Grace Archbishop P. A. Feehan, Rev. F. A. Noble, D. D., Rev. William M. Lawrence, D. D., Rev. F. M. Bristol, D. D., Rabbi E. G. Hirsch, Rev. A. J. Canfield, D. D., Rev. M. Ranseen, Rev. J. Berger, Mr. J. W. Plummer, Rev. J. Z. Torgersen, Rev. L. P. Mercer, Rev. Jenkin Lloyd Jones, Rt.-Rev. Bishop C. E. Cheney, D. D. The result is an imperishable monument to the zeal and efficiency of the chairman and coöperating members of this committee. Doctor Barrows entered with enthusiasm into the scheme, and brought his great abilities to the support of a faith in the world's response. The preliminary address of the committee, prepared by him and sent throughout the world, elicited the most gratifying responses, and proved that the proposed congress was not only practicable, but also that it was most earnestly demanded by the needs of the present age. The religious leaders of many lands, hungering and thirsting for a larger righteousness, gave the proposal their benedictions, and promised the congress their active coöperation and support. Opposition was encountered in many quarters, and not a few well-known Christian writers condemned what they called an attempt to congregate "the exponents and propagandists of all false and corrupt religions, on equal terms with the advocates of the Christian religion, for a competitive comparison of the merits of these beliefs." It was manifest from the outset, however, that the great popular sympathy of Christendom was with the movement, and that these narrow misconceptions were confined to a small, if zealous, minority. The position of Dr. John Henry Barrows as chairman of the General Committee, through the long period of strenuous toil which brought the preparations to completion, was not an enviable one. While his committee worked together in unbroken harmony, the burden of responsibility, and the correspondence necessary to any promise of success, and the executive energy and tact inevitable to the arrangement of so vast and varied a programme, fell upon him. At the same time, standing as the representative of an orthodox church which withheld its support from the movement, he became the target of bigoted criticism which must have often strained friendships and sometimes made his position little less than heroic. On the other hand, he received the benedictions and the generous coöperation of some of the foremost minds of Christendom, and the loyal assistance of the Woman's Committee and of the many local denominational committees, with their advisory councils, advanced the interest throughout the world.

The plan extended as the preparations advanced, and the programme itself of the religious congresses of 1893 constitutes what was with perfect propriety designated as one of the most remarkable publications of the century. The programme of this general parliament of religions directly represented England, Scotland, Sweden, Switzerland, France, Germany, Russia, Turkey, Greece, Egypt, Syria, India, Japan, China, Ceylon, New Zealand, Brazil, Canada, and the American States, and indirectly included many other countries. It presented, among other great themes to be considered in this congress, Theism, Judaism, Mohammedanism, Hinduism, Buddhism, Taoism, Confucianism, Shintoism, Zoroastrianism, Catholicism, the Greek church, Protestantism in many forms, and other religious systems.

This programme also announced for presentation the great subjects of revelation, immortality, the incarnation of God, the universal elements in religion, the ethical unity of different religious systems, the relations of religion to morals, marriage, education, science, philosophy, evolution, music, labor, government, peace and war, and many other themes of absorbing interest. The distinguished leaders of human progress by whom these great topics were presented constitute an unparalleled galaxy of eminent names. For the execution of this

INITIAMENT AND PREPARATION. 15

part of the general programme seventeen days were assigned. During substantially the same period the second part of the programme was executed in the adjoining Hall of Washington. This consisted of what are termed presentations of their distinctive faith and achievements by the different churches. These presentations were made to the world, as represented in the world's religious congresses of 1893.

The third part of the general programme for the congresses of this department consisted of separate and independent congresses of the different religious denominations, for the purpose of more fully setting forth their doctrines and the service they have rendered to mankind. These special congresses were held, for the most part, in the smaller halls of the memorial building. The denominational congresses were each held during the week in which the presentation of the denomination occurred.

The fourth and final part of the programme of the department of religion consisted of congresses of various kindred organizations, held between the close of the Parliament of Religions and October 15th, including Missions, Ethics, Sunday rest, the Evangelical Alliance, and similar associations.

Well might President Bonney in opening the parliament, contemplating with satisfaction and pride the event he had conceived with such daring, developed with so much labor to such elaborate completeness by the committees which he had called to his aid and intrusted with the responsibility, exclaim: "To this more than imperial feast I bid you welcome."

The great assembly has been held, the possibility of conference and fraternal respect demonstrated, the great deliverances made; and now the work of study, comparison, and honest criticism may begin.

CHAPTER II.

THE OPENING SPECTACLE AND SPEECHES.

AN unfinished art palace converted into reception chambers and assembly halls for a world's congress; eager and hospitable ladies offering cordial greetings and words of direction to the crowds who inquire for the Hall of Columbus, or seek to register as members of the Parliament of Religions; distinguished committeemen greeting and guiding, now a Roman Catholic cardinal, and now a stately Hindu in orange robe and turban, and again a group of Japanese Buddhist monks, to the president's reception-room, where they are welcomed by a Christian layman as the recognized official of a Christian nation, and by a Presbyterian clergyman as chairman of the occasion, and introduced to an archbishop of the Greek church in his high black cap, the black gown and jeweled ornaments of his order; everywhere Christians of many denominations are acting as hosts, welcoming distinguished visitors from China, Japan, India, Russia, Sweden, Germany, England, Australia, New Zealand, and introducing them to one another as brothers, worshiping the one only God, having a common goal! Surely the world moves. We have been boasting of a new age, an age of inquiry, expectation, and experiment. It is evident we have reached, also, a new era of fraternity and good-will, and that the "Fatherhood of God and the brotherhood of man" is to have henceforth a real interpretation among men

Gorgeous and imposing spectacles have been witnessed in every land, but nothing which inspires the heart and fires the imagination like this double file of the representatives of all religions headed by a Christian layman and a Presbyterian minister. The audience which filled Columbus Hall to its utmost capacity is deeply moved, and many who walk in the procession, who have had their hours of hope and hours of grave misgiving, are almost overpowered with a sense of the possible significance of the occasion. All know that at the hour of 10, on this 11th day of September, the new Liberty Bell struck ten strokes in honor of the ten great religions of the world, and many believed the bell proclaimed "a new liberty of thought and wider tolerance of opinion," and some devoutly pray as the procession moves to the platform for the Spirit that shall make them worthy links in a universal bond of brotherhood in God. But how shall these differences harmonize? If there is a common spirit of worship, how shall it find a common expression?

This is the first revelation of the memorable morning. Calling the assembly to its feet, President Bonney announces a brief moment of silent prayer, each offering the aspiration of his heart in the language of his thought; after which the whole multitude, Christian, Jew, and Gentile, led by Cardinal Gibbons, joined in the universal prayer "Our Father," and burst forth, with the organ's lead, into the doxology, "Praise God, from whom all blessings flow." In impressiveness and pregnant promise the occasion could not well be surpassed.

But how is this beginning to end? We know it ended well. "The Fatherhood of God and brotherhood of man" proved not only a watchword, but a sentiment impressive, respectful, and genuine. Vague and various the ideas of the significance of the phrase may have been with many, I am disposed to say with most, yet almost every speaker at the opening session expressed in some form what alone could give it reality of meaning. I asked myself, Why are these my brothers? Because they are scholars? Not that. Scholars there are from Christendom, and their peers in scholarship from the far-off East, on this platform, and the recognition of a common bond in knowledge of the history of opinion and in trained methods of study. But this alone would lead to debate and contest of opinion among intellectual peers. Something must hold this in check, and overshadow it in the recognition of a spiritual relationship, if our hopes are to be realized. Are these brothers because they are men? I asked. That fact will not bring the result hoped for unless there is a common sense of true manhood. And what should that be except the recognition of true humanity in a man's *faithfulness to what he believes to be divine in the hope of union with the*

All Good. Just that, I thought, expresses the universal bond of brotherhood in God. This man is my brother because he loves and lives up to what he believes to be from the divine, and in the hope of union with the divine. That in him is brother to that in me which seeks obedience to the divine. Diverse our readings of the divine may be, but faithfulness to what I read I know to be my highest and truly human quality, and because I recognize this faithfulness in another, also, I know him to be my brother. So I thought, and felt assured that if this sense of brotherhood were in the assembly, uttered or unexpressed, it would make itself felt.

Looking back now over the speeches of welcome and response on that opening day, I am profoundly impressed with the fact that this very recognition made the Parliament of Religions the inauguration of a new impulse among men.

"Worshipers of God and lovers of men," were the felicitous words in which President Bonney opened his inaugural.

"Let us rejoice," he continued, "that we have lived to see this glorious day; let us give thanks to the Eternal God, whose mercy endureth forever, that we are permitted to take part in the solemn and majestic event of a world's congress of religions. The importance of this event can not be overestimated. Its influence on the future relations of the various races of men can not be too highly esteemed.

"If this congress shall faithfully execute the duties with which it has been charged it will become a joy of the whole earth and stand in human history like a new Mount Zion, crowned with glory and marking the actual beginning of the new epoch of brotherhood and peace.

"For when the religious faiths of the world recognize each other as brothers, children of one Father, whom all profess to love and serve, then, and not till then, will the nations of the earth yield to the spirit of concord and learn war no more.

"It is inspiring to think that in every part of the world many of the worthiest of mankind, who would gladly join us here if that were in their power, this day lift their hearts to the Supreme Being in earnest prayer for the harmony and success of this congress. To them our own hearts speak in love and sympathy in this impressive and prophetic scene.

"In this congress the word 'religion' means the love and worship of God and the love and service of man. We believe the Scripture, that 'of a truth God is no respecter of persons, but in every nation he that feareth God and worketh righteousness is accepted of him.' We come together in mutual confidence and respect, without the least surrender or compromise of anything which we respectively believe to be truth or duty, with the hope that mutual acquaintance and a free and sincere interchange of views on the great questions of eternal life and human conduct will be mutually beneficial.

"As the finite can never fully comprehend the infinite, nor perfectly express its own view of the divine, it necessarily follows that individual opinions of the divine nature and attributes will differ.

But, properly understood, these varieties of view are not causes of discord and strife, but rather incentives to deeper interest and examination. Necessarily God reveals himself differently to a child than to a man; to a philosopher than to one who can not read. Each must see God with the eyes of his own soul; each must behold him through the colored glass of his own nature; each one must receive him according to his own capacity of reception. The fraternal union of the religions of the world will come when each seeks truly to know how God has revealed himself in the other, and remembers the inexorable law that with what judgment it judges it shall itself be judged.

"The religious faiths of the world have most seriously misunderstood and misjudged each other from the use of words in meanings radically different from those which they were intended to bear, and from a disregard of the distinctions between appearances and facts; between signs and symbols and the things signified and represented. Such errors it is hoped that this congress will do much to correct and to render hereafter impossible.

"He who believes that God has revealed himself more fully in his religion than in any other can not do otherwise than desire to bring that religion to the knowledge of all men, with an abiding conviction that the God who gave it will preserve, protect, and advance it in every expedient way; and hence he will welcome every just opportunity to come into fraternal relations with men of other creeds, that they may see in his upright life the evidence of the truth and beauty of his faith, and be thereby led to learn it, and be helped heavenward by it. When it pleased God to give me the idea of the world's congresses of 1893, there came with that idea a profound conviction that their crowning glory should be a fraternal conference of the world's religions. Accordingly, the original announcement of the world's congress scheme, which was sent by the Government of the United States to all other nations, contained, among other great themes to be considered, 'The grounds for fraternal union in the religions of different people.'"

Concluding, Mr. Bonney said: "This day the sun of a new era of religious peace and progress rises over the world, dispelling the dark clouds of sectarian strife. This day a new flower blooms in the gardens of religious thought, filling the air with its exquisite perfume. This day a new fraternity is born into the world of human progress, to aid in the upbuilding of the kingdom of God in the hearts of men. Era and flower and fraternity bear one name. It is a name which will gladden the hearts of those who worship God and love man in every clime. Those who hear its music joyfully echo it back to sun and flower.

"It is the brotherhood of religions.

"In this name I welcome the first parliament of the religions of the world."

This auspicious opening was received with an enthusiasm which was augmented and deepened when Doctor Barrows followed with his eloquent and catholic address. If the full significance of the occasion is to be measured, the circumstances must be frankly considered. Doctor Barrows was not merely the chairman of the Parliament of Religions; he was such as the representative of one of the denominations of Christendom. While his utterances were, of course, in no way intended to commit his denomination, they are to be considered as showing what a man in his position is free to say on an occasion in which not so very long ago he would not have been free to participate. While for conscientious boldness, as the utterance of a man who had been subjected to annoying sectarian criticism from many quarters, his words are admirable, they set a model of dignity and devout reliance upon the justifying providence of God that must silence opposition, quiet distrust, and stimulate generous impulses.

"If my heart did not overflow," he said, "with cordial welcome at this hour, which promises to be a great moment in history, it would be because I had lost the spirit of manhood and had been forsaken by the Spirit of God. The whitest snow on the sacred mount of Japan, the clearest water springing from the sacred fountains of India, are not more pure and bright than the joy of my heart and of many hearts here that this day has dawned in the annals of time, and that, from the farthest isles of Asia; from India, mother of religions; from Europe, the great teacher of civilization; from the shores on which breaks the 'long wash of Australasian seas'; that from neighboring lands and from all parts of this republic, which we love to contemplate as the land of earth's brightest future, you have come here at our invitation in the expectation that the world's first parliament of religions must prove an event of race-wide and perpetual significance.

"For more than two years the General Committee, which I have the honor to represent, working together in unbroken harmony, and presenting the picture of prophecy of a united Christendom, have carried their arduous and sometimes appalling task in happy anticipation of this golden hour. Your coming has constantly been in our thoughts, and hopes, and fervent prayers. I rejoice that your long voyages and journeys are over, and that here, in this young capital of our Western civilization, you find men eager for truth, sympathetic with the spirit of universal human brotherhood, and loyal, I believe, to the highest they know, glad and grateful to Almighty God that they see your faces and are to hear your words.

"Welcome, most welcome, O wise men of the East and of the West! May the star which has led you hither be like unto that luminary which guided the men of old, and may this meeting by the inland sea of a new continent be blessed of heaven to the redemption of men from error and from sin and despair. I wish you to understand that this great undertaking, which has aimed to house under one friendly roof in brotherly counsel the representatives of God's aspiring and believing children everywhere, has been conceived and carried on through strenuous and patient toil, with an unfaltering heart, with a devout faith in God, and with most signal and special evidences of his divine guidance and favor.

"Long ago I should have surrendered the task intrusted to me before the colossal difficulties looming ever in the way, had I not committed my work to the gracious care of that God who loves all his children, whose thoughts are long, long thoughts, who is patient and merciful as well as just, and who cares infinitely more for the souls of his erring children than for any creed or philosophy of human devising. If anything great and worthy is to be the outcome of this parliament, the glory is wholly due to him who inspired it, and who in the Scriptures, which most of us cherish as the word of God, has taught the blessed truths of divine fatherhood and human brotherhood.

"I should not use the word 'if' in speaking of the outcome of this congress of religions, since, were it decreed that our sessions should end this day, the truthful historian would say that the idea which has inspired and led this movement, the idea whose beauty and force have drawn you through these many thousand miles of travel, that this idea has been so flashed before the eyes of men that they will not forget it, and that our meeting this morning has become a new, great fact in the historic evolution of the race which will not be obliterated.

"What, it seems to me, should have blunted some of the arrows of criticism shot at the promoters of this movement is this other fact, that it is the representatives of that Christian faith which we believe has in it such elements and divine forces that it is fitted to the needs of all men who have planned and provided this first school of comparative religions, wherein devout men of all faiths may speak for themselves without hindrance, without criticism, and without compromise, and tell what they believe and why they believe it. I appeal to the representatives of the non-Christian faiths, and ask you if Christianity suffers in your eyes from having called this Parliament of Religions? Do you believe that its beneficent work in the world will be one whit lessened?"

"We are met together to-day," he continued, "as men, children of one God, sharers with all men in weakness, and guilt, and need, sharers with devout souls everywhere in aspiration, and hope, and longing. We are met as religious men, believing, even here in this capital of material wonders, in the presence of an exposition which displays the unparalleled marvels of steam and electricity, that there is a spiritual root to all human progress. We are met in a school of comparative theology, which I hope will prove more spiritual and ethical than theological. We are met, I believe, in the temper of love, determined to bury, at least for the time, our sharp hostilities, anxious to find out wherein we agree, eager to learn what constitutes the strength of other faiths and the weakness of our own; and we are met as conscientious and truth-seeking men in a council where no one is asked to surrender or abate his individual convictions, and where, I will add, no one would be worthy of a place if he did.

"We are met in a great conference, men and women of different minds, where the speaker will not be ambitious for short-lived verbal victories over others; where gentleness, courtesy, wisdom, and moderation will prevail far more than heated argumentation. I am confident that you appreciate the peculiar limitations which constitute the peculiar glory of this assembly. We are not here as Baptists and Buddhists, Catholics and Confucians, Parsees and Presbyterians, Methodists and Moslems. We are here as members of a parliament of religions, over which flies no sectarian flag, which is to be stampeded by no sectarian war-cries, but where for the first time in a large council is lifted up the banner of love, fellowship, brotherhood. We all feel that there is a spirit which should always pervade these meetings, and if any one should offend against this spirit let him not be rebuked publicly or personally. Your silence will be a graver and severer rebuke.

"We are not here to criticise one another, but each to speak out positively and frankly his own convictions regarding his own faith. The great world outside will review our work; the next century will review it. It is our high and noble business to make that work the best possible."

With earnest acknowledgment of the coöperation of men and women at home and abroad who had rendered assistance, with words of welcome to the representatives in their several orders, and with recognition of spiritual conditions and causes in the spirits of just and good men passed from earth, and forming "a great company of witnesses," Doctor Barrows concluded in these words:

"When, a few days ago, I met for the first time the delegates who have come to us from Japan, and shortly after the delegates who have come to us from India, I felt that the arms of human brotherhood had reached almost around the globe. But there is something stronger than human love and fellowship, and what gives us the most hope and happiness to-day is our confidence that —

> The whole round world is every way
> Bound by gold chains about the feet of God."

The key-note had been sounded, and the audience recognized it with sympathetic enthusiasm whenever it was approached in the varied addresses of the day. Whether it was the generosity of goodwill, or appreciation of the novelty of high official representatives of the Roman church pleading for "religious liberty," Archbishop Feehan and Cardinal Gibbons were received with especial interest. Perhaps it was not yet known to most that Bishop Keane, the eminent rector of the Catholic University at Washington, had taken a cordial and active part in the preliminary work, and that Catholics had shown from the outset a worthy interest in the parliament; but, whether from surprise or from expectation, the audience was eager to welcome the cardinal and archbishop. Their speeches were scarcely equal in dignity and catholicity to the addresses contributed by representatives of the Catholic church later in the sessions, and betrayed some restraint, as if unwilling too far to commit themselves. Archbishop Feehan noted "great diversities of opinion, but in all a great, high motive." Cardinal Gibbons that, notwithstanding diversities of belief, there is a "platform of charity, of humanity, and of benevolence" on which all may stand. Later in the day, Archbishop Redwood of New Zealand raised the opening voice of the Catholic church to a higher strain of faith, saying: "In her teaching there is an event which the human race shall never forget — that the Godhead took up our human nature to elevate and unite it with the divine nature, whence began a brotherhood of man never dreamed of by merely human beings." And pointing out that in all religions there must be an element of truth to account for their persistence, he recalled the saying of Christ, "I am the truth," and exclaimed, "Wherever there is truth there is something worthy the respect, not only of man, but of God, the Godman, the incarnate God."

When the Archbishop of Zante, Greece, the Most Reverend Dionysios Latus, was introduced, and arose with the dignity of manly strength, of great learning, of ripened age, and the bearing of official responsibility, curiosity gave place to profound respect before he had uttered a word. It was an object lesson — not so much in the power of presence as in the sphere of power. Through a certain labored ceremonial of manner there breathed a directness of purpose and intensity of feeling that made itself appreciated before he had articulated his thought:

C. C. BONNEY.
President of the World's Congress Auxiliary.

"Reverend ministers, most honorable gentlemen, the superiors of this congress, and honorable ladies and gentlemen: I consider myself very happy in having set my feet on this platform to take part in the congress of the different nations and peoples. I thank the great American nation, and especially the superiors of this congress, for the high manner in which they have honored me by inviting me to take part, and I thank the ministers of divinity of the different nations and peoples which, for the first time, will write their faiths together in the books of the history of the world."

Then, referring to the realization of his long-cherished hope to visit this country, and to the importance of the history and influence of the Greek church, which it was his privilege to represent, he turned to the dignitaries on the platform, and lifting his hands, he said:

"Reverend ministers of the eloquent name of God, the Creator of your earth and mine, I salute you on the one hand as my brothers in Jesus Christ, from whom, according to our faith, all good has originated in this world. I salute you in the name of the divinely inspired gospel, which, according to our faith, is the salvation of the soul of man and the happiness of man in this world.

"All men have a common Creator, without any distinction between the rich and the poor, the ruler and the ruled; all men have a common Creator without any distinction of clime or race, without distinction of nationality or ancestry, of name or nobility; all men have a common Creator, and consequently a common Father in God.

"I raise up my hands and I bless with heartfelt love the great country and the happy, glorious people of the United States."

The observer could not but notice that the eyes of the audience were fixed on the Orient, and as they listened to the salutations of evangelical Christianity, and Roman Christianity, and Eastern Christianity, in succession, expectation was raised to the point where relief seemed necessary; and when President Bonney presented P. C. Mozoomdar of India, author of the "Oriental Christ," and representative of the Brahmo Somaj, the audience greeted him with the wildest applause. Mozoomdar had been in this country ten years ago; many had heard him then, and added to their welcome to India greeting to a friend:

"Leaders of the Parliament of Religions, men and women of America: The recognition, sympathy, and welcome you have given to India to day are gratifying to thousands of liberal Hindu religious thinkers, whose representatives I see around me, and, on behalf of my countrymen, I cordially thank you. India claims her place in the brotherhood of mankind, not only because of her great antiquity, but equally for what has taken place there in recent times. Modern India has sprung from ancient India by a law of evolution, a process of continuity which explains some of the most difficult problems of our national life. In prehistoric times our forefathers worshiped the great living Spirit God, and, after many strange vicissitudes, we Indian theists, led by the light of ages, worship the same living Spirit God, and none other.

REV. JOHN HENRY BARROWS, D. D.,
Chairman of the Committee on Religious Congresses.

"Perhaps in other ancient lands this law of continuity has not been so well kept. Egypt aspired to build up the vast eternal in her elaborate symbolism and mighty architecture. Where is Egypt to-day? Passed away as a mystic dream in her pyramids, catacombs, and Sphinx of the desert.

"Greece tried to embody her genius of wisdom and beauty in her wonderful creations of marble, in her all-embracing philosophy; but where is ancient Greece to-day? She lies buried under her exquisite monuments and sleeps the sleep from which there is no waking.

"The Roman cohorts under whose victorious tramp the earth shook to its center, the Roman theaters, laws, and institutions — where are they? Hidden behind the oblivious centuries, or, if they flit across the mind, only point a moral or adorn a tale.

"The Hebrews, the chosen of Jehovah, with their long line of law and prophets, how are they? Wanderers on the face of the globe, driven by king and kaiser, the objects of persecution to the cruel or objects of sympathy to the kind. Mount Moria is in the hands of the Mussulman, Zion is silent, and over the ruins of Solomon's Temple a few men beat their breasts and wet their white beards with their tears.

"But India, the ancient among ancients, the elder of the elders, lives to-day with her old civilization, her old laws and her profound religion. The old mother of the nations and religions is still a power in the world; she has often risen from apparent death, and in the future will arise again. When the

Vedic faith declined in India the esoteric religion of the Vedantas arose; then the everlasting philosophy of the Darasanas. When these declined again the light of Asia arose and established a standard of moral perfection which will yet teach the world a long time. When Buddhism had its downfall the Shaiva and Vaish Rava revived and continued in the land down to the invasion of the Mohammedans. The Greeks and Scythians, the Turks and Tartars, the Monguls and Mussulman rolled over her country like torrents of destruction. Our independence, our greatness, our prestige — all had gone, but nothing could take away our religious vitality.

"We are Hindus still, and shall always be. Now sits Christianity on the throne of India, with the gospel of peace on one hand and the scepter of civilization on the other. Now it is not the time to despair and die. Behold the aspirations of modern India — intellectual, social, political — all awakened; our religious instincts stirred to the roots. If that had not been the case do you think Hindus, Jains, Buddhists, and others would have traversed these 14,000 miles to pay the tribute of their sympathy before this august Parliament of Religions?

"No individual, no denomination can more fully sympathize or more heartily join your conferences than we men of the Brahmo Somaj, whose religion is the harmony of all religions, and whose congregation is the brotherhood of all nations.

"Such, as our aspirations and sympathies, dear brethren, accept them. Let me thank you again for this welcome in the name of my countrymen, and wish every prosperity and success to your labors."

Perhaps the most remarkable scene of the day occurred when President Bonney introduced the representative of the Chinese government and of Confucianism. "We have not treated China very well in this country," remarked Mr. Bonney. "We have sometimes been severe toward her, and sometimes have persecuted her children, but the Emperor of China has responded in a Christian spirit to our call, and sent a delegate to this congress. This delegate is the Hon. Pung Quang Yu, secretary of the Chinese legation in Washington."

When Pung Quang Yu came forward he was greeted with a furor of applause. Men and women rose to their feet in the audience, and there was a wild waving of hats and handkerchiefs. The delegate's speech, translated by his secretary, was read in ringing tones by Doctor Barrows:

"On behalf of the imperial government of China I take great pleasure in responding to the cordial words which the chairman of the general committee and others have spoken to-day. This is a great moment in the history of nations and religions. For the first time men of various faiths meet in one great hall to report what they believe and the grounds for their belief. The great sage of China, who is honored not only by the millions of our own land, but throughout the world, believed that duty was summed up in reciprocity, and I think the word reciprocity finds a new meaning and glory in the proceedings of this historic parliament. I am glad that the great empire of China has accepted the invitation of those who have called this parliament and is to be represented in this great school of comparative religion. Only the happiest results will come, I am sure, from our meeting together in the spirit of friendliness. Each may learn from the other some lessons, I trust, of charity and good-will, and discover what is excellent in other faiths than his own. In behalf of my government and people I extend to the representatives gathered in this great hall the friendliest salutations, and to those who have spoken I give my most cordial thanks."

A representative of the Shinto faith, the state religion of Japan, Rt.-Rev. Reuchi Shibata, was next introduced. The bishop appeared in his full pontificals, and salaamed profoundly toward the audience and to the right and left when he came forward. Mr. Bonney, in his words of introduction, alluded in appropriate language to the rapidity with which Japan had advanced in the path of modern civilization and the peculiar kindness felt by the people of this country toward the people of the empire of the mikado. The Shinto bishop's address was read by Doctor Barrows. It was in these words:

"I can not help doing honor to the congress of religions held here in Chicago, as the result of the partial effort of those philanthropic brothers who have undertaken this, the greatest meeting ever held. It was fourteen years ago that I expressed, in my own country, the hope that there should be a friendly meeting between the world's religionists,

OPENING ADDRESSES. 37

and now I realize my hope with great joy in being able to attend these phenomenal meetings.

"In the history of the past we read of repeated and fierce conflicts between different religious creeds which sometimes ended in war. But that time has passed away and things have changed with advancing civilization. It is a great blessing, not only to the religions themselves, but also to human affairs, that the different religionists can thus gather in a friendly way and exchange their thoughts and opinions on the important problems of the age.

"I trust that these repeated meetings will gradually increase the fraternal relations between the different religionists in investigating the truths of the universe, and be instrumental in uniting all religions of the world, and in bringing all hostile nations into peaceful relations by leading them to the way of perfect justice."

When he had finished reading, Doctor Barrows introduced the delegation of Buddhist priests, who remained standing while Z. Noguchi, their interpreter, said: "I thank you on behalf of the Japanese Buddhist priests for the welcome you have given us and for the kind invitation to participate in the proceedings of this congress."

The Orient has been reached, and Buddhism has acknowledged its welcome, and all eyes turn to one of the most winning figures on the platform, tall, clad in white, soft and closely clinging robes, idealistic face, gentle eyes, waving black hair and scanty beard—the gentle and lovable Dharmapala of Ceylon.

"Friends: I bring to you the good wishes of 475,000,000 of Buddhists, the blessings and peace of the religious founder of that system which has prevailed so many centuries in Asia, which has made Asia mild, and which is to-day in its twenty-fourth century of existence, the prevailing religion of the country. I have sacrificed the greatest of all work to attend this parliament. I have left the work of consolidation — an important work which we have begun after 700 years — the work of consolidating the different Buddhist countries, which is the most important work in the history of modern Buddhism. When I read the programme of this Parliament of Religions I saw it was simply the reëcho of a great consummation which the Indian Buddhists accomplished twenty-one centuries ago.

"At that time Asoka, the great emperor, held a council in the city of Patna, of 1,000 scholars, which was in session for seven months. The proceedings were epitomized and carved on rock and scattered all over the Indian peninsula and the then known globe. After the consummation of that programme the great emperor sent the gentle teachers, the mild disciples of Buddha in the garb that you see on this platform, to instruct the world. In that plain garb they went across the deep rivers, the Himalayas, to the plains of Mongolia and the Chinese plains, and to the far-off beautiful isles, the empire of the rising sun; and the influence of that congress held twenty-one centuries ago is to-day a living power, because you everywhere see mildness in Asia.

"Go to any Buddhist country, and where do you

find such healthy compassion and tolerance as you find there? Go to Japan, and what do you see? The noblest lessons of tolerance and gentleness. Go to any of the Buddhist countries and you will see the carrying out of the programme adopted at the congress called by the Emperor Asoka.

"Why do I come here to day? Because I find in this new city, in this land of freedom, the very place where that programme can also be carried out. For one year I meditated whether this parliament would be a success. Then I wrote to Doctor Barrows that this would be the proudest occasion of modern history and the crowning work of nineteen centuries. Yes, friends, if you are serious, if you are unselfish, if you are altruistic, this programme can be carried out and the twentieth century will see the teachings of the meek and lowly Jesus accomplished.

"I hope in this great city, the youngest of all cities, but the greatest of all cities, this programme will be carried out, and that the name of Doctor Barrows will shine forth as the American Asoka. And I hope that the noble lessons of tolerance learned in this majestic assembly will result in the dawning of universal peace which will last for twenty centuries more."

A short but most pleasing address was made by Virchand A. Gandhi, a lawyer of Bombay, and one of the chief exponents of Jain religion of that oriental country. Mr. Gandhi spoke as follows:

"Mr. President, ladies and gentlemen: I will

not trouble you with a long speech. I, like my respected friends, Mr. Mozoomdar and others, come from India, the mother of religions. I represent Jainism, a faith older than Buddhism, similar to it in its ethics, but different from it in its psychology, and professed by 1,500,000 of India's most peaceful and law-abiding citizens. You have heard so many speeches from eloquent members, and as I shall speak later on at some length, I will therefore, at present, only offer on behalf of my community and their high priest, Moni Atma Ranji, whom I especially represent here, our sincere thanks for the kind welcome you have given us. This spectacle of the learned leaders of thought and religion meeting together on a common platform, and throwing light on religious problems, has been the dream of Atma Ranji's life. He has commissioned me to say to you that he offers his most cordial congratulations on his own behalf, and on behalf of the Jain community, for your having achieved the consummation of that grand idea of convening a parliament of religions."

Professor C. N. Chakravarti, a Theosophist, from Allahabad, India, responded in these words:

"I came here to represent a religion the dawn of which appeared in a misty antiquity which the powerful microscope of modern research has not yet been able to discover; the depth of whose beginnings the plummet of history has not been able to sound. From time immemorial spirit has been represented by white and matter has been represented by black, and the two sister streams which join at the town from which I came, Allahabad, represent two sources of spirit and matter, according to the philosophy of my people. And when I think that here, in this city of Chicago, this vortex of physicality, this center of material civilization, you hold a parliament of religions; when I think that, in the heart of the World's Fair, where abound all the excellencies of the physical world, you have provided also a hall for the feast of reason and the flow of soul, I am once more reminded of my native land.

"Why? Because here, even here, I find the same two sister streams of spirit and matter, of the intellect and physicality, joining hand and hand, representing the symbolical evolution of the universe. I need hardly tell you that, in holding this Parliament of Religions, where all the religions of the world are to be represented, you have acted worthily of the race that is in the vanguard of civilization — a civilization the chief characteristic of which, to my mind, is widening toleration, breadth of heart, and liberality toward all the different religions of the world. In allowing men of different shades of religious opinion, and holding different views as to philosophical and metaphysical problems, to speak from the same platform — aye, even allowing me, who, I confess, am a heathen, as you call me, to speak from the same platform with them — you have acted in a manner worthy of the motherland of the society which I have come to represent to-day. The fundamental principle of that society is universal tolerance; its cardinal belief that underneath the superficial strata runs the living water of truth.

"I have always felt that between India and America there was a closer bond of union in the times gone by, and I do think it is probable that there may be a subtler reason for the identity of our names than either the theory of Johnson or the mistake of Columbus can account for. It is true that I belong to a religion which is now decrepit with age, and that you belong to a race in the first flutter of life, bristling with energy. And yet you can not be surprised at the sympathy between us, because you must have observed the secret union that sometimes exists between age and childhood.

"It is true that in the East we have been accustomed to look toward something which is beyond matter. We have been taught for ages after ages and centuries after centuries to turn our gaze inward toward realms that are not those which are reached by the help of the physical senses. This fact has given rise to the various schools of philosophy that exist to-day in India, exciting the wonder and admiration, not only of the dead East, but of the living and rising West. We have in India, even to this day, thousands of people who give up as trash, as nothing, all the material comforts and luxuries of life with the hope, with the realization that, great as the physical body may be, there is something greater within man, underneath the universe, that is to be longed for and striven after.

"In the West you have evolved such a stupendous energy on the physical plane, such unparalleled vigor on the intellectual plane, that it strikes any stranger landing on your shores with a strange amazement. And yet I can read, even in this atmosphere of material progress, I can discern beneath this thickness of material luxury a secret and mystic aspiration to something spiritual.

"I can see that even you are getting tired of your steam, of your electricity, and the thousand different material comforts that follow these two great powers. I can see that there is a feeling of despondency coming even here — that matter pursued, however vigorously, can be only to the death of all, and it is only through the clear atmosphere of spirituality that you can mount up to the regions of peace and harmony. In the West, therefore, you have developed this material tendency. In the East we have developed a great deal of the spiritual tendency; but even in this West, as I travel from place to place, from New York to Cincinnati, and from Cincinnati to Chicago, I have observed an ever-increasing readiness of people to assimilate spiritual ideas, regardless of the source from which they emanate. This, ladies and gentlemen, I consider a most significant sign of the future, because through this and through the mists of prejudice that still hang on the horizon will be consummated the great event of the future, the union of the East and of the West.

"The East enjoys the sacred satisfaction of having given birth to all the great religions of the world, and even as the physical sun rises ever from the east, the sun of spirituality has always dawned in the East. To the West belongs the proud privilege of having advanced on the intellectual and on the moral plane and of having supplied to the world all the various contrivances of material luxuries and of physical comfort. I look, therefore, upon a union of the East and West as a most significant event, and I look with great hope upon the day when the East and the West will be like brothers helping each other, each supplying to the other what it wants — the West supplying the vigor, the youth, the power of organization, and the East opening up its inestimable treasures of a spiritual law, and which are now locked up in the treasure boxes grown rusty with age.

"And I think that this day, with the sitting of the Parliament of Religions, we begin the work of building up a perennial fountain from which will flow for the next century waters of life and light and of peace, slaking the thirst of the thousands of millions that are to come after us."

Swami Vivekananda of Bombay, India, arose, a magnificent figure of manly beauty, in his orange robe and turban, with striking, strong, and reposeful countenance, and said: "Sisters and brothers of America," whereupon there arose a peal of applause in acknowledgment of the originality of the salutation, and perhaps not less as testifying interest in the personality of the speaker.

"It fills my heart with joy unspeakable," he

OPENING ADDRESSES.   45

said, "to rise in response to the warm and cordial welcome which you have given us. I thank you in the name of the most ancient order of monks in the world; I thank you in the name of the mother of religions, and I thank you in the name of the millions and millions of Hindu people of all classes and sects.

"My thanks, also, to some of the speakers on this platform who have told you that these men from far-off nations may well claim the honor of bearing to the different lands the idea of toleration. I am proud to belong to a religion which has taught the world both tolerance and universal acceptance. We believe not only in universal toleration, but we accept all religions to be true. I am proud to tell you that I belong to a religion into whose sacred language, the Sanscrit, the word seclusion is untranslatable. I am proud to belong to a nation which has sheltered the persecuted and the refugees of all religions and all nations of the earth. I am proud to tell you that we have gathered in our bosom the purest remnant of the Israelites, a remnant which came to Southern India and took refuge with us in the very year in which their holy temple was shattered to pieces by Roman tyranny. I am proud to belong to the religion which has sheltered and is still fostering the remnant of the grand Zoroastrian nation. I will quote to you, brethren, a few lines from a hymn which I remember to have repeated from my earliest boyhood, which is every day repeated by millions of human beings: 'As the different streams having their sources in different places all mingle their waters in the sea, O Lord, so the different paths which men take through different tendencies, various though they appear, crooked or straight, all lead to thee.'

"The present convention, which is one of the most august assemblies ever held, is in itself a vindication, a declaration to the world of the wonderful doctrine preached in Gita, 'Whosoever comes to me, through whatsoever form I reach him, they are all struggling through paths that in the end always lead to me.' Sectarianism, bigotry, and its horrible descendant, fanaticism, have possessed long this beautiful earth. It has filled the earth with violence, drenched it often and often with human blood, destroyed civilization, and sent whole nations to despair. Had it not been for this horrible demon human society would be far more advanced than it is now. But its time has come, and I fervently hope that the bell that tolled this morning in honor of this convention will be the death-knell to all fanaticism, to all persecutions with the sword or the pen, and to all uncharitable feelings between persons wending their way to the same goal."

Many eyes have rested upon a sweet-faced woman in oriental dress, and when Doctor Barrows introduced Miss Jeanne Sorabji, from far-off India, many were surprised to learn that she was an earnest Christian convert with a sweet and simple faith to testify.

"Doctor Barrows just told you that I belonged to the order of Parsee. He is correct in one way and not in another. My people were fire-worshipers, but I am not now. Before I go on further I wish to thank all those who have extended their welcome to us. This morning as I looked around and saw the many faces that greeted a welcome I felt indeed that it was the best day I have seen in Chicago. I have been here for some time, and I have asked the question over and over again: 'Where is religious America to be found — Christian America?' To-day I see it all around me. You have given me a welcome. I will give you a greeting from my country. When we meet one another in our land the first thing we say to each other is 'Peace be with you.' I say it to you to-day in all sincerity, in all love. I feel to-day that the great banner over us is the banner of love. I feel to-day more than ever that it is beautiful to belong to the family of God, to acknowledge the Lord Christ.

"My father, at the age of eighteen, was brought to the knowledge of Christ by the light of an English missionary. He gave up friends and countrymen, rank, and wealth, and money, to be a disciple of the Lord Jesus Christ; and I tell you, friends, that it is a great privilege and a great honor to be able to stand here and say to you that I love that Lord Christ, and I will stand by him and under his banner until the end of my life.

"I would close with one little message from my countrywomen. When I was leaving the shores of Bombay the women of my country wanted to know where I was going, and I told them I was going to America on a visit. They asked me whether I would be at this congress. I thought then I would only come in as one of the audience, but I have the great privilege and honor given to me to stand here and speak to you, and I give you the message as it was given to me. The Christian women of my land said: 'Give the women of America our love and tell them that we love Jesus, and that we shall always pray that our countrywomen may do the same. Tell the women of America that we are fast being educated. We shall one day be able to stand by them and converse with them and be able to delight in all they delight in.'

"And so I have a message from each one of my countrywomen, and once more I will just say that I haven't words enough in which to thank you for the welcome you have given to all those who have come here from the East. When I came here this morning and saw my countrymen my heart was warmed, and I thought I would never feel homesick again, and I feel to-day as if I were at home. Seeing your kindly faces has turned away the heartache.

"We are all under the one banner, love. In the name of the Lord Jesus Christ, I thank you. You will hear possibly the words in his own voice saying unto you, 'Inasmuch as ye have done it unto the least of these, my brethren, ye have done it unto me.'"

Salutations and responses from many Christians I have omitted. They contained nothing new, and little that was strong in promise, beyond the fact of interest in what was to follow, except one, which

I have saved to conclude the review of the opening day because of its originality. When Prince Serge Wolkonsky of Russia was introduced he expressed thanks for the honor of the invitation, the more because he was not an ecclesiastic, nor a representative of his government at the parliament, and could only respond as a man — a true prince among men, many said of him.

"Those who during the last week have had the opportunity of attending not only the congresses of one single church, but who could witness different congresses of different churches and congregations, must have been struck with a noticeable fact. They went to the Catholic congress and heard beautiful words of charity and love. Splendid orators invoked the blessings of heaven upon the children of the Catholic church, and in eloquent terms the listeners were entreated to love their human brothers, in the name of the Catholic church. They went to the Lutheran congress and heard splendid words of humanity and brotherhood, orators inspired with love, and the blessing of God invoked on the children of the Lutheran church. Those who were present were taught to love their human brothers, in the name of the Lutheran church. They went to other more limited congresses, and everywhere they heard these same great words, proclaiming these same great ideas and inspiring these same great feelings. They saw a Catholic archbishop who went to a Jewish congress and with fiery eloquence brought feelings of brotherhood to his Hebraic sisters. Not in one of these congresses did a speaker forget that he belonged to humanity, and that his own church or congregation was but a starting-point, a center, for a further radiation.

"This is the noticeable fact that must have struck everybody, and everybody must have asked himself at the end of the week: 'Why don't they come together, all these people who all speak the same language? Why do not all these splendid orators unite their voices in one single chorus, and, if they preach the same ideas, why don't they proclaim them in the name of the same and single truth that inspires them all?' This seems to have been the idea of those who, in composing the programmes of the religious congresses, decided that the general religious congress should follow the minor ones. To-night, in fact, we see the representatives of different churches gathered together and actuated with one common desire of union.

"Being called to welcome it on the day of its opening, I will take the liberty of relating to you a popular legend of my country. The story may appear rather too humorous for the occasion, but one of our national writers says: 'Humor is an invisible tear through a visible smile,' and we think that human tears, human sorrow and pain are sacred enough to be brought even before a religious congress.

"There was an old woman who for many centuries suffered tortures in the flames of hell, for she had been a great sinner during her earthly life. One day she saw far away in the distance an angel taking his flight through the blue skies; and with the whole strength of her voice she called to him. The call must have been desperate, for the angel stopped in his flight, and coming down to her asked her what she wanted.

"'When you reach the throne of God,' she said, 'tell him that a miserable creature has suffered more than she can bear, and that she asks the Lord to be delivered from these tortures.'

"The angel promised to do so, and flew away. When he had transmitted the message, God said:

"'Ask her whether she has done any good to any one during her life.'

"The old woman strained her memory in search of a good action during her sinful past, and all at once: 'I've got one,' she joyfully exclaimed; 'one day I gave a carrot to a hungry beggar.'

"The angel reported the answer.

"'Take a carrot,' said God to the angel, 'and stretch it out to her. Let her grasp it, and if the plant is strong enough to draw her out from hell she shall be saved.'

"This the angel did. The poor old woman clung to the carrot. The angel began to pull, and, lo! she began to rise. But when her body was half out of the flames she felt a weight at her feet. Another sinner was clinging to her. She kicked, but it did not help. The sinner would not let go his hold, and the angel, continuing to pull, was lifting them both. But, oh! another sinner clung to them, and then a third, and more, and always more — a chain of miserable creatures hung at the old woman's feet. The angel never ceased pulling. It did not seem to be any heavier than a small carrot could support, and they all were lifted in the air. But the old woman suddenly took fright. Too many people were availing themselves of her last chance of salvation, and, kicking and pushing those who were clinging to her, she exclaimed: 'Leave me alone! hands off! the carrot is mine.'

"No sooner had she pronounced this word 'mine' than the tiny stem broke, and they all fell back to hell, and forever.

"In its poetical artlessness and popular simplicity this legend is too eloquent to need interpretation. If any individual, any community, any congregation, any church, possesses a portion of truth and of good, let that truth shine for everybody; let that good become the property of everyone. The substitution of the word 'mine' by the word 'ours' and that of 'ours' by the word 'everyone's'—this is what will secure a fruitful result to our collective efforts as well as to our individual activities.

"This is why we welcome and greet the opening of this congress, where, in a combined effort of the representatives of all churches, all that is great and good and true in each of them is brought together in the name of the same God and for the sake of the same man.

"We congratulate the president, the members, and all the listeners of this congress upon the tendency of union that has gathered them on the soil of the country whose allegorical eagle, spreading her mighty wings over the stars and stripes, holds in her talons those splendid words, 'E Pluribus Unum.'"

CHAPTER III.

A RELIGIOUS SYMPOSIUM.

THOSE who kept files of the full reports in the daily press of the addresses before the parliament, or who look forward to the official publication of the proceedings with the intention of reviewing these deliverances, are likely to be appalled at the magnitude of the undertaking when they shall seriously approach it. A lack of classification in the programme makes the systematic arrangement of opinion on the great subjects of religion a work of toil, even for an expert. Each man speaks as if he had the whole field before him, and therefore of many things which throw no light upon the specific system of thought which he represents. The popular interest in seeing and hearing many representative men doubtless determined the idea of the programme, but the permanent value of the result is greatly diminished by the excessive amount of redundant and indeterminate discourse.

My own idea of the most useful order of programme, proposed at the outset and urged throughout, was an arrangement of great subjects: God, Revelation, Sin and Reconciliation, Conduct of Life, Immortality, etc. "What have you to say of God?" Let the Hindu answer, the Buddhist, the Parsee, the Mohammedan, the Jew, the Greek

Christian, the Catholic, and so on, in brief, specific, and inclusive statements. Then propound the next subject and follow in the same order. If this dream of a religious symposium had been practicable, the result would have been a most complete cyclopedia of religious thought, showing at a glance what is common and what is distinctive in existing faiths on any subject. The interest centered, however, in great men rather than in great subjects; and the addresses, not having as an aim definite statements on specific questions, present a collection of ideas so vast as to almost defy the classification necessary to helpful comparison.

Whatever of permanent value is to result from the congress of religions, apart from coming together in friendly interchange and the breaking of prejudice, must come from comparison of views; and before there can be such comparison there must be some arrangement. I propose, therefore, in this chapter to attempt to bring into contrast some of the more important deliverances, first in general, and then more briefly under specific subjects.

We may for the purpose of a general comparison set over against each other some extended passages from representatives of Hinduism, orthodox and liberal Christianity, Buddhism, Judaism, Mohammedanism, and the Roman Catholic and Greek churches, together with some foreign criticism and appeal.

THE HINDU.

Swami Vivekananda may probably be considered as a fair exponent of what Hinduism is with the liberally educated men of India:

A RELIGIOUS SYMPOSIUM.

"Three religions now stand in the world which have come down to us from time prehistoric — Hinduism, Zoroastrianism, and Judaism. These all have received tremendous shocks, and all of them prove by their revival their internal strength; but Judaism failed to absorb Christianity, and was driven out of its place of birth by its all-conquering daughter. Sect after sect has arisen in India, and seemed to shake the religion of the Vedas to its very foundations, but, like the waters of the seashore in a tremendous earthquake, it has receded for awhile, only to return in an all-absorbing flood; and when the tumult of the rush was over these sects had been all sucked in, absorbed, and assimilated in the immense body of another faith.

"From the high spiritual flights of philosophy, of which the latest discoveries of science seem like echoes, from the atheism of the Jains to the low ideas of idolatry and the multifarious mythologies, each and all have a place in the Hindu's religion.

"Where then, the question arises, where then the common center to which all these widely diverging radii converge? Where is the common basis upon which all these seemingly hopeless contradictions rest? And this is the question which I shall attempt to answer.

"The Hindus have received their religion through the revelation of the Vedas. They hold that the Vedas are without beginning and without end. It may sound ludicrous to this audience how a book can be without beginning or end. But by the Vedas no books are meant. They mean the accumulated treasury of spiritual laws discovered by different persons in different times. Just as the law of gravitation existed before its discovery, and would exist if all humanity forgot it, so with the laws that govern the spiritual world; the moral, ethical, and spiritual relations between soul and soul, and between individual spirits and the Father of all spirits, were there before their discovery, and would remain even if we forgot them.

"The discoverers of these laws are called Rishis, and we honor them as perfected beings, and I am glad to tell this audience that some of the very best of them were women.

"Here it may be said that the laws, as laws, may be without end, but they must have had a beginning. The Vedas teach us that creation is without beginning or end. Science has proved to us that the sum total of the cosmic energy is the same throughout all time. Then, if there was a time when nothing existed, where was all this manifested energy? Some say it was in a potential form in God. But then God is sometimes potential and sometimes kinetic, which would make him mutable, and everything mutable is a compound, and everything compound must undergo that change which is called destruction. Therefore, God would die. Therefore, there never was a time when there was no creation.

"Well, then, the human soul is eternal and immortal, perfect and infinite, and death means only a change of center from one body to another. The present is determined by our past actions, and the future will be by the present. The soul will go on evolving up or reverting back from birth to birth and death to death, like a tiny boat in a tempest, raised one moment on the foaming crest of a billow and dashed down into a yawning chasm the next, rolling to and fro at the mercy of good and bad actions, a powerless, helpless wreck in an ever-raging, ever-rushing, uncompromising current of cause and effect; a little moth placed under the wheel of causation, which rolls on crushing everything in its way, and waits not for the widow's tears or the orphan's cry.

"The heart sinks at the idea, yet this is the law of nature. Is there no hope? Is there no escape? The cry that went up from the bottom of the heart of despair reached the throne of mercy, and words of hope and consolation came down and inspired a Vedic sage, and he stood up before the world and in trumpet voice proclaimed the glad tidings to the world: 'Hear, ye children of immortal bliss, even ye that resisted in higher spheres; I have found the ancient one, who is beyond all darkness, all delusion, and knowing him alone you shall be saved from death again.' 'Children of immortal bliss!' What a sweet, what a hopeful name! Allow me to call you, brethren, by that sweet name, 'heirs of immortal bliss'; yea, the Hindu refuses to call you sinners. . . .

"Thus it is the Vedas proclaim, not a dreadful combination of unforgiving laws, not an endless prison of cause and effect, but that, at the head of all these laws, in and through every particle of matter and force, stands one 'through whose command the wind blows, the fire burns, the clouds rain, and death stalks upon the earth.' And what is his nature?

"He is everywhere, the pure and formless one, the almighty, and the all-merciful. 'Thou art our father, thou art our mother, thou art our beloved friend, thou art the source of all strength. Thou art he that bearest the burdens of the universe; help me bear the little burden of this life.' Thus sang the Rishis of the Veda. And how to worship him? Through love. 'He is to be worshiped as the one beloved dearer than everything in this and the next life.'

"'This is the doctrine of love preached in the Vedas, and let us see how it is fully developed and preached by Krishna, whom the Hindus believe to have been God incarnate on earth.

"He taught that a man ought to live in this world like a lotus leaf, which grows in water but is never moistened by water; so a man ought to live in this world — his heart for God and his hands for work.

"It is good to love God for hope of reward in this or the next world, but it is better to love God for love's sake; and the prayer goes, 'Lord, I do not want wealth, nor children, nor learning. If it be thy will I will go to a hundred hells, but grant me this, that I may love thee without the hope of reward — unselfishly love for love's sake.' One of the disciples of Krishna, the then Emperor of India, was driven from his throne by his enemies and had to take shelter in a forest in the Himalayas with his queen, and there one day the queen was asking him how it was that he, the most virtuous of men, should suffer so much misery, and Yuchistera answered: 'Behold, my queen, the Himalayas, how grand and beautiful they are! I love them. They do not give me anything, but my nature is to love the grand, the beautiful, therefore I love them; similarly, I love the Lord. He is the source of all beauty, of all sublimity. He is the only object to be loved. My nature is to love him, and therefore I love. I do not pray for anything. I do not ask for anything. Let him place me wherever he likes. I must live for love's sake. I can not trade in love.'

"The Vedas teach that the soul is divine, only held under bondage of matter, and perfection will be reached when the bond shall burst, and the word they use is, therefore, Mukto — freedom — freedom from the bonds of imperfection; freedom from death and misery.

"And they teach that this bondage can only fall off through the mercy of God, and this mercy comes to the pure. So purity is the condition of his mercy. How that mercy acts! He reveals himself to the pure heart, and the pure and stainless man sees God, yea, even in this life; and then, and then only, all the crookedness of the heart is made straight. Then all doubt ceases. Man is no more the freak of a terrible law of causation. So this is the very center, the very vital conception, of Hinduism. The Hindu does not want to live upon words and theories — if there are existences beyond the ordinary sensual existence, he wants to come face to face with them. If there is a soul in him which is not matter, if there is an all-merciful universal soul, he will go to him direct. He must see him, and that alone can destroy all doubts. So the best proof a Hindu sage gives about the soul, about God, is, 'I have seen the soul, I have seen God.'

"And that is the only condition of perfection. The Hindu religion does not consist in struggles and attempts to believe a certain doctrine and dogma, but in realizing — not in believing, but in being and becoming. So the whole struggle in their system is a constant struggle to become perfect, to become divine, to reach God and see God; and in this reaching God, seeing God, becoming perfect, even as the Father in heaven is perfect, consists the religion of the Hindus. And what becomes of man when he becomes perfect? He lives a life of bliss, infinite. He enjoys infinite and perfect bliss, having obtained the only thing in which man ought to have pleasure — God — and enjoys the bliss with God.

"So far all the Hindus are agreed — this is the common religion of all the sects of India; but then the question comes — perfection is absolute, and the absolute can not be two or three. It can not have any qualities; it can not be an individual; and so when a soul becomes perfect and absolute it must become one with the Brahma, and he would only realize the Lord as the perfection, the reality, of his own nature and existence — existence absolute; knowledge absolute, and life absolute. We have often and often read about this being called the losing of individuality, as in becoming a stock or a stone. 'He jests at scars that never felt a wound '

"I tell you it is nothing of the kind. If it is happiness to enjoy the consciousness of this small body, it must be more happiness to enjoy the consciousness of two bodies, or three, four, five — and the ultimate of happiness would be reached when it would become a universal consciousness.

"Therefore, to gain this infinite universal individuality, this miserable little individuality must go. Then alone can death cease, when I am one with life. Then alone can misery cease, when I am with happiness itself. Then alone can all errors cease, when I am one with knowledge itself."

Speaking later of the religion of the simple-minded he said. "There is no polytheism in India," and the use of images "is not idolatry." Continuing, he said:

"Superstition is the enemy of man, but bigotry is worse. Why does a Christian go to church? Why is the cross holy? Why is the face turned toward the sky in prayer? Why are there so many images in the Catholic church? Why are there so many images in the minds of Protestants when they pray? My brethren, we can no more think about anything without a material image than we can live without breathing. And by the law of association the material image calls the mental idea up, and *vice versa*. Omnipresence, to almost the whole world, means nothing. Has God superficial area? If not, when we repeat the word we think of the extended earth, that is all.

"As we find that somehow or other, by the laws of our constitution, we have got to associate our ideas of infinity with the image of a blue sky or a sea, some cover the idea of holiness with an image of a church or a mosque, or a cross. The Hindus have associated the ideas of holiness, purity, truth, omnipresence, and all other ideas with different images and forms; but with this difference: Some devote their whole lives to their idol of a church and never rise higher, because with them religion means an intellectual assent to certain doctrines and doing good to their fellows. The whole religion of the Hindu is centered in realization. Man is to become divine, realizing the divine, and therefore idol or temple, or church or books, are only the supports, the helps, of his spiritual childhood; but on and on man must progress.

"He must not stop anywhere. 'External worship, material worship,' says the Vedas, 'is the lowest stage; struggling to rise high, mental prayer is the next stage; but the highest stage is when the Lord has been realized.' Mark the same earnest man who was kneeling before the idol tell you, 'Him the sun can not express, nor the moon, nor the stars; the lightning can not express him, nor the fire; through him they all shine.' He does not abuse the image or call it sinful. He recognizes in it a necessary stage of his life. 'The child is father of the man.' Would it be right for the old man to say that childhood is a sin, or youth a sin? Nor is it compulsory in Hinduism.

"If a man can realize his divine nature with the

help of an image, would it be right to call it a sin? Nor, even when he has passed that stage, should he call it an error. To the Hindu, man is not traveling from error to truth, but from truth to truth, from lower to higher truth. To him all the religions, from the lowest fetishism to the highest absolutism, mean so many attempts of the human soul to grasp and realize the infinite, each determined by the conditions of its birth and association, and each of these mark a stage of progress, and every soul is a young eagle soaring higher and higher, gathering more and more strength till it reaches the glorious sun."

Concluding, he said: "If there is ever to be a universal religion it must be one which will hold no location in place or time; which will be infinite, like the God it will preach; whose sun shines upon the followers of Krishna or Christ, saints or sinners, alike; which will not be the Brahmin or Buddhist, Christian or Mohammedan, but the sum total of all these, and still have infinite space for development; which in its catholicity will embrace in its infinite arms and find a place for every human being, from the lowest groveling man, from the brute, to the highest mind towering almost above humanity and making society stand in awe and doubt his human nature.

"It will be a religion which will have no place for persecution or intolerance in its polity, which will recognize a divinity in every man or woman, and whose whole scope, whose whole force, will be centered in aiding humanity to realize its divine nature.

"Asoka's council was a council of the Buddhist faith. Akbar's, though more to the purpose, was only a parlor meeting. It was reserved for America to proclaim to all quarters of the globe that the Lord is in every religion.

"May he who is the Brahma of the Hindus, the Ahura Mazda of the Zoroastrians, the Buddha of the Buddhists, the Jehovah of the Jews, the Father in heaven of the Christians, give strength to you to carry out your noble idea.

"The star arose in the east; it traveled steadily toward the west, sometimes dimmed and sometimes effulgent, till it made a circuit of the world, and now it is again rising on the very horizon of the east, the borders of the Tasifu, a thousand-fold more effulgent than it ever was before. Hail, Columbia, motherland of liberty! It has been given to thee, who never dipped hand in neighbor's blood, who never found out that shortest way of becoming rich by robbing one's neighbors — it has been given to thee to march on in the vanguard of civilization with the flag of harmony."

ORTHODOX CHRISTIANITY.

The chairman in introducing Joseph Cook referred to the undoubted quality of his orthodoxy; and on this ground his statement of "the certainties of religion" may be introduced into this comparison. His address has been very generally remarked upon, and often severely criticised; but the fact remains to the credit of Joseph Cook that, in its main statements, it stands out as a frank and manly dec-

RT.-REV. REUCHI SHIBATA,
High Priest of Zhikko Sect of Shintoism, Japan.

laration of what Protestant orthodoxy is committed to by creed and sermon; unnecessarily dramatic, it may be, and too much in the nature of challenge to suit the spirit of the occasion, but honest and clear:

"It is no more wonderful that we should live again than that we should live at all. It is less wonderful that we should continue to live than that we have begun to live; and even the most determined and superficial skeptic knows that we have begun. On the faces of this polyglot international audience I seem to see written, as I once saw chiseled on the marble above the tomb of the great Emperor Akbar in the land of the Ganges, the hundred names of God.

"Let us beware how we lightly assert that we are glad that those names are one. How many of us are ready for immediate, total, irreversible self-surrender to God as both Saviour and Lord? Only such of us as are thus ready can call ourselves in any deep sense religious. I care not what name you give to God if you mean by him a spirit omnipresent, eternal, omnipotent, infinite in holiness and every other operation. Who is ready for coöperation with such a God in life and death and beyond death? Only he who is thus ready is religious. William Shakespeare is supposed to have known something of human nature, and certainly was not a theological partisan. Now Shakespeare, you will remember, in 'The Tempest,' tells you of two characters who conceived for each other supreme affection as soon as they met. 'At the first glance they have changed eyes,' he says. The truly religious man is one who has 'changed eyes' with God under some one or another of his hundred names. It follows from this definition of religion, and as a certainty dependent on the unalterable nature of things, that only he who has changed eyes with God can look into his face in peace. A religion of delight in God, not merely as Saviour, but as Lord also, is scientifically known to be a necessity to the peace of the soul, whether we call God by this name or the other, whether we speak of him in the dialect of this or that of the four continents, or this or that of the 10,000 isles of the sea.

"What is the distinction between morality and religion, and how can the latter be shown by the scientific method to be a necessity to the peace of the soul? And now, though I do not understand morality and the philanthropies, I purpose to speak of the strategic certainties of religion from the point of view of comparative religion. First, from the very center of the human heart and in the presence of all the hundred names of God, conscience demands that what ought to be, be chosen by the will, and it demands this universally. Conscience is that faculty within us which tastes intentions. A man does unquestionably know whether he means to be mean, and he inevitably feels mean when he knows that he means to be mean. If we say to that still, small voice we call conscience, that proclaims 'thou oughtest,' 'I will not,' there is lack of peace in us, and until only we say 'I will,' and do like to say it, there is no harmony within our souls. The delight in saying 'I will' to the still, small voice 'thou oughtest' is religion. Merely calculating, selfish obedience to that still, small voice saves no man.

"This is the first commandment of absolute science: 'Thou shalt love the Lord thy God with all thy mind, and might, and heart, and strength.' When Shakespeare's two characters met, curiosity as to each other's qualities did not constitute the changing of eyes. That mighty capacity which exists in human nature to give forth a supreme affection was not the changing of eyes. Let us not mistake a capacity of religion which every man has for religion itself. We must not only have a capacity to love God, we must have adoration of God; and half the loose, limp, unscientific liberalisms of the world mistake mere admiration for adoration. It is narrowness to refuse mental hospitality for any single truth; but we, assembled in the name of science, in the name of every grave purpose, have an international breadth, and what we purpose to promote is such a self-surrender to God as shall amount to delight in all known duty and make us affectionately and irreversibly choose God under some one of his names — I care not what the name is if you mean by it all the Bible means by the word 'God' — choose him not as Saviour only but as God also, not as Lord only but as Saviour also.

"But choice in relation to persons means love. What we choose we love; but conscience reveals a holy person, the author of the moral law, and conscience demands that this law should not only be obeyed but loved, and that the holy person should be not only obeyed but loved. This is the unalterable demand of an unalterable portion of our nature. As personalities, therefore, must keep company with this part of our nature and with its demands while we exist in this world and in the next, the love of God by man is inflexibly required by the very nature of things. Conscience draws an unalterable distinction between loyalty and disloyalty to the ineffable, holy person whom the moral law reveals, and between the obedience of slavishness and that of delight. Only the latter is obedience to conscience.

"Religion is the obedience of affectionate gladness. Morality is the obedience of selfish slavishness. Only religion, therefore, and not mere morality, can harmonize the soul with the nature of things. A delight in obedience is not only a part of religion, but is necessary to peace in God's presence. A religion consisting in the obedience of gladness is, therefore, scientifically known to be according to the nature of things. It will not be to-morrow or the day after that these propositions will cease to be scientifically certain. Out of them multitudinous inferences flow as Niagaras from the brink of God's palm. Demosthenes once made the remark that every address should begin with an incontrovertible proposition. Now it is a certainty, and my topic makes my key-note a word of certainty, that a little while ago we were not in the world and a little while hence we shall be here no longer. Lincoln, Garfield, Seward, Grant, Beecher, Gough, Emerson, Longfellow, Tennyson, Lord

Beaconsfield, George Eliot, Carlyle — I know not how many Mahomets — are gone, and we are going. These are certainties that will endure in the four continents and on the isles of the sea —

> Till the heavens are old, and the stars are cold,
> And the leaves of the judgment book unfold.

"The world expects to hear from us this afternoon no drivel, but something fit to be professed face to face with the crackling artillery of the science of our time. I know I am going hence, and I know I wish to go in peace. Now, I hold that it is a certainty, and a certainty founded on truth absolutely self-evident, that there are three things from which I can never escape — my conscience, my God, and my record of sin in an irreversible past. How am I to be harmonized with that unescapable environment? Here is Lady Macbeth. See how she rubs her hands —

> Out, damned spot! Will these hands ne'er be clean?
> All the perfumes of Arabia could not sweeten this little hand.

And her husband, in a similar mood, says:

> This red right hand, it would the multitudinous seas incarnadine, making the green one red.

"What religion can wash Lady Macbeth's red right hand? That is a question I propose to the four continents and all the isles of the sea. Unless you can answer that, you have not come here with a serious purpose to a parliament of religions.

"I speak now to that branch of skeptics which is not represented here, and I ask who can wash Lady

Macbeth's red right hand, and their silence or their responses are as inefficient as a fishing-rod would be to span this vast lake or the Atlantic.

"I turn to Mohammedanism. Can you wash our red right hands? I turn to Confucianism and Buddhism. Can you wash our red right hands? So help me God, I mean to ask a question this afternoon that shall go in some hearts across the seas and to the antipodes, and I ask it in the name of what I hold to be absolutely self-evident truth, that unless a man is washed from the old sin and the guilt of mankind he can not be at peace in the presence of infinite holiness.

"Old and blind Michael Angelo in the Vatican used to go to the torso, so called — a fragment of the art of antiquity — and he would feel along the marvelous lines chiseled in bygone ages, and tell his pupils that thus and thus the study should be completed. I turn to every faith on earth except Christianity and I find every such faith a torso. I beg pardon. The occasion is too grave for mere courtesy and nothing else. Some of the faiths of the world are marvelous as far as they go, but if they were completed along the lines of the certainties of the religions themselves they would go up and up and up to an assertion of the necessity of the new purpose to deliver the soul from a life of sin, and of atonement made of God's grace, to deliver the soul from guilt.

"Take the ideas which have produced the torsos of the earthly faiths and you will have a universal religion, under some of the names of God, and it will be a harmonious outline with Christianity. There is no peace anywhere in the universe for a soul with bad intentions, and there ought not to be. Ours is a transitional age, and we are told we are all sons of God; and so we are, in a natural sense, but not in a moral sense. We are all capable of changing eyes with God, and until we do change eyes with him it is impossible for us to face him in peace. No transition in life or death or beyond death will ever deliver us from the necessity of good intentions to the peace of the soul with its environments, nor from exposure to penalty for deliberately bad intentions. I hold that we not only can not escape from conscience and God and our records of sins, but that it is a certainty, and a strategic certainty, that except Christianity there is no religion under heaven or among men that effectively provides for the peace of the soul by its harmonization with this environment."

Here also should be cited the equally plain and emphatic declaration of Prof. W. C. Wilkinson of Chicago University, who concluded an extended discussion of the "Attitude of Christianity toward Other Religions" as follows:

"It is much if a religion, such as the Bible thus teaches Christianity to be, leaves us any chance at all for entertaining hope concerning those remaining to the last involved in the prevalence of false religion surrounding them. But chance there seems indeed to be of hope justified by Christianity, for some among these unfortunate men. Peter, the straightened Peter, the one apostle perhaps most inclined to be unalterably Jewish, he it was who, having been hitherto specially instructed, said:

"'Of a truth I perceive that God is no respecter of persons, but in every nation he that feareth him and worketh righteousness is acceptable to him.'

"To fear God first, and then also to work righteousness, these are the traits characterizing ever and everywhere the man acceptable to God. But evidently to fear God is not, in the idea of Christianity, to worship another than he. It will accordingly be in degree as a man escapes the ethnic religion dominant about him, and rises — not by means of it, but in spite of it — into the transcending element of the true divine worship, that the man will be acceptable to God.

"Of any ethnic religion, therefore, can it be said that it is a true religion, only not perfect? Christianity says no. Christianity speaks words of undefined, unlimited hope concerning those, some of those, who shall never have heard of Christ. These words Christians, of course, will hold and cherish according to their inestimable value. But let us not mistake them as intended to bear any relation whatever to the erring religions of mankind. Those religions the Bible nowhere represents as pathetic and partly successful gropings after God. They are one and all represented as groping downward, not groping upward. According to Christianity they hinder, they do not help. Their adherents' hold on them is like the blind grasping of drowning men on roots or rocks that only tend to keep them to the bottom of the river. The truth that is in the false religion may help, but it will be the truth, not the false religion.

"According to Christianity the false religion exerts all its force to choke and to kill the truth that is in it. Hence the historic degeneration represented in the first chapter of Romans as effecting false religions in general. If they were upward reachings they would grow better and better. If, as Paul teaches, they in fact grow worse and worse, it must be because they are downward reachings. The indestructible instinct to worship, that is in itself a saving power. Carefully guarded, carefully cultivated, it may even save. But the worshiping instinct, misused or disused, that is, depraved to idolatry or extinguished in atheism — 'held down,' as Paul graphically expresses it — is in swift process of becoming an irresistible destroying power. The light that is in the soul turns swiftly into darkness. The instinct to worship lifts Godward. The issue of that instinct, its abuse in idolatry, its disuse in atheism, is evil, only evil, and that continually.

"The attitude, therefore, of Christianity toward religions other than itself is an attitude of universal, absolute, eternal, unappeasable hostility, while toward all men, everywhere, the adherents of false religion by no means excepted, its attitude is an attitude of grace, mercy, peace, for whosoever will. How many may be found that will is a problem which Christianity leaves unsolved. Most welcome hints and suggestions, however, it affords, encouraging Christians joyfully and gratefully to entertain on behalf of the erring that relieved and sympathetic sentiment which the poet has taught us to call 'the larger hope.'"

More generous and inviting is the "Message of Christianity to Other Religions," as voiced by the Rev. James S. Dennis, D. D., secretary of the Presbyterian Board of Missions. He gives the message in a series of "code words," as he calls them:

"The initial word which we place in this signal code of Christianity is fatherhood. This may have a strange sound to some ears, but to the Christian it is full of sweetness and dignity. It simply means that the creative act of God, so far as our human family is concerned, was done in the spirit of fatherly love and goodness. He created us in his likeness, and to express this idea of spiritual resemblance and tender relationship the symbolical term of fatherhood is used. When Christ taught us to pray 'Our Father' he gave us a lesson which transcends human philosophy, and has in it so much of the height and depth of divine feeling that human reason has hardly dared to receive, much less to originate, the conception.

"A second word which is representative in the Christian message is brotherhood. This exists in two senses — there is the universal brotherhood of man to man, as children of one father, in whose likeness the whole family is created, and the spiritual brotherhood of union in Christ. Here again is the suggestion of love as the rule and sign of human as well as Christian fellowship. The world has drifted far away from this ideal of brotherhood; it has been repudiated in some quarters even in the name of religion, and it seems clear that it will never be fully recognized and exemplified except as the Spirit of Christ assumes its sway over the hearts of men.

"The next code word of Christianity is redemption. We use it here in the sense of a purpose on God's part to deliver man from sin, and to make a universal provision for that end, which, if rightly used, insures the result. I need not remind you that this purpose is conceived in love. God, as Redeemer, has taken a gracious attitude toward man from the beginning of history, and he is 'not far from every one' in the immanence and omnipresence of his love. Redemption is a world-embracing term. It is not limited to any age or class. Its potentiality is world-wide; its efficiency is unrestrained except as man limits it; its application is determined by the sovereign wisdom of God, its Author, who deals with each individual as a possible candidate for redemption, and decides his destiny in accordance with his spiritual attitude toward Christ.

"Where Christ is unknown God still exercises his sovereignty, although he has been pleased to maintain a significant reserve as to the possibility, extent, and spiritual tests of redemption where trust is based on God's mercy in general rather than upon his mercy as specially revealed in Christ. We know from his word that Christ's sacrifice is infinite. God can apply its saving benefits to one who intelligently accepts it in faith, or to an infant who receives its benefits as a sovereign gift, or to one who, not having known of Christ, so casts himself upon God's mercy that divine wisdom sees good reason to exercise the prerogative of compassion and apply to the soul the saving power of the great sacrifice.

"Another cardinal idea in the Christian system is incarnation — God clothing himself in human form and coming into living touch with mankind. This he did in the person of Jesus of Nazareth. It is a mighty mystery, and Christianity would never dare assert it except as God has taught its truth. Granted the purpose of God to reveal himself in visible form to man, and he must be free to choose his own method. He did not consult human reason. He did not seek the permission of ordinary laws. He came in his spiritual chariot, in the glory of the supernatural, but he entered the realm of human life through the humble gateway of nature. He came not only to reveal God, but to bring him into contact with human life. He came to assume permanent relations to the race. His brief life among us on earth was for a purpose, and when that was accomplished, still retaining his humanity, he ascended to assume his kingly dominions in the heavens.

"We are brought now to another fundamental truth in Christian teaching — the mysterious doctrine of atonement. Sin is a fact which is indisputable. It is universally recognized and acknowledged. It is its own evidence. It is, moreover, a barrier between man and his God. The divine holiness and sin, with its loathsomeness, its rebellion, its horrid degradation, and its hopeless ruin, can not coalesce in any system of moral government. God can not tolerate sin, or temporize with it, or make a place for it in his presence. He can not parley with it; he must punish it. He can not treat with it; he must try it at the bar. He can not overlook it; he must overcome it. He can not give it a moral status; he must visit it with the condemnation it deserves.

"Atonement is God's marvelous method of vindicating, once for all, before the universe, his eternal attitude toward sin, by the voluntary self assumption, in the spirit of sacrifice, of its penalty. This he does in the person of Jesus Christ, who came as God incarnate upon this sublime mission. The facts of Christ's birth, life, death, and resurrection take their place in the realm of veritable history, and the moral value and propitiatory efficacy of his perfect obedience and sacrificial death in a representative capacity become a mysterious element of limitless worth in the process of readjusting the relation of the sinner to his God.

"Christ is recognized by God as a substitute. The merit of his obedience and the exalted dignity of his sacrifice are both available to faith. The sinner, humble, penitent, and conscious of unworthiness, accepts Christ as his redeemer, his intercessor, his saviour, and simply believes in him, trusting in his assurances and promises, based as they are upon his atoning intervention, and receives from God, as the gift of sovereign love, all the benefits of Christ's mediatorial work. This is God's way of reaching the goal of pardon and reconciliation. It is his way of being himself just and yet accomplishing the justification of the sinner. Here again we have the mystery of love in its most intense form and the mystery of wisdom in its most august exemplification.

"This is the heart of the gospel. It throbs with mysterious love. It pulsates with ineffable throes of divine feeling; it bears a vital relation to the whole scheme of government; it is in its hidden activities beyond the scrutiny of human reason; but it sends the life-blood coursing through history and it gives to Christianity its superb vitality and its undying vigor. It is because Christianity eliminates sin from the problem that its solution is complete and final.

"We pass now to another word which is of vital importance — it is character. God's own attitude to the sinner being settled, and the problem of moral government solved, the next matter which presents itself is the personality of the individual man. It must be purified, transformed into the spiritual likeness of Christ, trained for immortality. It must be brought into harmony with the ethical standards of Christ. This Christianity insists upon, and for the accomplishment of this end it is gifted with an influence and impulse, a potency and winsomeness, an inspiration and helpfulness, which is full of spiritual mastery over the soul. Christianity uplifts, transforms, and eventually transfigures the personal character. It is a transcendent school of incomparable ethics. It honors the rugged training of discipline; it uses it freely but tenderly. It accomplishes its purpose by exacting obedience, by teaching submission, by helping to self-control, by insisting upon practical righteousness as a rule of life, and by introducing the golden rule as the law of contact and duty between man and man.

"In vital connection with character is a word of magnetic impulse and unique glory which gives to Christianity a sublime practical power in history. It is service. There is a forceful meaning in the double influence of Christianity over the inner life and the outward ministry of its followers. Christ, its founder, glorified service and lifted it in his own experience to the dignity of sacrifice. In the light of Christ's example, service becomes an honor, a privilege, and a moral triumph; it is consummated and crowned in sacrifice.

"Christianity, receiving its lesson from Christ, subsidizes character in the interest of service. It lays its noblest fruitage of personal gifts and spiritual culture upon the altar of philanthropic sacrifice. It is unworthy of its name if it does not reproduce this spirit of its master; only by giving itself to benevolent ministry, as Christ gave himself for the world, can it vindicate its origin. Christianity recognizes no worship which is altogether divorced from work for the weal of others; it indorses no religious professions which are unmindful of the obligations of service; it allows itself to be tested not simply by the purity of its motives, but by the measure of its sacrifices. The crown and goal of its followers is, 'Well done, good and faithful servant.'

"One other word completes the code. It is fellowship. It is a word which breathes the sweetest hope and sounds the highest destiny of the Christian. It gives the grandest possible meaning to eternity, for it suggests that it is to be passed with God. It illumines and transfigures the present, for it brings God into it, and places him in living touch with our lives, and makes him a helper in our moral struggles, our spiritual aspirations, and our heroic though imperfect efforts to live the life of duty. It is solace in trouble, consolation in sorrow, strength in weakness, courage in trial, help in weariness, and cheer in loneliness. It becomes an unfailing inspiration when human nature, left to its own resources, would lie down in despair and die. Fellowship with God implies and secures fellowship with each other in a mystical spiritual union of Christ with his people, and his people with each other. An invisible society of regenerate souls, which we call the kingdom of God among men, is the result. This has its visible product in the organized society of the Christian church, which is the chosen and honored instrument of God for the conservation and propagation of Christianity among men.

"This, then, is the message which Christianity signals to other religions as it greets them to-day: Fatherhood, brotherhood, redemption, incarnation, atonement, character, service, fellowship."

If we pause here to compare, we find the Hindu looking up to the Almighty and the All-merciful One, who was incarnate on earth, as Krishna, and taught the love of God for its own sake; believing that the pure in heart see him, and that purity is attained by crucifying all selfish desire, and in the constant struggle to become perfect, even as the Father in heaven is perfect. In what that perfection consists is not definitely set forth; nor does the means of reaching it appear clear, except as a continual struggle, through no matter how many conditions of life, to rise above selfishness. One might suggest here, that however defective this view may be to the intellect aspiring to a knowledge of the origins and issues of life and death, yet, as a practical religion, it teaches the acknowledgment of the divine in shunning the evils of self-love as sins against him. And here one is reminded of the voice of Jehovah, by the prophet, "If a man turn from the evil he hath done and doeth righteousness he shall live," and of the word in the gospel, that "whosoever will do his will shall know," and "he that hath my commandments and keepeth them, he it is that loveth me," and "he that is not against us is for us."

Orthodox Christianity, on the other hand, sees the great fact of sin as a bar to the love of God, and finds in the gospel no hope for any until the old sin and the guilt of mankind is blotted out from the mind of God by a substitutional sacrifice, accepted by faith on the part of the sinner. It sees in Christianity only an attitude of absolute, eternal, and unappeasable hostility toward other religions, while it holds out to all men grace and mercy, and pleads for the acceptance of redemption and atonement, through faith in the sacrifice of Christ as acceptable with God, with inclination toward a "larger hope."

LIBERAL CHRISTIANITY.

Of course there is the broader view, with which all are familiar in this day, as voiced by Dr. Lyman Abbott, who said, "Religion is essential to humanity," the "religion" that is "the mother of all religions, not the child," which he defined as the power to apprehend the infinite and the eternal.

Tracing some of the ways in which the children of God are necessitated to seek after him, Doctor Abbott concludes:

"Thus we get out of religion religions — religions that vary with one another, according as curiosity, or fear, or hope, or the ethical element, or the personal reverence predominates. Religious curiosity wants to know about the infinite and eternal, and it gives us creeds and theologies; the religion of fear gives us the sacrificial system, with its atonements and propitiations; the religion of hope expects some reward or recompense from the great Infinite, and expresses itself in services and gifts, with the expectation of rewards here or in some Elysium hereafter. Then there is the religion which, although it can never learn the nature of the law-giver, still goes on trying to understand the nature of his laws; and, finally, the religion which more or less clearly sees behind all this that there is One who is the ideal of humanity, the infinite and eternal Ruler of humanity, and therefore reveres and worships, and last of all learns to love.

"If, in this very brief summary, I have carried you with me, you will see that the object of man's search is not merely religion; he is seeking to know the infinite and the eternal, not merely the priests and the hierarchies, not merely the men and women, with their services, and their rituals, and their prayer-books, but the whole current and tendency of human life is a search for the infinite and the divine. All science, all art, all sociology, all business, all government, as well as all worship, is in the last analysis an endeavor to comprehend the meaning of the great words, honesty, justice, truth, pity, mercy, love. In vain does the atheist or the agnostic try to stop our search to know the infinite and eternal; in vain does he tell us it is a useless quest. Still we press on, and must press on. The incentive is in ourselves, and nothing can blot it out of us and still leave us men and women.

"God made us out of himself and God calls us back to himself. It would be easier to kill the appetite of man and let us feed by merely shoveling in carbon as into a furnace; it would be easier to blot ambition out of man and to consign him to endless and nerveless content; easier to blot love out of man and banish him to live the life of a eunuch in the wilderness than to blot out of the soul of man those desires and aspirations which knit him to the infinite and the eternal, give him love for his fellowman and reverence for God. In vain does the philosopher of the barnyard say to the egg, 'You are made of egg; you always were an egg; you always will be an egg; don't try to be anything but an egg.' The chicken pecks and pecks until he breaks the shell and comes out to the sunlight of the world.

"We welcome here to-day, in this most cosmopolitan city of the most cosmopolitan race on the globe, the representatives of all the various forms of religious life from east to west and north to south. We are glad to welcome them. We are glad to believe that they, as we, have been seeking to know something more and better of the divine from which we issue, of the divine to which we are returning. We are glad to hear the message they have to bring to us. We are glad to know what they have to tell us, but what we are gladdest of all about is that we can tell them what we have found in our search, and that we have found the Christ.

"I do not stand here as an exponent, the apologist, or the defender of Christianity. In it there have been the blemishes and the marks of human handiwork. It has been too intellectual, too much a religion of creeds. It has been too fearful, too much a religion of sacrifices. It has been too selfishly hopeful; there has been too much a desire of reward here or hereafter. It has been too little a religion of unselfish service and unselfish reverence. No! It is not Christianity that we want to tell our brethren across the sea about; it is the Christ.

"What is it that this universal hunger of the human race seeks? Is it not these things — a better understanding of our moral relations, one to another, a better understanding of what we are and what we mean to be, that we may fashion ourselves according to the idea of the ideal being in our nature, a better appreciation of the infinite one who is behind all phenomena, material and spiritual? Is it not more health and added strength and clearer light in our upward tendency to our everlasting Father's arms and home? Are not these the things that most we need in the world? We have found the Christ, and loved him and revered him and accepted him, for nowhere else, in no other prophet, have we found the moral relations of men better represented than in the golden rule, 'Do unto others that which you would have others do unto you.' We do not think that he furnishes the only ideal the world has ever had. We recognize the voice of God in all prophets and in all time. But we do think we have found in this Christ, in his patience, in his courage, in his heroism, in his self-sacrifice, in his unbounded mercy and love an idea that transcends all other ideals written by the pen of poet, painted by the brush of artist, or graven into the life of human history.

"We do not think that God has spoken only in Palestine and to the few in that narrow province. We do not think he has been vocal in Christendom and dumb everywhere else. No! We believe that he is a speaking God in all times and in all ages. But we believe no other revelation transcends and none other equals that which he has made to man in the one transcendental human life that was lived eighteen centuries ago in Palestine. And we think we find in Christ one thing that we have not been able to find in any other of the manifestations of the religious life of the world. All religions are the result of man's seeking after God. If what I have portrayed to you this morning so imperfectly has any truth in it the whole human race seeks to know its eternal and divine Father; the message of the Incarnation—that is the glad tidings we have to give to Africa, to Asia, to China, to the isles of the sea.

"The everlasting Father is also seeking the children who are seeking him. He is not an unknown, hiding himself behind a veil impenetrable. He is not a being dwelling in the eternal silence; he is a speaking, revealing, incarnate God. He is not an absolute justice, sitting on the throne of the universe and bringing before him imperfect, sinful man and judging him with the scales of unerring justice; he is a father coming into human life and coming into one transcendental human life, coming into all human life for all time. Perhaps we have sometimes misrepresented our own faith respecting this Christ. Perhaps, in our metaphysical definitions, we have sometimes been too anxious to be accurate and too little anxious to be true. He himself has said it. He is a door. We do not stand merely to look at the door for the beauty of the carving upon it. We push the door open and go in. Through that door God enters into human life; through that door humanity enters into the divine life; man seeking after God, the incarnate God seeking after man; the end in that great future after life's troubled dream shall be o'er, and we shall awake satisfied because we awake in his likeness."

BUDDHISM.

Buddhism rivals Christianity in the number and characteristic differences of its sects; but with better reason in the intent of its original teacher, according to Banriu Yatsabuchi of Japan, from whose paper we quote the following:

"Buddhism is the doctrine taught by Buddha Sakyamuni. The word Buddha is Sanscrit, and in the Japanese it is Satoru, which means understanding, or comprehension. It has three meanings — self-comprehension, to let others comprehend, and perfect comprehension. When wisdom and humanity are attained thoroughly by one he may be called Buddha, which means perfect comprehension. In Buddhism we have Buddha as our Saviour, the spirit incarnate of perfect self-sacrifice and divine compassion, and the embodiment of all that is pure and good. Although Buddha was not a creator and had no power to destroy the law of the universe, he had the power of knowledge to know the origin of nature and end of each revolving manifestation of the universal phenomena. He suppressed the craving and passions of his mind until he could reach no higher spiritual and moral plane. As every object of the universe is one part of the truth, of course it may become Buddha, according to a natural reason. . . .

"The complete doctrines of Buddha, who spent fifty years in elaborating them, were preached precisely and carefully, and their meanings are so profound and deep that I can not explain at this time an infinitesimal part of them. His preaching was a compass to point out the direction to the bewildered spiritual world. He taught his disciples just as the doctor cures his patient, by giving several medicines according to the different cases. Twelve divisions of Sutras and 84,000 laws made to meet the different cases of Buddha's patients in the suffering world are minute classifications of Buddha's teachings. Why are there so many sects and preachings in Buddhism? Simply because of the differences in human character. His teaching may be divided under four heads: Thinking about the general state of the world; thinking about the individual character simply; conquering the passions; giving up the life to the sublime first principle.

"There is no room for censure because Buddhism has many sects which were founded on Buddha's teachings, because Buddha considered it best to preach according to the spiritual needs of his hearers and leave to them the choice of any particular set. We are not allowed to censure other sects, because the teaching of each guides us all to the same place at last. The necessity for separating the many sects arose from the fact that the people of different countries were not alike in dispositions and could not accept the same truths in the same way as others. One teaching of Buddha contains many elements which are to be distributed and separated; but as the object as taught by Buddha is one, we teach the ignorant according to the conditions that arise through our different sects."

The teachings of Buddhism were more particularly set forth in a paper by H. R. H. Prince Chandradat Chudhadharn, on "The Buddhism of Siam," explaining that all things in the universe are made up from Dharma, defined as "the essence of nature," and presenting the three following phenomena, namely: 1st, the accomplishment of eternal evolution; 2d, sorrow and suffering, according to human ideas; and 3d, a separate power uncontrollable by the desire of man, and not belonging to man. He continued:

"Man, who is an aggregate of Dharma, is, however, unconscious of the fact, because his will either receives impressions and becomes modified by mere visible things, or because his spirit has become identified with appearances, such as man, animal, deva, or any other beings that are also but modified spirits and matter. Man becomes, therefore, conscious of separate existence. But all outward forms, man himself included, are made to live or to last for a short space of time only. They are soon to be destroyed and recreated again and again by an eternal evolution. He is first body and spirit, but, through ignorance of the fact that all is Dharma, and of that which is good and evil, his spirit may become impressed with evil temptation. Thus, for instance, he may desire certain things with that force peculiar to a tiger, whose spirit is modified by craving for lust and anger. In such a case he will be continually adopting, directly or indirectly, in his own life, the wills and acts of that tiger, and thereby is himself that animal in spirit and soul. Yet outwardly he appears to be a man, and is as yet unconscious of the fact that his spirit has become endowed with the cruelties of the tiger.

"If this state continues until the body be dissolved

or changed into other matter, be dead, as we say, that same spirit which has been endowed with the cravings of lust and anger of a tiger, of exactly the same nature and feelings as those that have appeared in the body of the man before his death, may reappear now to find itself in the body of a tiger, suitable to its nature. Thus, so long as man is ignorant of that nature of Dharma, and fails to identify that nature, he continues to receive different impressions from beings around him in this universe, thereby sufferings, pains, sorrows, disappointments of all kinds, death.

"If, however, his spirit be impressed with the good qualities that are found in a superior being, such as the deva, for instance, by adopting in his own life the acts and wills of that superior being man becomes spiritually that superior being himself, both in nature and soul, even while in his present form. When death puts an end to his physical body a spirit of the very same nature and quality may reappear in the new body of a deva, to enjoy a life of happiness not to be compared to anything that is known in this world.

"However, to all beings alike, whether superior or inferior to ourselves, death is a suffering. It is, therefore, undesirable to be born into any being that is a modification of Dharma, to be sooner or later, again and again, dissolved by the eternal phenomenon of evolution. The only means by which we are able to free ourselves from sufferings and death is, therefore, to possess a perfect knowledge of Dharma, and to realize by will and acts that nature only obtainable by adhering to the precepts given by Lord Buddha in the four Noble Truths. The consciousness of self-being is a delusion, so that, until we are convinced that we ourselves and whatever belongs to ourselves is a mere nothingness, until we have lost the idea or impression that we are men, until that idea be completely annihilated and we have become united to Dharma, we are unable to reach spiritually the state of Nirvana, and that is only attained when the bodies dissolve both spiritually and physically. So that one should cease all petty longing for personal happiness, and remember that one life is as hollow as the other, that all is transitory and unreal.

"The true Buddhist does not mar the purity of his self-denial by lusting after a positive happiness which he himself shall enjoy here or hereafter. Ignorance of Dharma leads to sin, which leads to sorrow; and under these conditions of existence each new birth leaves man ignorant and finite still. What is to be hoped for is the absolute repose of Nirvana, the extinction of our being, nothingness. Allow me to give an illustration: A piece of rope is thrown in a dark road; a silly man passing by can not make out what it is. In his natural ignorance the rope appears to be a horrible snake, and immediately creates in him alarm, fright, and suffering. Soon light dwells upon him; he now realizes that what he took to be a snake is but a piece of rope. His alarm and fright are suddenly at an end; they are annihilated, as it were. The man now becomes happy and free from the suffering he has just experienced through his own folly.

"It is precisely the same with ourselves, our lives, our deaths, our alarms, our cries, our lamentations, our disappointments, and all other sufferings. They are created by our own ignorance of eternity, of the knowledge of Dharma to do away with and annihilate all of them.

"I shall now refer to the four Noble Truths as taught by our merciful and omniscient Lord Buddha; they point out the path that leads to Nirvana, or to the desirable extinction of self.

"The first noble truth is suffering; it arises from birth, old age, illness, sorrow, death, separation, and from what is loved, association with what is hateful, and, in short, the very idea of self in spirit and matters that constitute Dharma. The second Noble Truth is the cause of suffering which results from ignorance, creating lust for objects of a perishable nature. If the lust be for sensual objects it is called, in Pali, Kama Tanha. If it be for supersensual objects, belonging to the mind but still possessing a form in the mind, it is called Bhava Tanha. If the lust be pure for supersensual objects that belong to the mind, but are devoid of all form whatever, it is called Wibhava Tanha. The third Noble Truth is the extinction of sufferings, which is brought about by the cessation of the three kinds of lust, together with their accompanying evils, which all result directly from ignorance. The fourth Noble Truth is the means of paths that lead to the cessation of lusts and other evils. This Noble Truth is divided into the following eight paths: Right understanding, right resolutions, right speech, right acts, right way of earning a livelihood, right efforts, right meditation, right state of mind. A few words of explanation on these paths may not be out of place:

"By right understanding is meant proper comprehension, especially in regard to what we call sufferings. We should strive to learn the cause of our sufferings and the manner to alleviate and even to suppress them. We are not to forget that we are in this world to suffer; that wherever there is pleasure there is pain, and that, after all, pain and pleasure only exist according to human ideas.

"By right resolutions is meant that it is our imperative duty to act kindly to our fellow-creatures. We are to bear no malice against anybody and never seek revenge. We are to understand that in reality we exist in flesh and blood only for a short time, and that happiness and sufferings are transient or idealistic, and therefore we should try to control our desires and cravings and endeavor to be good and kind toward our fellow-creatures.

"By right speech is meant that we are always to speak the truth, never to incite one's anger toward others, but always to speak of things useful, and never use harsh words destined to hurt the feelings of others. By right acts is meant that we should never harm our fellow-creatures, neither steal, take life, nor commit adultery. Temperance and celibacy are also enjoined. By right way of earning a livelihood is meant that we are always to be honest and never to use wrongful or guilty means to attain an end. By right efforts is meant that we are to persevere in our endeavors to do good and to mend our conduct should we ever have strayed from the path of virtue. By right meditation is meant that we should always look upon life as being temporary, consider our existence as a source of suffering, and therefore endeavor always to calm our minds that may be excited by the sense of pleasure or pain. By right state of mind is meant that we should be firm in our belief, and be strictly indifferent both to the sense or feeling of pleasure and pain.

"It would be out of place here to enter into further details on the four Noble Truths; it would require too much time. I will, therefore, merely summarize their meanings and say that sorrow and sufferings are mainly due to ignorance, which creates in our minds lust, anger, and other evils. The extermination of all sorrow and suffering, and of all unhappiness, is attained by the eradication of ignorance and its evil consequences, and by replacing it with cultivation, knowledge, contentment, and love.

"Now comes the question, What is good and what is evil? Every act, speech, or thought derived from falsehood, or that which is injurious to others, is evil. Every act, speech, or thought derived from truth, and that which is not injurious to others, is good. Buddhism teaches that lust prompts avarice, anger creates animosity, ignorance produces false ideas. These are called evils because they cause pain. On the other hand, contentment prompts charity, love creates kindness, knowledge produces progressive ideas. These are called good because they give pleasure.

"The teachings of Buddhism on morals are numerous, and are divided into three groups of advantages: The advantage to be obtained in the present life, the advantage to be obtained in the future life, and the advantage to be obtained in all eternity. For each of these advantages there are recommended numerous paths to be followed by those who aspire to any one of them. I will only quote a few examples. To those who aspire to advantages in the present life Buddhism recommends diligence, economy, expenditure suitable to one's income, and association with the good. To those who aspire to the advantages of the future life are recommended charity, kindness, knowledge of right and wrong. To those who wish to enjoy the everlasting advantages in all eternity are recommended purity of conduct, of mind, and of knowledge.

"Allow me now to say a few words on the duties of man toward his wife and family, as preached by the Lord Buddha himself to the lay disciples in different discourses, or Sutras, as they are called in Pali. They belong to the group of advantages of present life. A good man is characterized by seven qualities. He should not be loaded with faults, he should be free from laziness, he should not boast of his knowledge, he should be truthful, benevolent, content, and should aspire to all that is useful.

"A husband should honor his wife, never insult her, never displease her, make her mistress of the house, and provide for her. On her part, a wife ought to be cheerful toward him when he works, entertain his friends and care for his dependents, to never do anything he does not wish, to take good care of the wealth he has accumulated, not to be idle, but always cheerful when at work herself.

"Parents in old age expect their children to take care of them, to do all their work and business, to maintain the household, and, after death, to do honor to their remains by being charitable. Parents help their children by preventing them from doing sinful acts, by guiding them in the path of virtue, by educating them, by providing them with husbands and wives suitable to them, by leaving them legacies. When poverty, accident, or misfortune befalls man, the Buddhist is taught to bear it with patience, and if these are brought on by himself it is his duty to discover their causes and try, if possible, to remedy them. If the causes, however, are not to be found here in this life he must account for them by the wrongs done in his former existence. Temperance is enjoined upon all Buddhists, for the reason that the habit of using intoxicating things tends to lower the mind to the level of that of an idiot, a madman, or an evil spirit.

"These are some of the doctrines and moralities taught by Buddhism, which I hope will give you an idea of the scope of the Lord Buddha's teachings. In closing this brief paper I earnestly wish you all, my brother religionists, the enjoyment of long life, happiness, and prosperity."

The gentle Dharmapala of Ceylon, who won all hearts by his refined intelligence, affectionate and uniform charity, and his zeal to lift all men out of

P. C. MOZOOMDAR,
Brahmo-Somaj, Calcutta, India.

gross selfishness, read on several occasions from an extended exposition of the teachings and influence of Buddhism. We quote here from his address the following showing of some points of difference and of resemblance between Buddhism and Christianity:

"Max Müller says: 'When a religion has ceased to produce champions, prophets, and martyrs, it had ceased to live in the true sense of the word, and the decisive battle for the dominion of the world would have to be fought out among the three missionary religions which are alive—Buddhism, Mohammedanism and Christianity.' Sir William W. Hunter, in his 'Indian Empire' (1893), says: 'The secret of Buddha's success was that he brought spiritual deliverance to the people. He preached that salvation was equally open to all men, and that it must be earned, not by propitiating imaginary deities, but by our own conduct. His doctrines thus cut away the religious basis of caste, and that of the efficiency of the sacrificial ritual, and assailed the supremacy of the Brahmans (priests) as the mediators between God and man.' Buddha taught that sin, sorrow, and deliverance, the state of man in this life, in all previous and in all future lives, are the inevitable results of his own acts (Karma). He thus applied the inexorable law of cause and effect to the soul. What a man sows he must reap.

"As no evil remains without punishment and no good deed without reward, it follows that neither priest nor God can prevent each act bearing its own consequences. Misery or happiness in this life is the unavoidable result of our conduct in a past life, and our actions here will determine our happiness or misery in the life to come. When any creature dies he is born again, in some higher or lower state of existence, according to his merit or demerit. His merit or demerit, that is, his character, consists of the sum total of his actions in all previous lives.

"By this great law of Karma Buddha explained the inequalities and apparent injustice of man's estate in this world as the consequence of acts in the past, while Christianity compensates those inequalities by rewards in the future. A system in which our whole well-being, past, present, and to come, depends on ourselves, theoretically, leaves little room for the interference, or even existence, of a personal God. But the atheism of Buddha was a philosophical tenet, which, so far from weakening the functions of right and wrong, gave them new strength from the doctrine of Karma, or the metempsychosis of character. To free ourselves from the thralldom of desire and from the fetters of selfishness was to attain to the state of the perfect disciple in this life and to the everlasting rest after death.

"The great practical aim of Buddha's teaching was to subdue the lusts of the flesh and the cravings of self, and this could only be attained by the practice of virtue. In place of rites and sacrifices Buddha prescribed a code of practical morality as the means of salvation. The four essential features of that code were: Reverence to spiritual teachers and parents, control over self, kindness to other men, and reverence for the life of all creatures. He urged on his disciples that they must not only follow the true path themselves, but that they should teach it to all mankind.

"The life and teachings of Buddha are also beginning to exercise a new influence on religious thought in Europe and America. Buddhism will stand forth as the embodiment of the eternal verity that as a man sows he will reap, associated with the duties of mastery over self and kindness to all men, and quickened into a popular religion by the example of a noble and beautiful life.

"Here are some Buddhist teachings as given in the words of Jesus and claimed by Christianity:

"'Whosoever cometh to me and heareth my sayings and doeth them, he is like a man which built a house and laid the foundation on a rock.

"'Why call ye me lord and do not the things which I say?

"'Judge not, condemn not, forgive.

"'Love your enemies and do good, hoping for nothing again, and your reward shall be great.

"'Blessed are they that hear the word of God and keep it.

"'Be ready, for the Son of Man cometh at an hour when ye think not.

"'Sell all that ye have and give it to the poor.

"'Soul, thou hast much goods laid up for many years; take thine ease, eat, drink, and be merry. But God said unto him, Thou fool, this night thy soul shall be required of thee, then whose shall these things be which thou hast provided?

"'The life is more than meat and the body more than raiment. Whosoever he be of you that forsaketh not all that he hath he can not be my disciple.

"'He that is faithful in that which is least is faithful in much.

"'Whosoever shall save his life shall lose it, and whosoever shall lose his life shall preserve it.

"'For behold the kingdom of God is within you.

"'There is no man that hath left house or parents, or brethren, or wife, or children for the kingdom of God's sake who shall not receive manifold more in this present time.

"'Take heed to yourselves lest at any time your hearts be overcharged with surfeiting and drunkenness and cares of this life. Watch ye, therefore, and pray always.'

"Here are some Buddhist teachings for comparison: 'Hatred does not cease by hatred at any time. Hatred ceases by love. This is an ancient law. Let us live happily, not hating those who hate us. Among men who hate us, let us live free from hatred. Let one overcome anger by love. Let him overcome evil by good. Let him overcome the greedy by liberality. Let the liar be overcome by truth.

"'As the bee, injuring not the flower, its color or scent, flies away, taking the nectar, so let the wise man dwell upon the earth.

"'Like a beautiful flower, full of color and full of scent, the fine words of him who acts accordingly are full of fruit.

"'Let him speak the truth, let him not yield to anger, let him give when asked, even from the little he has. By these things he will enter heaven.

"'The man who has transgressed one law and speaks lies and denies a future world, there is no sin he could not do.

"'The real treasure is that laid up through charity and piety, temperance and self-control; the treasure thus hid is secured, and passes not away.

"'He who controls his tongue, speaks wisely and is not puffed up, who holds up the torch to enlighten the world, his word is sweet.

"'Let his livelihood be kindness, his conduct righteousness; then in the fullness of gladness he will make an end of grief.

"'He who is tranquil and has completed his course, who sees truth as it really is, but is not partial when there are persons of different faith to be dealt with, who with firm mind overcomes ill will and covetousness, he is a true disciple.

"'As a mother, even at the risk of her own life, protects her son, her only son, so let each one cultivate good-will without measure among all beings.'

"Nirvana is a state to be realized here on this earth. He who has reached the fourth stage of holiness consciously enjoys the bliss of Nirvana. But it is beyond the reach of him who is selfish, skeptical, realistic, sensual, full of hatred, full of desire, proud, self-righteous, and ignorant. When by supreme and unceasing effort he destroys all selfishness and realizes the oneness of all beings; is free from all prejudices and dualism; when he by patient investigation discovers truth, the stage of holiness is reached.

"Among Buddhist ideals are self-sacrifice for the sake of others, compassion based on wisdom, joy in the hope that there is final bliss for the pure-minded, altruistic individual. The student of Buddha's religion takes the burden of life with sweet contentment; uprightness is his delight; he encompasses himself with holiness in word and deed; he sustains his life by means that are quite pure; good is his conduct; guarded the door of his senses; mindful and self-possessed, he is altogether happy.

"H. T. Buckle, the author of the 'History of Civilization,' says: 'A knowledge of Buddhism is necessary to the right understanding of Christianity. Buddhism is, besides, a most philosophical creed. Theologians should study it.'

"In his inaugural address delivered at the Congress of Orientals last year, Max Müller remarked: 'As to the religion of Buddha being influenced by foreign thought, no true scholar now dreams of that. The religion of Buddha is the daughter of the old Brahman religion, and a daughter in many respects more beautiful than the mother. On the contrary, it was through Buddhism that India, for the first time, stepped forth from its isolated position and became an actor in the historical drama of the world.'

"Doctor Hoey, in his preface to Doctor Oldberg's excellent work on Buddha, says: 'To thoughtful men who evince an interest in the comparative study of religious belief, Buddhism, as the highest effort of pure intellect to solve the problem of being, is attractive. It is not less so to the metaphysician and the sociologist who study the philosophy of the modern German pessimistic school and observe its social tendencies.'

"Dr. Rhys David says that Buddhism is a field of inquiry in which the only fruit to be gathered is knowledge. R. C. Dutt says: 'The moral teachings and precepts of Buddhism have so much in common with those of Christianity that some connection between the two systems of religion has long been suspected. Candid inquirers who have paid attention to the history of India and of the Greek world during the centuries immediately preceding the Christian era, and noted the intrinsic relationship which existed between these countries in scientific, religious, and literary ideas, found no difficulty in believing that Buddhist ideas and precepts penetrated into the Greek world before the birth of Christ. The discovery of the Asoka inscription of Hirnar, which tells us that that enlightened emperor of India made peace with five Greek kings, and sent Buddhist missionaries to preach his religion in Syria, explains to us the process by which the ideas were communicated. Researches into doctrines of the Therapeuts in Egypt and of the Essenes in Palestine leave no doubt, even in the minds of such devout Christian thinkers as Dean Mansel, that the movement which those sects embodied was due to Buddhist missionaries who visited Egypt and Palestine within two generations of the time of Alexander the Great. A few writers, like Benson, Seydal, and Lillie, maintain that the Christian religion has sprung directly from Buddhism.'"

JUDAISM.

Judaism was amply represented in its historic relation to the past and to the future; but for the purposes of this comparison by no one more ably, and on no occasion more fully, than in the address of Dr. Emil G. Hirsch of Chicago, on the last day of the congress, upon "The Elements of Universal Religion."

"The day of national religions," he said, "is past. The God of the universe speaks to all mankind. He is not the God of Israel alone, not that of Moab, of Egypt, Greece, or America. He is not domiciled in Palestine. The Jordan and the Ganges, the Tiber and the Euphrates hold water wherewith the devout may be baptized unto his service and redemption. 'Whither shall I go from thy spirit? whither flee from thy presence?' exclaims the old Hebrew bard. And before his wondering gaze unrolled itself the awful certainty that the heavenly divisions of morning and night were obliterated in the all-embracing sweep of divine law and love. If the wide expanses of the skies and abysses of the deep can not shut out from the divine presence, can the pigmy barriers erected by man and protected by political intrigues and national pride dam in the mighty stream of divine love? The prophet of Islam repeats the old Hebrew singer's joy when he says: 'The east is God's and the west is his,' as indeed the apostle, true to the spirit of the prophetic message of Messianic Judaism, refused to tolerate the line of cleavage marked by language or national affinity. Greek and Jew are invited by him to the citizenship of the kingdom to come.

"The church universal must have the pentecostal gift of the many flaming tongues in it, as the rabbis say was the case at Sinai. God's revelation must be sounded in every language, in every land. But, and this is essential as marking a new advance, the universal religion for all the children of Adam will not palisade its courts by the pointed and forbidding stakes of a creed. Creeds in time to come will be recognized to be indeed cruel barbed-wire fences, wounding those that would stray to broader pastures and hurting others who would come in. Will it for this be a Godless church? Ah, no; it will have much more of God than the churches and synagogues with their dogmatic definitions now possess. Coming man will not be ready to resign the crown of his glory which is his by virtue of his feeling himself to be the son of God. He will not exchange the church's creed for that still more presumptuous and deadening one of materialism which would ask his acceptance of the hopeless perversion that the world which sweeps by us in such sublime harmony and order is not cosmos, but chaos — is the fortuitous outcome of the chance play of atoms producing consciousness by the interaction of their own unconsciousness. Man will not extinguish the light of his own higher life by shutting his eyes to the telling indications of purpose in history, a purpose which when revealed to him in the outcome of his own career he may well find reflected also in the interrelated life of nature. But for all this man will learn a new modesty now wofully lacking to so many who honestly deem themselves religious. His God will not be a figment, cold and distant, of metaphysics, nor a distorted caricature of embittered theology. 'Can man by searching find out God?' asks the old Hebrew poet. And the ages so flooded with religious strife or vocal with the stinging rebuke to all creed-builders say that man can not. Man grows unto the knowledge of God, but not to him is vouchsafed that fullness of knowledge which would warrant his arrogance to hold that his blurred vision is the full light and that there can be none other.

"Says Maimonides, greatest thinker of the many Jewish philosophers of the middle ages: 'Of God we may merely assert that he is; what he is in himself we can not know. "My thoughts are not your thoughts and my ways are not your ways."' This prophetic caution will resound in clear notes in the ears of all who will worship in the days to come at the universal shrine. They will cease their futile efforts to give a definition of him who can not be defined in human symbols. They will certainly be astonished at our persistence — in their eyes very blasphemy — to describe by article of faith God, as though he were a fugitive from justice and a Pinkerton detective should be enabled to capture him by the identification laid down in the catalogue of his attributes. The religion universal will not presume to regulate God's government of this world by circumscribing the sphere of his possible salvation and declaring, as though he had taken us into his counsel, whom he must save and whom he may not save. The universal religion will once more make the God idea a vital principle of human life. It will teach men to find him in their own hearts and to have him with them in whatever they may do. No mortal has seen God's face, but he who opens his heart to the message will, like Moses on the lonely rock, behold him pass and hear the solemn proclamation.

"It is not in the storm of fanaticism nor in the fire of prejudice, but in the still, small voice of conscience, that God speaks and is to be found. He believes in God who lives a godlike, *i. e.*, a goodly, life. Not he that mumbles his credo, but he who lives it, is accepted. Were those marked for glory by the great Teacher of Nazareth who wore the largest phylacteries? Is the sermon on the mount a creed? Was the decalogue a creed? Character and conduct, not creed, will be the key-note of the gospel in the Church of Humanity Universal.

"But what then about sin? Sin as a theological imputation will perhaps drop out of the vocabulary of this larger communion of the righteous. But as a weakness to be overcome, an imperfection to be laid aside, man will be as potently reminded of his natural shortcomings as he is now of that of his first progenitor, over whose conduct he certainly had no control, and for whose misdeed he should not be held accountable. Religion will then, as now, lift man above his weaknesses by reminding him of his responsibilities. The goal before is Paradise. Eden is to rise. It has not yet been. .And the life of the great and good and saintly, who went about doing good in their generations, and who died that others might live, will for very truth be pointed out as the spring from which have flowed the waters of salvation, by whose magic efficacy all men may be washed clean, if baptized in the spirit which was living within these God-appointed redeemers, of their infirmities.

"This religion will indeed be for man to lead him to God. Its sacramental word will be duty. Labor is not the curse but the blessing of human life. For as man was made in the image of the Creator, it is his to create. Earth was given him for his habitation. He changed it from Tohu into his home. A theology and a monotheism which will not leave room in this world for man's free activity and dooms him to passive inactivity will not harmonize with the truer recognition that man and God are the correlates of a working plan of life. Sympathy and resignation are indeed beautiful flowers grown in the garden of many a tender and noble human heart. But it is active love and energy which alone can push on the chariot of human progress, and progress is the gradual realization of the divine spirit which is incarnate in every human being. This principle will assign to religion once more the place of honor among the redeeming agencies of society from the bondage of selfishness. On this basis every man is every other man's brother, not merely in misery, but in active work. 'As you have done to the least of these you have unto me' will be the guiding principle of human conduct in all the relations into which human life enters. No more than Cain's enormous excuse, a scathing accusation of himself, 'Am I my brother's keeper?' no longer will be tolerated or condoned the double standard of morality, one for Sunday and the church and another diametrically opposed for week-days and the counting-room. Not as now will be heard the cynic insistence that 'business is business' and has as business no connection with the decalogue or the sermon on the mount. Religion will, as it did in Jesus, penetrate into all the relations of human society. Not then will men be rated as so many hands to be bought at the lowest possible price, in accordance with a deified law of supply and demand, which can not stop to consider such sentimentalities as the fact that these hands stand for souls and hearts.

"An invidious distinction obtains now between secular and sacred. It will be wiped away. Every thought and every deed of man must be holy or it is unworthy of men. Did Jesus merely regard the temple as holy? Did Buddha merely have religion on one or two hours of the Sabbath? Did not an earlier prophet deride and condemn all ritual religion? 'Wash ye, make ye clean.' Was this not the burden of Isaiah's religion? The religion universal will be true to these, its forerunners.

"But what about death and hereafter? This religion will not dim the hope which has been man's since the first day of his stay on earth; but it will be most emphatic in winning men to the conviction that a life worthily spent here on earth is the best.

is the only preparation for heaven. Said the old rabbis: 'One hour spent here in truly good works and in the true intimacy with God is more precious than all life to be.' The egotism which now mars so often the aspirations of our souls, the scramble for glory which comes while we forget duty, will be replaced by a serene trust in the eternal justice of him 'in whom we live and move and have our being.' To have done religiously will be a reward sweeter than which none can be offered. Yea, the religion of the future will be impatient of men who claim that they have the right to be saved, while they are perfectly content that others shall not be saved, and while not stirring a foot or lifting a hand to redeem brother men from hunger and wretchedness, in the cool assurance that this life is destined or doomed to be a free race of haggling, snarling competitors in which by some mysterious will of Providence the devil takes the hindmost.

"Will there be prayer in the universal religion? Man will worship, but in the beauty of holiness his prayer will be the prelude to his prayerful action. Silence is more reverential and worshipful than a wild torrent of words breathing forth not adoration but greedy requests for favors to self. Can an unforgiving heart pray, 'Forgive as we forgive?' Can one ask for daily bread when he refuses to break his bread with the hungry? Did not the prayer of the great Master of Nazareth thus teach all men and all ages that prayer must be the stirring to love? Had not that little waif caught the inspiration of our universal prayer who, when first taught its sublime phrases, persisted in changing the opening words to 'Your father which is in heaven?' Rebuked time and again by the teacher, he finally broke out, 'Well, if it is our father, why, I am your brother.' Yea, the gates of prayer in the church to rise will lead to the recognition of the universal brotherhood of man.

"Will this new faith have its Bible? It will. It retains the old Bibles of mankind, but gives them a new luster by remembering that 'the letter killeth, but the spirit giveth life.' Religion is not a question of literature, but of life. God's revelation is continuous, not contained in tablets of stone or sacred parchment. He speaks to-day yet to those that would hear him. A book is inspired when it inspires. Religion made the Bible, not the book religion.

"And what will be the name of this church? It will be known not by its founders, but by its fruits God replies to him who insists upon knowing his name: 'I am he who I am.' The church will be. If any name it will have, it will be 'the church of God,' because it will be the church of man.

"When Jacob, so runs an old rabbinical legend, weary and footsore the first night of his sojourn away from home, would lay him down to sleep under the canopy of the star-set skies, all the stones of the field exclaimed: 'Take me for thy pillow.' And because all were ready to serve him all were miraculously turned into one stone. This became Beth El, the gate of heaven. So will all religions, because eager to become the pillow of man, dreaming of God and beholding the ladder joining earth to heaven, be transformed into one great rock which the ages can not move, a foundation-stone for the all-embracing temple of humanity united to God's will with one accord."

This address, most enthusiastically received, shows not only the new spirit of Judaism, but represents the popular discontent with artificial, traditional, and formal religions, and the demand for reality. It was notable, not for its definitions, or the new light thrown upon religious questions, but for its demand that a man shall be and do what he believes. Christians and men of the world, listening, each defining "religion" for himself, yet enthusiastically applauded this appeal for reality and genuineness; and this the more because uttered by a representative of Judaism.

MOHAMMEDANISM.

A religion which holds influence over such multitudes, whole tribes and nations having been reclaimed by it from idolatry, naturally received a prominent place, and awakened much interest. There has been noticeable in recent years, moreover, a change in the attitude of Christians toward Mohammedanism. Whereas it was formerly attributed to satanic agency, recently there has grown up a spirit of tolerance, not only, but a recognition in it of a mission from above, called for by the state of the Eastern nations, and brought forth 'in the Divine Providence. One feels some disappointment in the papers of Mohammed Webb on "The Spirit of Islam" and "The Influence of Islam on Social Conditions," which are confined almost exclusively to the superficial features of the Moslem religion. Some passages brought together from the two addresses delivered by him may serve our present purpose. Defining Islam, he said:

"Now let us see what the word Islam means. It is the most expressive word in existence for a religion. It means simply and literally resignation to the will of God. It means aspiration to God. The Islam system is designed to cultivate all that is purest and noblest and grandest in the human character. Some people say Islam is impossible in a high state of civilization. Now that is the result of ignorance. Look at Spain in the eighth century, when it was the center of all the arts and sciences, when Christian Europe went to Moslem Spain to learn all that there was worth knowing — languages, arts, all the new discoveries were to be found in Moslem Spain, and in Moslem Spain alone. There was no civilization in the world as high as that of Moslem Spain.

"With this spirit of resignation to the will of God is inculcated the idea of individual responsibility, that every man is responsible, not to this man, or that man, or the other man, but responsible to God for every thought and act of his life. He must pay for every act that he commits; he is rewarded for every thought he thinks. There is no mediator, there is no priesthood, there is no ministry.

"The Moslem brotherhood stands upon a perfect

equality, recognizing only the fatherhood of God and the brotherhood of man. The emir, who leads in prayer, preaches no sermon. He goes to the mosque every day at noon and reads two chapters from the holy Koran. He descends to the floor, upon a perfect level with the hundreds, or thousands, of worshipers, and the prayer goes on, he simply leading it. The whole system is calculated to inculcate that idea of perfect brotherhood.

"The subject is so broad, there is so much of it that I can only touch upon it. There is so much unfamiliar to Americans and Englishmen in Islam that I regret exceedingly I have not more time to speak of it. A man said to me in New York the other day: 'Must I give up Jesus and the Bible if I become a Mohammedan?' No, no! There is no Mussulman on earth who does not recognize the inspiration of Jesus. The system is one that has been taught by Moses, by Abraham, by Jesus, by Mohammed, by every inspired man the world has ever known. You need not give up Jesus, but assert your manhood. Go to God.

"Now, let us look at the practical side of Islam in reference to the application of the spirit of Islam to daily life. A Mussulman is told that he must pray. So is everyone else; so are the followers of every other religion. But the Mussulman is not told to pray when he feels like it, if it does not interfere with business, with his inclinations, or some particular engagement. Some people do not pray at such times; they say it does not make very much difference, we can make it up some other time. A little study of human nature will show that there are people who pray from a conscientious idea of doing a duty, but there are a great many others who shirk a duty at every chance if it interferes with pleasure or business. The wisdom of Mohammed was apparent in the single item of prayer. He did not say, 'Pray when you feel like it,' but 'Pray five times a day at a certain time.' Stated in the briefest manner possible, the Islamic system requires belief in the unity of God and in the inspiration of Mohammed. Its pillars of practice are physical and mental cleanliness, prayer, fasting, fraternity, almsgiving, and pilgrimage. There is nothing in it that tends to immorality, social degradation, nor fanaticism. On the contrary, it leads on to all that is purest and noblest in the human character; and any professed Mussulman who is unclean in his person or habits, or is cruel, untruthful, dishonest, irreverent, or fanatical, fails utterly to grasp the meaning of the religion he professes.

"But there is something more in the system than the mere teaching of morality and personal purity. It is thoroughly practical, and the results, which are plainly apparent among the more intelligent Moslems, show how well the prophet understood human nature. It will not produce the kind of civilization that we Americans seem to admire so much, but it will make a man sober, honest, and truthful, and will make him love his God with all his heart and all his mind, and his neighbor as himself. Every Mussulman who has not become demoralized by contact with British civilization prays five times a day; not whenever he happens to feel like it, but at fixed periods. His prayer is not a servile, cringing petition for some material benefit, but a hymn of praise to the one incomprehensible, unknowable God, the omnipotent, omniscient, omnipresent ruler of the universe. He does not believe that by argument and entreaty he can sway the judgment and change the plans of God; but with all the force of his soul he tries to soar upward in spirit to where he can gain strength to be pure and good and holy, and worthy of the happiness of the future life. His purpose is to rise above the selfish pleasures of earth, and strengthen his spirit wings for a lofty flight when he is at last released from the body.

"Before every prayer he is required to wash his face, nostrils, mouth, hands, and feet, and he does it. During youth he acquires the habit of washing himself five times a day, and this habit clings to him through life and keeps him physically clean. He comes in touch with his religion five times a day in a manner which produces results proportionate to the intelligence and spiritual development of the man. His religion is not a thing apart from his daily life, to be put on once a week, and thrown aside when it threatens to interfere with his business or pleasure. It is a fixed and inseparable part of his existence, and exerts a direct and potent influence on his every thought and act. Is it to be wondered at that his idea of civilization differs from that of the West? That it is less active and progressive, less grand and imposing, and dazzling and noisy? I will confess that when I went to live among the intelligent Mussulmans I was astonished beyond measure at the social conditions I encountered. I had acquired the idea that prevails generally in this country and Europe, and was prepared to find the professed followers of Islam selfish, treacherous, untruthful, intolerant, sensual, and fanatical. I was very agreeably disappointed. I saw the practical results of Islam manifested in honesty, truthfulness, sobriety, tolerance, gentleness, and a degree of true brotherly love that was a surprise to me. The evils that we Americans complain of in our social system — drunkenness, prostitution, marital infidelity, and cold selfishness — were almost entirely absent."

THE ROMAN CATHOLIC CHURCH.

Throughout the series of congresses the interest and activity of the Catholic church was conspicuous; and in the deliverances before the parliament none surpassed its representatives in the generosity of love for the good of all men, combined with the quiet dignity of faith in its divine authority and mission to help men. If the individual, as Prince Wolkonsky said, in proportion to the strength of his individual qualities, seeks the more to merge himself in the church, it is because he has persuaded himself that the church is of God, and that he speaks through it as an organic whole. This was the conclusion presented by Bishop Keane, rector of the Catholic University of America, in his address on "The Center and Character of the Ultimate

Religion," at the last session of the parliament. If the conclusion was to be expected, it may surprise some to observe the breadth of his recognition of good and truth in all religions.

Starting out with congratulations at the meeting of God's long-separated children to clasp hands in friendship and in brotherhood, he said: "We have had practical and experimental evidence of the truth of the old saying that 'there is truth in all religions.'" And he stated explicitly what was none too often remembered: "It is because the human family started from unity, from one undivided treasury of truth, and when the separations and wanderings came they carried with them what they could of the treasure. No wonder that we all recognize the common possession of the olden truth when we come together at last.

"Then we have heard repeated and multifarious, yet concordant definitions of what religion really is, viewed in all its aspects; we have seen how true is the old definition that religion means the union of man with God. This, we have seen, is the great goal toward which all aim, whether walking in the fullness of the light or groping in the dimness of the twilight. And therefore we have seen how true it is that religion is a reality back of all religions. Religions are orderly or disorderly systems for the attainment of that great end, the union of man with God. Any system not having that for its aim may be a philosophy, but can not be a religion!

"And therefore, again, we have clearly recognized that religion, in itself and in the system for its attainment, necessarily implies two sides, two constitutive elements — the human and the divine, man's side to God's side, in the union and in the way or means to it. The human side of it, the craving, the need, the aspiration, is, as here testified, universal among men. And this is a demonstration that the author of our nature is not wanting as to his side; that the essential religiousness of man is not a meaningless trick of nature; that the craving is not a Tantalus in man's heart meant only for his delusion and torture. This parliament has thus been a weighty blow to atheism, to deism, to antagonism, to naturalism, to mere humanism. While the utterances of these various philosophies have been listened to with courage and charity, yet its whole meaning and moral has been to the contrary; the whole drift of its practical conclusion has been that man and the world never could, and in the nature of things never can, do without God, and so it is a blessing.

"From this standpoint, therefore, on which our feet are so plainly and firmly planted by this parliament, we look forward and ask, Has religion a future, and what is that future to be like? Again in the facts which we have been studying during these seventeen days we find the data to guide us to the answer. Here we have heard the voice of all the nations, yea, and of all the ages, certifying that the human intellect must have the great first cause and last end as the alpha and omega of its thinking; that there can be no philosophy of things without God.

"Here we have heard the cry of the human heart

all the world over that without God life would not be worth living. We have heard the verdict of human society in all its ranks and conditions, the verdict of those who have most intelligently and most disinterestedly studied the problem of the improvement of human conditions, that only the wisdom and power of religion can solve the mighty social problems of the future, and that in proportion as the world advances toward the perfection of self-government, the need of religion as a balance-power in every human life, and in the relations of man with man and of nation with nation, becomes more and more imperative. Next we must ask, Shall the future tendency of religion be to greater unity, or to greater diversity?

"This parliament has brought out in clear light the old familiar truth that religion has a two-fold aim — the improvement of the individual and, through that, the improvement of society and of race; that it must, therefore, have in its system of organization and its methods of action a two-fold tendency and plan on the one side to what might be called religious individualism, on the other side what may be termed religious socialism or solidarity; on the one side, adequate provision for the dealings of God with the individual soul; on the other, provision for the order, the harmony, the unity, which is always a characteristic of the works of God, and which is equally the aim of wisdom in human things, for 'order is heaven's first law.'

"The parliament has also shown that, if it may be truly alleged that there have been times when solidarity pressed too heavily on individualism, at present the tendency is to an extreme of individualism threatening to fill the world more and more with religious confusion and distract the minds of men with religious contradictions.

"But on what basis, what method, is religious unity to be attained or approached? Is it to be by a process of elimination, or by a process of synthesis? Is it to be by laying aside all disputed elements, no matter how manifestly true and beautiful and useful, so as to reach at last the simplest form of religious assertion, the protoplasm of the religious organism? Or, on the contrary, is it to be by the acceptance of all that is manifestly true, and good, and useful, of all that is manifestly from the heart of God as well as from the heart of humanity, so as to attain to the developed and perfected organism of religion? To answer this momentous question wisely let us glance at analogies.

"First, in regard to human knowledge, we are, and must be, willing to go down to the level of uninformed or imperfectly informed minds; not, however, to make that the intellectual level of all, but in order that from that low level we may lead up to the higher and higher levels which knowledge has reached. In like manner as to civilization, we are willing to meet the barbarian or the savage on his own low level, not in order to assimilate our condition to his, but in order to lead him up to better conditions. So also in scientific research we go down to the study of the protoplasm and of the cell, but only in order that we may trace the process of differentiation, of accretion, of development by which higher and higher forms of organization lead to the highest. In the light, therefore, of all the facts here placed before us, let us ask to what result gradual development will lead us.

"In the first place, this comparison of all the principal religions of the world has demonstrated that the only worthy and admissible idea of God is that of monotheism. It has shown that polytheism in all its forms is only a rude degeneration. It has proved that pantheism in all its modifications, obliterating as it does the personality both of God and of man, is no religion at all, and therefore inadmissible as such. That it can not even be admitted as a philosophy, since its very first postulates are metaphysical contradictions. Hence, the basis of all religion is the belief in the one living God.

"Next, this parliament has shown that humanity repudiates the gods of the Epicureans, who were so taken up with their own enjoyment that they had no thought for poor man, and nothing to say to him for his instruction and no care to bestow on him for his welfare. It has shown that the god of agnosticism is only the god of the Epicureans dressed up in modern garb and that he cares nothing for humanity, but leaves it in the dark; humanity cares nothing for him and is willing to leave him to his unknowableness. As the first step in the solid ascent of the true religion is belief in the one living God, so the second must be the belief that the great Father has taught his children what they need to know and what they need to be in order to attain their destiny, that is, belief in divine revelation.

"Again, the parliament has shown that all the attempts of the tribes of earth to recall and set forth God's teaching, all their endeavors to tell of the means provided by the Almighty God for uniting man with himself, logically and historically lead up to and culminate in Jesus Christ. The world longing for the truth points to him who brings its fullness. The world's sad wail over the wretchedness of sin points not to despairing escape from the thralls of humanity — a promise of escape which is only an impossibility and a delusion — but to humanity's cleansing, and uplifting, and restoration in his redemption. The world's craving for union with the divine finds its archetypal glorious realization in his incarnation, and to a share in that wondrous union all are called as branches of the mystical vine, members of the mystical body, which lifts humanity above its natural state and pours into it the life of love.

"Therefore does the verdict of the ages proclaim in the words of the apostle of the Gentiles, who knew him and knew all the rest: 'Other foundation can no man lay but that which God hath laid, which is Christ Jesus.' As long as God is God and man is man, Jesus Christ is the center of religion forever.

"But, still further, we have seen that Jesus Christ is not a myth, not a symbol, but a personal reality. He is not a vague, shadowy personality, leaving only a dim, vague, mystical impression behind him; he is a clear and definite personality, with a clear and definite teaching as to truth, clear and definite command as to duty, clear and definite ordaining as to the means by which God's life is imparted to man and by which man receives it, corresponds to it, and advances toward perfection.

"The wondrous message he sent 'to every creature,' proclaiming, as it had never been proclaimed before, the value and the rights of each individual soul, the sublimest individualism the world has ever heard of. And then, with the heavenly balance and equilibrium which brings all individualities into order, and harmony, and unity, he calls all to be sheep of one fold, branches of one vine, members of one body, in which all, while members of one head, are also 'members one of another,' in which is the fulfillment of his own sublime prayer and prophecy: 'That all may be one, as thou, Father, in me, and I in thee, that they also may be one in us, that they may be made perfect in one.'

"Thus he makes his church a perfect society, both human and divine; on its human side the most perfect multiplicity in unity and unity in multiplicity, the most perfect socialism and solidarity that the world could ever know; on its divine side, the instrumentality devised by the Saviour of the world for imparting, maintaining, and operating the action of the divine life in each soul; in its entirety, the body, the vine, both divine and human, a living organism, imparting the life of God to humanity. This is the way in which the church of

Christ is presented to us by the apostles and by our Lord himself. It is a concrete individuality, as distinct and unmistakable as himself. It is no mere aggregation, no mere coöperation or confederation of distinct bodies; it is an organic unity, it is the body of Christ, our means of being ingrafted in him and sharing in his life."

Many who felt the bishop mistaken in his conclusion that the Catholic church is the organic body of Christ, presented by the apostles and kept in living integrity by the spirit of the Lord from the beginning for its ultimate perfection, could not but feel the majesty of the conception, and the ultimate certainty of some such realization, even if only in a spiritual and invisible bond, when he concluded with these words: "Jesus Christ is the ultimate center of religion. He has declared that his one organic church is equally ultimate. Because I believe him, here must be my stand forever."

THE GREEK CHURCH.

One of the most eloquent and every way remarkable of the addresses before the parliament was the oration of Archbishop Latus, on the part of Greece and the Greek church in the history of Christianity. It set forth in noble review the intellectual preparation of the world for Christianity through the influence of Grecian learning and philosophy.

"Ancient Greece prepared the way for Christianity, and rendered smooth the path for the diffusion and propagation of it in the world Greece undertook to develop Christianity, and formed and systematized a Christian church; that is the church of the East, the original Christian church, which for this reason historically and justly may be called the mother of the Christian churches. The original establishment of the Greek church is directly referred to the presence of Jesus Christ and his apostles. The coming of the Messiah, from which the kingdom of God was to originate in this world, was at a fixed point of time, as the Apostle Paul said. The fullness of this point of time ancient Greece was predestined to point out and determine. Greece had so developed letters, arts, sciences, philosophy, and every other form of progress, that in comparison with it all other nations were exhausted. For this reason the inhabitants of that happy land used rightly and properly to say: 'Whoever is not a Greek is a barbarian.' But while at that time, under Plato and Aristotle, Greek philosophy had arrived at the highest phase of its development, Greece at that very period, after these great philosophers, began to decline and fall. The Macedonian and Roman armies gave a definite blow to the political independence and national liberty of Greece, but at the same time opened up to Greece a new career of spiritual life, and brought them into immediate contact and intercommunication with other nations and peoples of the earth."

Tracing then the development of Grecian philosophy in Alexandria, and its contact there with Judaism, and the reflex effect upon Grecian thought, the archbishop proceeded to show the relation of this intellectual preparation to the reception of Christianity.

"When the Roman Empire began to fall Christianity had to undertake the great struggle of acquiring superiority over all other religions that it might demolish the partition walls which separated race from race, nation from nation. It is the work of Christianity to bring all men into one spiritual family, into the love of one another, and into the belief of one supreme God. Mary, the most blessed of all human kind, appears and brings forth the expected divine nature, revealed to Plato. She brings forth the fulfillment of the ideals of the Gods of the different peoples and nations of the ancient world. She brings forth at last that one whose name, whose shadow came down into the world and overshadowed the souls, the minds, the hearts of all men, and removed the mystery from every philosophy and philosophic system.

"In this permanent idea and the tendencies of the different peoples in such a time and religion, I may say two voices are heard. One, though it is from Palestine, reëchoed into Egypt, and especially to Alexandria and through parts of Greece and Rome. Another voice from Egypt reëchoed through Palestine, and through it over all the other countries and peoples of the East. And the voices from Palestine, having Jerusalem as their focus and center, reëchoed the voice back again to the Grecians and the Romans. And there it was that his doctrine fell amidst the Greek nations, the Grecian elements of character, Greek letters, and the sound reasoning of different systems of Greek philosophy.

"Surely in the regeneration of the different peoples there had been a divine revelation in the formation of all human kind into one spiritual family through the goodness of God. In one family equal, without any distinctions between the mean and the great, without distinction of climate or race, without distinction of national destiny or inspiration, of name or nobility, or family ties. And all the beauties which ever clustered around the ladder of Jacob, or were given to it by the men of Judea, were given by the prophets to the Virgin Mary in the cave of Bethlehem. But Greece gave Christianity the letters, gave the art, gave, as I may say, the enlightenment with which the Gospel of Christianity was invested, and presented itself then and now presents itself before all nations."

Following the history of the introduction of Christianity into Greece, reciting in magnificent declamation Paul's sermon on Mars Hill, translating and applying it in scarcely less remarkable English, he concluded:

"It suffices me to say that no one of you, I believe, in the presence of these historical documents will deny that the original Christian, the first Christan church was the church of the East, and that is the Greek church. Surely the first Christian churches in Asia Minor, Egypt, and Assyria were instituted by the apostles of Christ and for the most part in Greek communities. All those are the foundation-stones on which the present Greek

MOST REV. DIONYSIOS LATUS,
Archbishop of Zante, Greece.

church is based. The apostles themselves preached and wrote in the Greek letters, and all the teachers and writers of the gospel in the East, the contemporaries and the successors of the apostles, were teaching, preaching, and writing in the Greek language. Especially the two great schools, that of Alexandria and that of Antioch, undertook to develop Christianity and form and systematize a Christian church. The great teachers and writers of these two schools, whose names are very well known, labored courageously to defend and determine forever the Christian doctrine and to constitute under divine rules and forms a Christian church. At last the Greek church, therefore, may be called historically and justly the treasurer of the first Christian doctrine, fundamental evangelical truths. It may be called the ark which bears the spiritual manna and feeds all those who look to it in order to obtain from it the richness of the ideas and the unmistakable reasoning of every Christian doctrine, of every evangelical truth, of every ecclesiastical sentiment.

"After this my oration about the Greek church I have nothing more to add than to extend my open arms and embrace all those who attend this congress of the ministers of the world. I embrace, as my brothers in Jesus Christ, as my brothers in the divinely inspired gospel, as my friends in eminent ideas and sentiments, all men; for we have a common creator, and consequently a common father and God. And I pray you lift with me for a moment the mind toward the divine presence, and say with me, with all your minds and hearts, a prayer to Almighty God."

Here the grand old churchman lifted his hands and his eyes heavenward, and said:

"Most High, Omnipotent King, look down upon human kind; enlighten us that we may know thy will, thy ways, thy holy truths. Bless and magnify the reunited peoples of the world and the great people of the United States of America, whose greatness and kindness has invited us from the remotest parts of the earth in this their Columbian year to see with them an evidence of their progress in the wonderful achievements of the human mind and the human soul."

JAPANESE CRITICISM AND APPEAL.

On more than one occasion Christendom and Christianity, as represented by missionaries and Christian civilization, came in for severe criticism from the representatives of other religions.

Kinza Riuge Hirai of Japan created quite a sensation by an earnest assault upon the treatment of Japan by so-called Christian nations. Among other things in his arraignment he said:

"Admitting, for the sake of argument, that we are idolaters and heathen, is it Christian morality to trample upon the rights and advantages of a non-Christian nation, coloring all their natural happiness with the dark stain of injustice? I read in the Bible, 'Whosoever shall smite thee on thy right cheek, turn to him thy left also'; but I can not discover there any passage which says, 'Whosoever shall demand justice of thee smite his right cheek, and when he turns smite the other also.' Again I read in the Bible, 'If any man will sue thee at law, and take away thy coat, let him have thy cloak also'; but I can not discover there any passage which says, 'If thou shalt sue any man at the law, and take away his coat, let him give thee his cloak also.' You send your missionaries to Japan and they advise us to be moral and believe Christianity. We like to be moral; we know that Christianity is good; and we are very thankful for this kindness; but at the same time our people are rather perplexed and very much in doubt about this advice. For we think that the treaty stipulated in the time of feudalism, when we were yet in our youth, is still clung to by the powerful nations of Christendom; when we find that every year a good many western vessels engaged in the seal fishery are smuggled into our seas; when legal cases are decided by the foreign authorities in Japan unfavorably to us; when some years a Japanese was not allowed to enter a university on the Pacific Coast of America because of his being of a different race; when a few months ago the school board of San Francisco enacted a regulation that no Japanese should be allowed to enter the public school there; when last year the Japanese were driven out in wholesale from one of the territories of the United States of America; when our business men in San Francisco were compelled by some union not to employ the Japanese assistants or laborers, but the Americans; when there are some in the same city who speak on the platforms against those of us who are already here; when there are many men who go in processions hoisting lanterns marked 'Jap must go'; when the Japanese in the Hawaiian Islands are deprived of their suffrage; when we see some western people in Japan who erect before the entrance of their houses a special post upon which is the notice, 'No Japanese is allowed to enter here,' just like a board upon which is written, 'No dogs allowed'; when we are in such a situation is it unreasonable — notwithstanding the kindness of the western nations, from one point of view, who send their missionaries to us — for us intelligent heathen to be embarrassed and hesitate to swallow the sweet and warm liquid of the heaven of Christianity? If such be the Christian ethics, well, we are perfectly satisfied to be heathen.

"If any person should claim that there are many people in Japan who speak and write against Christianity, I am not a hypocrite and I will frankly state that I was the first in my country who ever publicly attacked Christianity — no, not real Christianity, but false Christianity, the wrongs done toward us by the people of Christendom. If any reprove the Japanese because they have had strong anti-Christian societies, I will honestly declare that I was the first in Japan who ever organized a society against Christianity — no, not against real Christianity, but to protect ourselves from false Christianity and the injustice which we receive from the people of Christendom. Do not think that I took such a stand on account of my being a Buddhist, for this was my position many years before I entered the Buddhist temple; but at the same time I will proudly state that if any one discussed the affinity of all religions before the public, under the title of Synthetic Religion, it was I. I say this to you because I do not wish to be understood as a bigoted Buddhist sectarian.

"Really there is no sectarian in my country. Our people well know what abstract truth is in Christianity, and we, or at least I, do not care about the names if I speak from the point of teaching. Whether Buddhism is called Christianity or Christianity is named Buddhism, whether we are called Confucianists or Shintoists, we are not particular; but we are very particular about the truth taught and its consistent application. Whether Christ saves us or drives us into hell, whether Gautama Buddha was a real person or there never was such a man, it is not a matter of consideration to us, but the consistency of doctrine and conduct is the point on which we put the greater importance. Therefore unless the inconsistency which we observe is renounced, and especially the unjust treaty by which we are entailed is revised upon an equitable basis, our people will never cast away their prejudices about Christianity, in spite of the eloquent orator who speaks its truth from the pulpit. We are very often called barbarians, and I have heard and read that Japanese are stubborn and can not understand the truth of the Bible. I will admit that this is true in some sense, for, though they admire the eloquence of the orator and wonder at his courage, though they approve his logical argument, yet they are very stubborn and will not join Christianity as long as they think it is a western morality to preach one thing and practice another."

Far more significant than this criticism of the breach between Christian theory and practice is an appeal made at a later day from the Christianity of the sects to the Christianity of the gospels. N. Kishimoto, speaking of the future of religion in Japan, pointed out that "that country is the battlefield between religion and no religion, and also between Christianity and other systems of religion," and in concluding said:

"In my mind there is no doubt that Christianity will survive in this struggle for existence and become the future religion of the land of the rising sun. My reasons for this are numerous, but I must be brief. In the first place, Christianity claims to be and is the universal religion. It teaches one God, who is the father of all mankind, but is so pliable that it can adapt itself to any environment, and then it can transform and assimilate the environment to itself. This is amply proved by its history. In the second place, Christianity is inclusive. It is a living organism, a seed or germ which is capable of growth and development and which will leaven all the nations of the world. In growing it draws and can draw its nutritious elements from any sources. It survives the struggle of existence and feeds and grows on the flesh of the fallen.

"In the third place, Christianity teaches that man was created in the image of God. The human is divine and the divine is human. Here lies the merit of Christianity, in uplifting man, all human beings — young and old, men and women, the governing and the governed — to their proper position. In the fourth place, Christianity teaches love to God and love to men as its fundamental teaching. The golden rule is the glory of Christianity, not because it was originated by Christ — this rule was also taught by Buddha and Lao-tsee many centuries before — but because he properly emphasized it by his words and by his life. In the fifth place, Christianity requires every man to be perfect, as the Father in heaven is perfect. Here lies the basis for the hope of man's infinite development in science, in art, and in character — in one word, in perfection. In brief these are some of the reasons which make me think that sooner or later Christianity will, as it ought to, become the future religion of Japan.

"If Christianity will triumph and become the religion of Japan, which form of Christianity, or Christianity of which denomination, will become the religion of Japan? Catholic Christianity or Protestant Christianity? We do not want Catholic Christianity, nor do we want Protestant Christianity. We want the Christianity of the Bible, nay, the Christianity of Christianity. We do not want the Christianity of England nor the Christianity of America; we want the Christianity of Japan. On the whole, it is better to have different sects and denominations than to have lifeless monotony. The Christian church should observe the famous saying of St. Vincent: 'In essentials, unity;

in non-essentials, liberty; in all things charity.' We Japanese want the Christianity of the Christ. We want the truth of Christianity; nay, we want the truth pure and simple. We want the spirit of the Bible and not its letter. We hope for the union of all Christians, at least in spirit if not possible in form. But we Japanese Christians are hoping more; we are ambitious to present to the world one new and unique interpretation of Christianity as it is presented in our Bible, which knows no sectarian controversy and which knows no heresy hunting. Indeed, the time is coming, and ought to come, when God shall be worshiped, not by rites and ceremonies, but he shall be worshiped in spirit and in truth."

This voice from the Orient will be hailed by many as a hopeful portent. If some despair of anything better in the effort of native churches to find in the Gospels the religion of Jesus Christ, others, more hopeful and more faithful, will see in that effort the promise of a true Christian church that may yet become the teacher of a Christendom that has lost its teaching power through the falsities of centuries' inventing. And this aspiration after a new and native form of Christianity, free from the dogmas of Western theologies, and suited to the genius of the oriental mind, recalls another form of faith; a reform in the religion of India which its founder, Cheshub Chunder Senn, proclaimed as "The New Dispensation in India."

THE BRAHMO-SOMAJ.

Much interest attaches to this development of Hinduism, because, started as a reform movement in India, it became in its development under the leadership of Cheshub Chunder Senn in some degree a native Christian church. Since the death of Chunder Senn, P. C. Mozoomdar, who was present and spoke often at the congresses, has been the acknowledged leader of the movement. The Rev. B. B. Nagarkar of Bombay furnished in his address the following simple and beautiful exposition of "The Ideals of the Brahmo-Somaj":

"The fundamental spiritual ideal of the Brahmo-Somaj is belief in the existence of one true God. Now, the expression belief in the existence of God is nothing new to you. In a way you all believe in God, but to us of the Brahmo-Somaj that belief is a stern reality; it is not a logical idea; it is nothing arrived at after an intellectual process. It must be our aim to feel God, to realize God in our daily spiritual communion with him. We must be able, as it were, to feel his touch — to feel as if we were shaking hands with him. This deep, vivid, real, and lasting perception of the Supreme Being is the first and foremost ideal of the theistic faith.

"You in the Western countries are too apt to forget this ideal. The ceaseless demand on your time and energy, the constant worry and hurry of your business activity, and the artificial conditions of your Western civilization are all calculated to make you forgetful of the personal presence of God. You are too apt to be satisfied with a mere belief — perhaps at the best a notional belief in God. The Eastern does not live on such a belief, and such a belief can never form the life of a life-giving faith. It is said that the way to an Englishman's heart is through his stomach; that is, if you wish to reach his heart you must do so through the medium of that wonderful organ called the stomach. The stomach, therefore, is the life of an Englishman, and all his life rests in his stomach.

"Wherein does the heart of a Hindu lie? It lies in his sight. He is not satisfied unless and until he has seen God. The highest dream of his spiritual life is God-vision — the seeing and feeling in every place and at every time the presence of a Supreme Being. He does not live by bread but by sight.

"The second spiritual ideal of the Brahmo-Somaj is the unity of truth. We believe that truth is born in time but not in a place. No nation, no people, or no community has any exclusive monopoly of God's truth. It is a misnomer to speak of truth as Christian truth, Hindu truth, or Mohammedan truth. Truth is the body of God. In his own providence he sends it through the instrumentality of a nation or a people, but that is no reason why that nation or that people should pride themselves for having been the medium of that truth. Thus we must always be ready to receive the gospel truth from whatever country and from whatever people it may come to us. We all believe in the principle of free trade or unrestricted exchange of goods. And we eagerly hope and long for the golden day when people of every nation and of every clime will proclaim the principle of free trade in spiritual matters as ardently and as zealously as they are doing in secular affairs or in industrial matters.

"It appears to me that it is the duty of us all to put together the grand and glorious truths believed in and taught by different nations of the world. This synthesis of truth is a necessary result of the recognition of the principle of the unity of truth. Owing to this character of the Brahmo-Somaj the church of Indian theism has often been called an eclectic church; yes, the religion of the Brahmo-Somaj is the religion of eclecticism, of putting together the spiritual truths of the entire humanity and of earnestly striving after assimilating them with our spiritual being. The religion of the Brahmo-Somaj is inclusive and not exclusive.

"The third spiritual ideal of the Brahmo-Somaj is the harmony of prophets. We believe that the prophets of the world — spiritual teachers such as Vyas and Buddha, Moses and Mohammed, Jesus and Zoroaster, all form a homogeneous whole. Each has to teach mankind his own message. Every prophet was sent from above with a distinct message, and it is the duty of us who live in these advanced times to put these messages together and thereby harmonize and unify the distinctive teachings of the prophets of the world. It would not do to accept the one and reject all the others, or to accept some and reject even a single one. The general truths taught by these different prophets are nearly the same in their essence; but in the midst of all these universal truths that they taught each has a distinctive truth to teach, and it should be our earnest purpose to find out and understand this particular truth. To me Vyas teaches how to understand and apprehend the attributes of divinity. The Jewish prophets of the Old Testament teach the idea of the sovereignty of God; they speak of God as a king, a monarch, a sovereign who rules over the affairs of mankind as nearly and as closely as an ordinary human king. Mohammed, on the other hand, most emphatically teaches the idea of the unity of God. He rebelled against the trinitarian doctrine imported into the religion of Christ through Greek and Roman influences. The monotheism of Mohammed is hard and unyielding, aggressive, and almost savage. I have no sympathy with the errors or erroneous teachings of Mohammedanism, or of any religion, for that matter. In spite of all such errors Mohammed's ideal of the unity of God stands supreme and unchallenged in his teachings. Buddha, the great teacher of morals and ethics, teaches in most sublime strains the doctrine of Nirvana, or self-denial and self-effacement. This principle of extreme self-abnegation means nothing more than the subjugation and conquest of our carnal self. For you know that man is a composite being. In him he has the angelic and the animal, and the spiritual training of our life means no more than subjugation of the animal and the setting free of the angelic. So, also, Christ Jesus of Nazareth taught a sublime truth when he inculcated the noble idea of the fatherhood of God. He taught many other truths, but the fatherhood of God stands supreme above them all. The brotherhood of man is a mere corollary, or a conclusion, deduced from the idea of the fatherhood of God. Jesus taught this truth in the most emphatic language, and therefore that is the special message that he has brought to fallen humanity. In this way, by means of an honest and earnest study of the lives and teachings of different prophets of the world, we can find out the central truth of each faith. Having done this it should be our highest aim to harmonize all these and to build up our spiritual nature on them.

"The religious history of the present century has most clearly shown the need and necessity of the recognition of some universal truths in religion. For the last several years there has been a ceaseless yearning, a deep longing after such a universal religion. The present parliament of religions, which we have been for the last few days celebrating with so much edification and ennoblement, is the clearest indication of this universal longing, and whatever the prophets of despondency or the champions of orthodoxy may say or feel, every individual who has the least spark of spirituality alive in him must feel that this spiritual fellowship that we have enjoyed for the last several days within the precincts of this noble hall can not but be productive of much that leads toward the establishment of universal peace and good-will among men and nations of the world.

"To us of the Brahmo-Somaj this happy consummation, however partial and imperfect it may be for the time being, is nothing short of a sure foretaste of the realization of the principle of the harmony of prophets. In politics and in national government it is now an established fact that in future countries and continents on the surface of the earth will be governed, not by mighty monarchies or aristocratic autocracies, but by the system of universal federation. The history of political progress in your own country stands in noble evidence of my statement; and I am one of those who strongly believe that at some future time every country will be governed by itself as an independent unit, though in some respects may be dependent on some brother power or sister kingdom. What is true in politics will also be true in religion; and nations will recognize and realize the truths taught by the universal family of the sainted prophets of the world.

"In the fourth place, we believe that the religion of the Brahmo-Somaj is a dispensation of this age; it is a message of unity and harmony, of universal amity and unification, proclaimed from above. We do not believe in the revelation of books and men, of histories and historical records. We believe in the infallible revelation of the Spirit—in the message that comes to man by the touch of the human spirit with the supreme Spirit. And can we even for a moment ever imagine that the Spirit of God has ceased to work in our midst? No, we can not. Even to-day God communicates his will to mankind as truly and as really as he did in the days of Christ or Moses, Mohammed or Buddha.

"The dispensations of the world are not isolated units of truth, but, viewed as a whole, and followed out from the earliest to the latest in their historical sequence, they form a continuous chain, and each dispensation is only a link in this chain. It is our bounden duty to read the message of each dispensation in the light that comes from above, and not according to the dead letter that might have been recorded in the past. The interpretation of letters and words, of books and chapters, is a drag behind on the workings of the Spirit. Truly hath it been said that the letter killeth. Therefore, brethren, let us seek the guidance of the Spirit, and interpret the message of the supreme Spirit by the help of his holy Spirit.

"Thus the Brahmo-Somaj seeks to Hinduize Hinduism, Mohammedanize Mohammedanism, and Christianize Christianity. And whatever the champions of the old Christian orthodoxy may say to the contrary, mere doctrine, mere dogma can never give life to any country or community. We are ready and most willing to receive the truths of the religion of Christ as truly as the truths of the religions of other prophets, but we shall receive these from the life and teachings of Christ himself, and not through the medium of any church or the so-called missionary of Christ. If Christian missionaries have in them the meekness and humility and the earnestness of purpose that Christ lived in his own life, and so pathetically exemplified in his glorious death on the cross, let our missionary friends show it in their lives.

"We are wearied of hearing the dogmas of Christendom reiterated from Sunday to Sunday from hundreds of pulpits in India, and evangelists and revivalists of the type of Doctor Pentecost, who go to our country to sing to the same tune, only add to the chaos and confusion presented to the natives of India by the dry and cold lives of hundreds and thousands of his Christian brethren. They come to India on a brief sojourn, pass through the country like birds of passage, moving at a whirlwind speed, surrounded by Christian fanatics and dogmatists; and to us it is no matter of wonder that they do not see any good, or having seen it do not recognize it, in any of the ancient or modern religious systems of India. Mere rhetoric is no reason, nor is abuse an argument, unless it be the argument of a want of common sense. And we are not disposed to quarrel with any people if they are inclined to indulge in these two instruments generally used by those who have no truth on their side. For these our only feeling is a feeling of pity — unqualified, unmodified, earnest pity — and we are ready to ask God to forgive them, for they know not what they say.

"The fifth ideal of the Brahmo-Somaj is the ideal of the motherhood of God. I do not possess the powers, nor have I the time to dwell at length on this most sublime ideal of the church of Indian Theism. The world has heard of God as the almighty creator of the universe, as the omnipotent sovereign that rules the entire creation, as the protector, the saviour and the judge of the human race; as the supreme being, vivifying and enlivening the whole of the sentient and insentient nature.

"We humbly believe that the world has yet to

understand and realize, as it never has in the past, the tender and loving relationship that exists between mankind and their supreme, universal, divine mother. Oh, what a world of thought and feeling is centered in that one monosyllabic word *ma*, which in my language is indicative of the English word mother. Words can not describe, hearts can not conceive of the tender and self-sacrificing love of a human mother. Of all human relations the relation of mother to her children is the most sacred and elevating relation. And yet our frail and fickle human mother is nothing in comparison with the divine mother of the entire humanity, who is the primal source of all love, of all mercy and all purity. Let us, therefore, realize that God is our mother, the mother of mankind, irrespective of the country or the clime in which men and women may be born. The deeper the realization of the motherhood of God the greater will be the strength and intensity of our ideas of the brotherhood of man and the sisterhood of woman. Once we see and feel that God is our mother, all the intricate problems of theology, all the puzzling quibbles of church government, all the quarrels and wranglings of the so-called religious world will be solved and settled. We of the Brahmo-Somaj family hold that a vivid realization of the motherhood of God is the only solution of the intricate problems and differences in the religious world.

"May the universal mother grant us all her blessings to understand and appreciate her sweet relationship to the vast family of mankind. Let us approach her footstool in the spirit of her humble and obedient children."

One is inclined to speculate as to the origin and real force of this conception of the divine motherhood, as to how far it is an appeal in behalf of divine attributes heretofore undervalued in the religious experiences of the Hindus, or as to how far it may be an aspiration after the realization of what has been known to Christians as the Spiritual Mother; that is, heaven and the church, through which the Lord mediates his love and nurture to the feebleness of his children. The confidence expressed that the realization of the divine motherhood would resolve conflicts and bring in universal charity would indicate a faith in what all Christians have believed in, and too often sought to realize in human ecclesiastical orders in the name of God, when the divine of the Lord was not in them. In that case this ideal of the Brahmo-Somaj is simply faith in a universal church from the triumph sometime of the universal love of God. And it is at least evident that the plan of procedure, as Mr. Nagarkar says, "to Hinduize Hinduism, to Christianize Christianity," or in other words to make the subjects of any religion more faithful to its fundamental truths, is a witness to their belief that religious life and faith are from God alone; and being genuine from him, will make all worshipers one in him. This recalls the teaching of Swedenborg concerning the universal church of the Lord, that "the Lord's church is neither here nor there, but is everywhere, both within

those kingdoms where the church is and outside of
the same, wherever men lead a life according to the
precepts of charity;" and that all in the whole world
who are in love to the Lord, and charity toward
the neighbor, are really one universal communion or
church, "conjoined with the Lord's kingdom in the
heavens, and thus conjoined with the Lord himself."
Though he taught that of this universal church,
which is as one grand man in the Lord's sight, the
church where the Word is known and loved, is as
the heart and lungs; and that when the Lord would
revive and restore the health of the church universal, and institute a new dispensation, he does so
by opening revelation and life afresh where the
Word is, and that he has done so even at this day
in Christendom. It is obvious, at least, that something has occurred to open the minds of all profess-
ors of religion, and that influences are operative
which are not very well understood, but which
incite to a more free and tolerant, not to say charitable and loving, search for fundamental principles.
We may, therefore, close this general comparison
with the writer's presentation of this position, on
the last day of the parliament, in a paper on "Swedenborg and the Harmony of Religion."

THE NEW CHRISTIAN CHURCH.

"Before the closing of this grand historic assembly, with its witness to the worth of every form of
faith by which men worship God and seek communion with him, one word more needs be spoken.
one more testimony defined, one more hope recorded.

"Every voice has witnessed to the recognition of a new age. An age of inquiry, expectation, and experiment has dawned. New inventions are stirring men's hearts, new ideals inspire their arts, new physical achievements beckon them on to one marvelous mastery after another of the universe. And now we see that the new freedom of 'willing and thinking' has entered the realm of religion, and the faiths of the world are summoned to declare and compare not only the formulas of the past, but the movements of the present and the forecasts of the future.

"One religious teacher, who explicitly heralded the new age before yet men had dreamed of its possibility, and referred its causes to great movements in the centers of influx in the spiritual world, and described it as incidental to great purposes in the providence of God, needs to be named from this platform — one who ranks with prophets and seers rather than with inquirers and speculators; a revelator rather than a preacher and interpreter; one whose exalted personal character and transcendent learning are eclipsed in the fruits of his mission as a herald of a new dispensation in religion, as the revealer of heavenly arcana, and 'restorer of the foundations of many generations'; who, ignored by his own generation, and assaulted by its successor, is honored and respected in the present, and awaits the thoughtful study which the expansion and culmination of the truth and the organic course of events will bring with to-morrow; 'the permeating and formative influence' of whose teachings in the religious belief and life of to-day in Christendom is commonly admitted; who subscribed with his name on the last of his Latin quartos — Emanuel Swedenborg, 'servant of the Lord Jesus Christ.'"

The address then proceeded to set forth Swedenborg's claim of seership, his account of a last judgment accomplished in the spiritual world, and of the influences which would descend from new sources of influx in that world to bring in a new dispensation of the church among men, and that this new dispensation is inaugurated and defined among men by the revelation of the spiritual sense and divine meaning of the sacred Scriptures, and that the Lord by this means makes his second advent, which is spiritual and universal.

"The Christian world is incredulous of such an event, and for the most part heedless of its announcement; but that does not much signify, except as it makes one with the whole course of history as to the reception of divine announcements. What prophet was ever welcomed until the event had proved his message? The question is not whether it meets the expectation of men; not whether it is what human prudence would forecast; but whether it reveals and meets the needs and necessities of the nations of the earth. 'My thoughts are not your thoughts, saith the Lord, neither are your ways my ways.' The great movements of divine providence are never what men anticipate, but they always provide what men need. And the appeal to the Parliament of Religions in behalf of the revelation announced from heaven is in its ability to prove its divinity by outreaching abundantly all human forecast whatsoever. Does it throw its light over the past and into the present, and project its promise into the future? Does it illuminate and unify history, elucidate the conflicting movements of to-day, and explain the hopes and yearnings of the heart in every age and clime?

"There is not time at this hour for exposition and illustration, only to indicate the catholicity of Swedenborg's teachings in their spirit, scope, and purpose. There is one God and one church. As God is one, the human race, in the complex movements of its growth and history, is before him as one greatest man. It has had its ages in their order, corresponding to infancy, childhood, youth, and manhood in the individual. As the one God is the Father of all, he has witnessed himself in every age according to its state and necessities. The divine care has not been confined to one line of human descent, nor the revelation of God's will to one set of miraculously given Scriptures.

"The great religions of the world have their origin in that same Word or mind of God which wrote itself through Hebrew law-giver and prophet and became incarnate in Jesus Christ. He, as 'the Word which was in the beginning with God, and was God,' was the light of every age in the spiritual development of mankind, preserving and carrying over the life of each into the several streams of tradition in the religions of men, conserving and embodying all in the Hebrew Scriptures, fulfilling that in his own person, and now opening his divine mind in all that Scripture, the religions of the world are to be restored to unity, purified and perfected in him.

"Nor is this with Swedenborg the liberal sentiment of good-will and the enthusiasm of hope, but the discovery of divine fact and the rational insight of spiritual understanding. He has shown that the sacred Scriptures are written according to the correspondence of natural with spiritual things, and that they contain an internal spiritual sense treating of the providence of God in the dispensations of the church, and of the regeneration and spiritual life of the soul. Before Abraham there was the church of Noah, and before the word of Moses there was an ancient word, written in allegory and correspondences, which the ancients understood and loved, but in process of time turned into magic and idolatry. The ancient church scattered into Egypt and Asia, carried fragments of that ancient word, and preserved something of its representatives and allegories in scriptures and mythologies, from which have come the myths and fables of the oriental religions, modified according to nations and peoples, and revived from time to time in the teachings of leaders and prophets.

"From the same ancient word Moses derived, under divine direction, the early chapters of Genesis, and to this in the order of providence was added the law and the prophets, the history of the incarnation, and the prophecy of a final kingdom of God, all so written as to contain an internal spiritual sense, corresponding with the letter, but distinct from it, as the soul corresponds with the body and is distinct and transcends it. It is the opening of this internal sense in all the holy Scriptures, and not any addition to their letter, which constitutes the new and needed revelation of our day. The science of correspondences is the key which unlocks the Scriptures and discloses their internal contents. The same key opens the Scriptures of the Orient and traces them back to their source in primitive revelation.

"If it shows that their myths and representatives have been misunderstood, misrepresented, and misapplied, it shows also that the Hebrew and Christian Scriptures have been likewise perverted and falsified. It is that very fact which necessitates the revelation of their internal meaning, in which resides their divine inspiration and the life of rational understanding for the separation of truth from error. The same rational light and science of interpretation separates the great primitive truths from the corrupting speculations and traditions in all the ancient religions, and furnishes the key to unlock the myths and symbols in ancient Scriptures and worship.

"If Swedenborg reveals errors and superstitions in the religions out of Christendom, so does he also show that the current Christian faith and worship is largely the invention of men and falsifying to the Christian's Bible. If he promises and shows true faith and life to the Christian from the Scriptures, so does he also to the Gentiles in leading them back to primitive revelation and showing them the meaning of their own aspirations for the light of life. If he sets the Hebrew and Christian word above all other sacred Scripture, it is because it brings, as now opened in its spiritual depths, the divine sanction to all the rest, and gathers their strains into its sublime symphony of revelation.

"So much for the indication of what Swedenborg does for catholic enlightenment in spiritual wisdom. As for salvation, he teaches that God has provided with every nation a witness of himself and means of eternal life. He is present by his Spirit with all. He gives the good of his love, which is life, internally and impartially to all. All know that there is a God, and that he is to be loved and obeyed; that there is a life after death, and that there are evils which are to be shunned as sins against God. So far as any one so believes and so lives from a principle of religion he receives eternal life in his soul, and after death instruction and perfection according to the sincerity of his life.

"No teaching could be more catholic than this, showing that, 'Whosoever in any nation feareth God and worketh righteousness is accepted of him.' If he sets forth Jesus Christ as the only wise God, in whom is the fullness of the Godhead, it is Christ glorified and realizing to the mind the infinite and eternal Lover and Thinker and Doer, a real and personal God, our Father and Saviour. If he summons all prophets and teachers to bring their honor and glory unto him, it is not as to a conquering rival, but as to their inspiring life, whose word they have spoken and whose work they have wrought. If he brings all good spirits in the other life to the acknowledgment of the glorified Christ as the only God, it is because they have in heart and essential faith believed in him and lived for him, in living according to the precepts of their religion. He calls him a Christian who lives as a Christian; and he lives as a Christian who looks to the one God and does what he teaches, as he is able to know it. If he denies reincarnation, so also does he deny sleep in the grave and the resurrection of the material body. If he teaches the necessity of regeneration and union with God, so also does he show that the subjugation and quiescence of self is the true 'Nirvana,' opening consciousness to the divine life, and conferring the peace of harmony with God. If he teaches that man needs the Spirit of God for the subjugation of self, he teaches that this Spirit is freely imparted to whosoever will look to the Lord and shun selfishness as sin. If he teaches, thus, that faith is necessary to salvation, he teaches that faith alone is not sufficient, but faith which worketh by love. If he denies that salvation is of favor or immediate mercy, and affirms that it is vital and the effect of righteousness, he also teaches that the divine righteousness is imparted vitally to him who seeks it first and above all; and if he denies that several probations on earth are necessary to the working out of the issues of righteousness, it is because man enters a spiritual world after death in a spiritual body and personality, and in an environment in which his ruling love is developed, his ignorance enlightened, his imperfections removed, his good beginnings perfected, until he is ready to be incorporated in the Grand Man of heaven, to receive and functionate his measure of the divine life and participate in the divine joy. And so I might go on.

"My purpose is accomplished if I have won your respect, and interest in the teachings of this great apostle, who, claiming to be called of the Lord to open the Scriptures, presents a harmony of truths that would gather into its embrace all that is of value in every religion, and open out into a career of illimitable spiritual progress.

"The most unimpassioned of men, perhaps because he so well understood that his mission was not his own but the concern of Him who builds through the ages, Swedenborg wrote and published. The result is a library that calmly awaits the truth-seekers. If the religions of the world become disciples there, it will not be proselytism that will take them there, but the organic course of events in that providence which works on, silent but mighty, like the forces that poise planets and gravitate among the stars.

"Present history shows the effect of unsuspected causes. The Parliament of Religions is itself a testimony to unseen spiritual causes, and should at least incline to belief in Swedenborg's testimony, that a way is open, both in the spiritual world and on earth, for a universal church in the faith of one visible God in whom is the Invisible, imparting eternal life and enlightenment to all from every nation who believe in him and work righteousness."

CHAPTER IV.

A RELIGIOUS SYMPOSIUM — CONTINUED.

HAVING now passed in review some of the best things the representatives of the several religions had to declare for themselves, and to prophesy for men, we may compare the positive declarations of various speakers upon the great subjects of religious thought.

Central in every religion is the idea of God, for God to every man is what he regards as best and highest, what gives him the law of his being, and what he inwardly obeys in his doing. We begin, therefore, with the idea of God as interpreted by students of the ancient religions and by the teachers of the living religions represented in the World's Religious Congress.

GOD.

The first thing to remark is the universality of the idea that there is a God and that he is one. As Prince Momolu Massaquoi, of the Vey Nation in West Africa, a Christian, and educated in this country, but just returned from his own people, who are pagans, said in speaking of their religion, "They worship the same God that you do. The missionaries see them bow down before some natural object and report that they are idolaters. But they do not worship such things. They know that God is the creator of the universe, and they speak to him when they bow before what he has made, and think of him as a great spirit in the man form." And Swami Vivekananda, in speaking of the worship of the simple in India, said their idols are only symbols and reminders, and called attention to the fact that Christians, in common with all men, sought to make their spiritual ideas sensual by some symbolic object of sight. It is demonstrable that all idolatry originated in this tendency, confirmed by evils with the mass, but never obliterating the idea of one God so completely as to hide it from the innocent and good. And if this be true, it admonishes us to look behind the doctrinal developments of every religion for the great primitive concept that underlies them and constitutes for the good "the secret of the Lord with them that fear him."

Prof. N. Vallentine, in his paper on "The Harmonies and Distinctions in the Theistic Teachings of the Various Historic Faiths," remarks that "at the outset we need to remind ourselves of the exceeding difficulty of the comparison or of precise and firm classification of the theistic faiths of mankind. They are all — at least all the ethnic faiths — developments or evolutions, having undergone various and immense changes. Their evolutions amount to revolutions in some cases. They are not permanently marked by the same features, and will not admit the same predicates at different times. Some are found to differ more from themselves in their history than from one another."

He finds, however, at the basis of them all the idea of God, unless Buddhism be excepted, and the absence of positive theistic teaching in this system he regards as negative failure to emphasize the idea, which certainly is not denied. "But," he adds, "if these various religions be compared in the light of a second principle in theistic teaching — that of monotheism — it is startling to find how terribly the idea of God, whose existence is so unanimously owned, has been misconceived and distorted. For taking the historic faiths in their fully developed form, only two, Christianity and Mohammedanism, present a pure and maintained monotheism. Zoroastrianism can not be counted in here; though at first its Ahriman, or evil spirit, was not conceived of as a God, it afterward lapsed into theological dualism and practical polytheism. All the rest are prevailingly and discordantly polytheistic. They move off into endless multiplicity of divinities and grotesque degradations of their character. This fact does not speak well for the ability of the human mind, without supernatural help, to formulate and maintain the necessary idea of God worthily.

"This dark and regretful phenomenon is, however, much relieved by several modifying facts. One is that the search-lights of history and philology reveal for the principal historic faiths, back of their stages and conditions of luxuriantly developed polytheism, the existence of an early, or possibly though not certainly primitive, monotheism. This point, I know, is strongly contested, especially by many whose views are determined by acceptance of the evolutionist hypothesis of the derivative origin of the human race; but it seems to me that the evidence, as made clear through the true historical method of investigation, is decisive for monotheism as the earliest known form of theistic conception in the religions of Egypt, China, India, and the original Druidism, as well as of the two faiths already classed as asserting the divine unity.

"Polytheisms are found to be actual growths. Tracing them back they become simpler and simpler. 'The younger the polytheism the fewer the gods,' until a stage is reached where God is conceived of as one alone This accords, too, as has been well pointed out, with the psychological genesis of ideas — the singular number preceding the plural, the idea of a god preceding the idea of gods, the affirmation 'There is a God' going before the affirmation 'There are two or many gods.'

"Another fact of belief is that the polytheisms have not held their fields without dissent and revolt. Over against the tendency of depraved humanity to corrupt the idea of God and multiply imaginary and false divinities, there are forces that act for correction and improvement. The human soul has been formed for the one true and only God. Where reason is highly developed and the testing powers of the intellect and conscience are earnestly applied to the problems of existence and duty, these grotesque and gross polytheisms prove unsatisfactory."

Passing to another point of comparison, the principle of personality, he notes that "under this principle the religions of the world fall into two classes: those which conceive of God as an intelligent being, acting in freedom, and those that conceive of him pantheistically as the sum of nature or the impersonal energy or soul of all things. In Christian teaching God is a personal being, with all the attributes or predicates that enter into the concept of such being. In the Christian Scriptures of the Old and New Testaments this conception is never for a moment lowered or obscured. God, though immanent in nature, filling it with his presence and power, is yet its creator and preserver, keeping it subject to his will and purposes, never confounded nor identified with it. He is the infinite, absolute personality.

"In the early belief of Egypt, of China, of India, in the teaching of Zoroaster, of Celtic Druidism, of Assyrian and Babylonian faith, and in the best intuition of the Greek and Roman philosophers, without doubt God was apprehended as a personal God. Indeed, in almost the whole world's religious thinking this element of true theistic conception has had more or less positive recognition and maintenance. It seems to have been spontaneously and necessarily demanded by the religious sense and life.

"The human feeling of helplessness and need called for a God who could hear and understand, feel and act. And whenever thought rose beyond the many pseudo-gods to the existence of the one true God as a creator and ruler of the world, the ten thousand marks of order, plan, and purpose in nature speaking to men's hearts and reason led up to

H. DHARMAPALA.
Buddhist, Ceylon.

the grand truth that the Maker of all is a thinker and both knows and wills. And so a relation of trust, fellowship, and intercourse was found and recognized. None of the real feelings of worship, love, devotion, gratitude, consecration, could live and act simply in the presence of an impersonal, unconscious, fateful energy or order of nature. No consistent hope of a conscious personal future life can be established except as it is rooted in faith in a personal God.

"And yet the personality of God has often been much obscured in the historic faiths. The obscuration has not come as a natural and spontaneous product of the religious impulse or consciousness, but of mystic speculative philosophies. The phenomenon presented by Spinozaism and later pantheisms, in the presence of Christianity, was substantially anticipated again and again ages ago, in the midst of various religious faiths, despite their own truer visions of the eternal God. As we understand it, the philosophy of religion with Hinduism, the later Confucianism, developed Parseeism and Druidism is substantially pantheistic, reducing God to impersonal existence or the conscious factors and forces of cosmic order."

The important points here are these: that at the root of all the historic faiths is the idea that there is a God and that he is one divine person, a lover, and thinker, and doer; but that this primitive idea is variously obscured by the sensuous persuasions on the one hand, and by speculative thinking on the other; and that these developments, and revolts, and revivals, at different periods in their history, and on the part of their different sects, make any simple positive statement as the faith of any one of them difficult.

The prevailing prepossessation on the part of Christian scholars who contribute papers on comparative theology being the theory of progressive evolution, too much importance can not be given to facts like these presented by Professor Vallentine, which directly discredit the theory. The showing of one of the papers, for instance, that in the ancient Egyptian religion the one central religious notion was the nearness of the divine, and that in the Babylonian-Assyrian, on the other hand, the central idea was the separateness and transcendence of the divine, with the argument that these two elemental truths have been conveyed from Egypt and Babylonia to the nations of men, favors in such form the evolutionary leaning of thinkers. But it is not shown that the less-emphasized truth was absent from the religion which made the other prominent; nor is it necessary to conclude that either Egypt or Babylonia exercised any more than a modifying effect upon other religions, which together with them possessed both ideas as an inheritance from primitive revelation.

Belief in primitive revelation as the origin of the idea of God was not prominent, however, though it might be confirmed by most of the facts cited in support of the natural development of the idea of God. An exception to the rule was the argument of the Rev. Maurice Phillips of Madras, India, that the primitive Hindu religion was from primitive revelation.

In harmony with Professor Vallentine, quoted above, he contended that—

"Two things are evident. That the higher we push our inquiries into the ancient religion of India the purer and simpler we find the conception of God, and that in proportion as we come down the stream of time the more corrupt and complex it becomes. We conclude, therefore, that the ancient Hindus did not acquire their knowledge of the divine attributes and functions empirically, for in that case we should find at the end what we now find at the beginning. Hence we must seek for a theory that will account alike for the acquisition of that knowledge, the godlike conception of Varuna and its gradual depravation which culminated in Brahma.

"And what theory will cover these facts as well as the doctrine of a 'primitive revelation'? If we admit on the authority of the Bible that God revealed himself originally to man, the knowledge of the divine functions and attributes possessed by the ancient Hindus would be a reminiscence. And if we admit, on both the authority of the Bible and consciousness, the sinful tendency of human nature which makes the retention of divine knowledge either a matter of difficulty or aversion, it is easy to conceive that the idea of God as a spiritual personal being would gradually recede and ultimately disappear from the memory, while his attributes and functions would survive like broken fragments of a once united whole."

The same theory will explain satisfactorily the fact that ancient tradition of the true God in Egypt should take on rather than grow out of the natural characteristic of its people, and the same primitive truth receive a different bent and emphasis in the Babylonian mind. And this alone will explain the undeniable fact that, in proportion as the simple idea of a heavenly Father, the Creator of the universe, is revolved in sensuous and speculative thought with any people the more "corrupt and complex it becomes." Still, as remarked before, it is not entirely lost, and is from time to time, in the history of every faith, grasped and asserted anew by some one "pure in heart" who "sees God." It would be interesting, indeed, as showing to what the idea has come, to set side by side the answers of the several faiths, and sects even, to the direct question, "What have you to say of God?" It is impossible to gather more than general answers from the discussions before the parliament.

Swami Vivekananda, the Hindu monk, quoting a Vedic sage, who he says was inspired from the throne of mercy, and proclaimed in words of hope and consolation, 'I have found the Ancient One,' thus expounds the Hindu faith in God: "The Vedas proclaim, not a dreadful combination of unforgiving laws, not an endless prison of cause and effect, but that at the head of all these laws, in and through every particle of matter and force, stands one 'through whose command the wind blows, the fire burns, the clouds rain, and death stalks upon the earth.' And what is his nature?

"He is everywhere, the pure and formless one, the almighty and the all-merciful. 'Thou art our father, thou art our mother, thou art our beloved friend, thou art the source of all strength. Thou art he that bearest the burdens of the universe; help me bear the little burden of this life.' Thus sang the Rishis of the Veda. And how to worship him? Through love. 'He is to be worshiped as the one beloved, dearer than everything in this and the next life.'" And he adds, as giving definiteness to this idea, that the Hindus believe Krishna to have been "God incarnate on earth."

As a Christian estimate of the Hindu thought of God the following from Rev. R. A. Hume may be illustrative:

"Both Christian and Hindu thought recognize an infinite being with whom is bound up man's rational and spiritual life. Both magnify the indwelling of this infinite being in every part of the universe. Both teach that this great being is ever revealing itself; that the universe is a unit, and that all things come under universal laws of the infinite.

"To Christianity God is the heavenly Father, always and infinitely good; God is love.

"To philosophical Hinduism man is an emanation from the infinite, which, in the present stage of existence, is the exact result of this emanation in previous stages of existence. His moral sense is an illusion, for he can not sin.

"To popular Hinduism man is partially what he is to philosophical Hinduism, determined by fate; partially he is thought of as a created being more or less sinful, dependent on God for favor or disfavor.

"To Christianity man is the child of his heavenly Father, sinful and often erring, yet longed for and sought after by the Father."

In a remarkably definite and explicit paper on "Zoroastrianism," by Jinanji Jamshodji Modi, we are told of the idea of God among the Parsees:

"Zoroastrianism, or Parseeism — by whatever name the system may be called — is a monotheistic form of religion. It believes in the existence of one God, whom it knows under the names of Mazda, Ahura, and Ahura-Mazda, the last form being one that is most commonly met with in the latter writings of the Avesta. The first and the greatest truth that dawns upon the mind of a Zoroastrian is that the great and the infinite universe, of which he is an infinitesimally small part, is the work of a powerful hand — the result of a master-mind. The first and the greatest conception of that master-mind, Ahura-Mazda, is that, as the name implies, he is the Omniscient Lord, and as such he is the ruler of both the material and immaterial world, the corporeal and the incorporeal world, the visible and the invisible world. The regular movements of the sun and the stars, the periodical waxing and waning of the moon, the regular way in which the sun and the clouds are sustained, the regular flow of waters and the gradual growth of vegetation, the rapid movements of the winds and the regular succession of light and darkness, of day and night, with their accompaniments of sleep and wakefulness; all these grand and striking phenomena of nature point to and bear ample evidence of the existence of an almighty power, who is not only the creator but the preserver of this great universe, who has not only launched that universe into existence with a premeditated plan of completeness, but who, with the controlling hand of a father, preserves by certain fixed laws harmony and order here, there, and everywhere.

"As Ahura-Mazda is the ruler of the physical world, so he is the ruler of the spiritual world. His distinguished attributes are good mind, righteousness, desirable control, piety, perfection, and immortality. He is the beneficent Spirit from whom emanate all good and all piety. He looks into the hearts of men, and sees how much of the good and of the piety that have emanated from him has made its home there, and thus rewards the virtuous and punishes the vicious. Of course one sees at times in the plane of this world moral disorders and want of harmony, but then the present state is only a part, and that a very small part, of his scheme of moral government. As the ruler of the world, Ahura-Mazda hears the prayers of the ruled. He grants the prayers of those who are pious in thoughts, pious in words, and pious in deeds. 'He not only rewards the good, but punishes the wicked. All that is created, good or evil, fortune or misfortune, is his work.'"

He combats the misunderstanding that Zoroaster

preaches dualism. Ahura-Mazda is supreme; the good and evil principles which contend in the world and in man are under him. He cites in explanation the Christian doctrine of the devil and hell, and continues: "Consequently, though the Almighty is the creator of all, a part of the creation is said to be created by the good principle and a part by the evil principle. Thus, for example, the heavenly bodies, the earth, water, fire, horses, dogs, and such other objects are the creation of the good principle, and serpents, ants, locusts, etc., are the creation of the evil principle. In short, those things that conduce to the greatest good of the greatest number of mankind fall under the category of the creations of the good principle, and those that lead to the contrary result, under that of the creations of the evil principle. This being the case, it is incumbent upon men to do actions that would support the cause of the good principle and destroy that of the evil one. Therefore, the cultivation of the soil, the rearing of the domestic animals, etc., on the one hand, and the destruction of wild animals and other noxious creatures on the other, are considered meritorious actions by the Parsees.

"As there are two primeval principles under Ahura-Mazda that produce our material world, so there are two principles inherent in the nature of man, which encourage him to do good or tempt him to do evil. One asks him to support the cause of the good principle, the other to support that of the evil principle."

The idea of God in orthodox Judaism, according

to Rabbi Mendes, is "expressed in the creeds formulated by Maimonides, as follows:

"We believe in God the creator of all, a unity, a spirit who never assumed corporeal form, eternal, and he alone ought to be worshiped.

"We unite with Christians in the belief that revelation is inspired. We unite with the founder of Christianity that not one jot or tittle of the law should be changed. Hence we do not accept a first-day Sabbath, etc.

"We unite in believing that God is omniscient and just, good, loving, and merciful.

"We unite in the belief in the coming Messiah.

"We unite in our belief in immortality. In these Judaism and Christianity agree."

The definitions of Rabbi Wise, less specific in statement, are explicit as giving authority of revelation to only such passages in the Hebrew Scriptures as represent God to have spoken of himself, his name, or his attributes.

"Judaism is the complex of Israel's religious sentiments ratiocinated to conceptions in harmony with its Jehovistic God-cognition.

"These conceptions made permanent in the consciousness of this people are the religious knowledges which form the substratum to the theology of Judaism. The Thorah maintains that its 'teaching and canon' are divine. Man's knowledge of the true and the good comes directly to human reason and conscience (which is unconscious reason) from the supreme and universal reason, the absolutely true and good; or it comes to him indirectly from the same source by the manifestations of nature, the facts of history, and man's power of induction. This principle is in conformity with the second postulate of theology, and its extension in harmony with the standard of reason.

"All knowledge of God and his attributes, the true and the good, came to man by successive revelations of the indirect kind first, which we may call natural revelation, and the direct kind afterward, which we may call transcendental revelation. Both these revelations concerning God and his substantial attributes, together with their historical genesis, are recorded in the Thorah in the seven holy names of God, to which neither prophet nor philosopher in Israel added even one, and all of which constantly recur in all Hebrew literature.

"What we call the God of revelation is actually intended to designate God as made known in the transcendental revelations, including the successive God-ideas of natural revelation. His attributes of relation are made known only in such passages of the Thorah in which he himself is reported to have spoken to man of himself, his name, and his attributes, and not by any induction or reference from any law, story, or doing ascribed to God anywhere. The prophets only expand or define those conceptions of deity which these passages of direct transcendental revelation in the Thorah contain. There exists no other source from which to derive the cognition of the God of revelation."

It is known that Mohammedanism was a revolt against idolatry, and that its founder claimed that in so doing he had returned to the pure religion of Abraham. Still, "Mohammedanism is no more a reformed Judaism than it is a form of Christianity. It was essentially a new religion." It is worthy of notice that the best account of Mohammedanism presented to the congress was by Doctor Washburn, president of Roberts College, Constantinople, and not by the disciple of Islam. Doctor Washburn gives the doctrine of God as stated by a Mohammedan authority as follows:

"God is one and eternal. He lives, and is almighty. He knows all things, hears all things, sees all things. He is endowed with will and action. He has neither form nor feature, neither bounds, limits, or numbers, neither parts, multiplications, or divisions, because he is neither body nor matter. He has neither beginning nor end. He is self-existent, without generation, dwelling, or habitation. He is outside the empire of time, unequaled in his nature as in his attributes, which, without being foreign to his essence, do not constitute it."

Doctor Washburn continues: "It has often been said that the God of Islam is simply a God of almighty power, while the God of Christianity is a God of infinite love and perfect holiness; but this is not a fair statement of truth. The ninety-nine names of God which the good Moslem constantly repeats assign these attributes to him. The fourth name is 'The Most Holy'; the twenty-ninth, 'The Just'; the forty-sixth, 'The All Loving'; the first and most common is 'The Merciful,' and the moral attributes are often referred to in the Koran. In truth there is no conceivable perfection which the Moslem would neglect to attribute to God.

"Their conception of him is that of an absolute oriental monarch, and his unlimited power to do what he pleases makes entire submission to his will the first, most prominent duty. The name which they gave to their religion implies this. It is Islam, which means submission or resignation; but a king may be good or bad, wise or foolish, and the Moslem takes as much pains as the Christian to attribute to God all wisdom and all goodness.

"The essential difference in the Christian and Mohammedan conception of God lies in the fact that the Moslem does not think of this great King as having anything in common with his subjects, from whom he is infinitely removed. The idea of the incarnation of God in Christ is to them not only blasphemous but absurd and incomprehensible; and the idea of fellowship with God, which is expressed in calling him our Father, is altogether foreign to Mohammedan thought."

Confucianism in its modern disciples seems to have little definite idea of God, though a central thought of spirits and of a supreme spirit answers to them for the divine, which they denominate heaven. Confucianism was represented in the congress by a prize essay, and also by an address from Pung Quang Yu, a disciple, and secretary of the Chinese legation at Washington. The prize essay says:

"The most important thing in the superior man's learning is to fear disobeying heaven's will. Therefore in our Confucian religion the most important thing is to follow the will of heaven. The book of Yik King says: 'In the changes of the world there is a great supreme which produces two principles, and these two principles are Yin and Yang. By supreme is meant the spring of all activity. Our sages regard Yin and Yang and the five elements as acting and reacting on each other without ceasing, and this doctrine is all-important, like as the hinge of a door.

"The incessant production of all things depends on this as the tree does on the root. Even all human affairs and all good are also dependent on it; therefore it is called the supreme, just as we speak of the extreme points of the earth as the north and south poles.

"By great supreme is meant that there is nothing above it. But heaven is without sound or smell, therefore the ancients spoke of the infinite and the great supreme. The great supreme producing Yin and Yang is law-producing forces. When Yin and Yang unite they produce water, fire, wood, metal, earth. When these five forces operate in harmony the four seasons come to pass. The essences of the infinite, of Yin and Yang, and of the five elements, combine, and the heavenly become male, and the earthly become female. When these powers act on each other all things are produced and reproduced and developed without end.

"As to man, he is the best and most intelligent of all. This is what is meant in the book of Chung Yung when it says that what heaven has given is the spiritual nature. This nature is law. All men are thus born and have this law. Therefore it is Mencius says that all children love the parents and when grown up all respect their elder brethren. If men only followed the natural bent of this nature, then all would go the right way; hence, the Chung Yung says: 'To follow nature is the right way.'

"The choicest product of Yin, Yang, and the five elements in the world is man; the rest are refuse products. The choicest among the choice ones are the sages and worthies, and the refuse among them are the foolish and the bad. And as man's body comes from the Yin and man's soul from the Yang he can not be perfect. This is what the Lung philosophers called the material nature. Although all men have at birth a nature for goodness, still if there is nothing to fix it, then desires arise and passions rule, and men are not far from being like beasts; hence Confucius says: 'Men's nature is originally alike, but in practice men become very different.' The sages, knowing this, sought to fix the nature with the principles of moderation, uprightness, benevolence, and righteousness. Heaven appointed rulers and teachers, who in turn established worship and music to improve men's disposition and set up governments and penalties in order to check men's wickedness. The best among the people are taken into schools where they study wisdom, virtue, benevolence, and righteousness, so that they may know beforehand how to conduct themselves as rulers or ruled.

"And lest, after many generations, there should be degeneration and difficulty in finding the truth, the principles of heaven and earth, of men and of all things, have been recorded in the Book of Odes for the use of after generations The Chung Yung calls the practice of wisdom religion. Our religion well knows heaven's will; it looks on all under heaven as one family, great rulers as elder branches in their parents' clan, great ministers as chief officers of this clan, and people at large as brothers of the same parents; and it holds that all things should be enjoyed in common, because it regards heaven and earth as the parents of all alike. And the commandment of the Confucian is, 'Fear greatly lest you offend against heaven.'"

It thus appears that the disciples of Confucius have given less attention to definition of the divine than to practice in harmony with "heaven's will." Pung Quang Yu in his address gives some account of worship, as follows:

"'My prayers,' says Confucius, 'were offered up long ago.' The meaning he wishes to convey is that he considers his prayers to consist in living a virtuous life and in constantly obeying the dictates of conscience.

"He therefore looks upon prayers as of no avail to deliver any one from sickness. 'He who sins against heaven,' again he says, 'has no place to pray.' What he means is that even spirits have no power to bestow blessings on those who have sinned against the decrees of heaven.

"The wise and the good, however, make use of offerings and sacrifices simply as a means of purifying themselves from the contamination of the world, so that they may become susceptible of spiritual influences and be in sympathetic touch with the invisible world, to the end that calamities may be averted and blessings secured thereby. Still, sacrifices can not be offered by all persons without distinction. Only the emperor can offer sacrifices to heaven. Only governors of provinces can offer sacrifices to the spirits of mountains and rivers, land and agriculture. Lower officers of the government can offer sacrifices only to their ancestors of the five preceding generations, but are not allowed to offer sacrifices to heaven. The common people, of course, are likewise denied this privilege. They can offer sacrifices only to their ancestors.

"All persons, from the emperor down to the common people, are strictly required to observe the worship of ancestors. The only way in which a virtuous man and a dutiful son can show his sense of obligation to the authors of his being is to serve them when dead as when they were alive, when departed as when present. It is for this reason that the most enlightened rulers have always made filial duty the guiding principle of government. Observances of this character have nothing to do with religious celebrations and ceremonies."

It is commonly believed that there is no theism in the teachings of Buddha. H. Dharmapala, in his extended exposition of Buddhism, said that "to guide humanity in the right path a Messiah appears from time to time," but adds:

"In the sense of a supreme creator, Buddha says that there is no such being, accepting the doctrine of evolution as the only true one, with its corollary, the law of cause and effect. He condemns the idea of a creator, but the supreme God of the Brahmins and minor Gods are accepted; but they are subject to the law of cause and effect. This supreme God is all love, all merciful, all gentle, and looks upon all beings with equanimity. Buddha teaches men to practice these four supreme virtues. But there is no difference between the perfect man and this supreme God of the present world.

"The teachings of the Buddha on evolution are clear and expansive. We are asked to look upon the cosmos 'as a continuous process unfolding itself in regular order in obedience to natural laws. We see in it all not a yawning chaos restrained by the constant interference from without of a wise and beneficent external power, but a vast aggregate of original elements perpetually working out their own fresh redistribution in accordance with their own inherent energies. He regards the cosmos as an almost infinite collection of material, animated by an almost infinite sum total of energy, which is called Akasa. I have used the above definition of evolution as given by Grant Allen in his 'Life of Darwin,' as it beautifully expresses the generalized idea of Buddhism. We do not postulate that man's evolution began from the protoplasmic stage; but we are asked not to speculate on the origin of life, on the origin of the law of cause and effect, etc. So far as this great law is concerned we say that it controls the phenomena of human life as well as those of external nature; the whole knowable universe forms one undivided whole.

"Buddha promulgated his system of philosophy after having studied all religions. And in the Brahma-jola sutra sixty-two creeds are discussed. In the Kalama, the sutra, Buddha says:

"'Do not believe in what ye have heard. Do not believe in traditions, because they have been handed down for many generations. Do not believe in anything because it is renowned and spoken of by many. Do not believe merely because the written statement of some old sage is produced. Do not believe in conjectures. Do not believe in that as truth to which you have become attached by habit. Do not believe merely on the authority of your teachers and elders. Often observation and analysis, when the result agrees with reason, are conducive to the good and gain of one and all. Accept and live up to it.'"

One looks to the gentle Dharmapala for precepts of righteousness and purity rather than for philosophical insight; but this quotation here cited expresses just the one mission of Buddhism, to make such men full of the spirit of purity and love, which "accepts and lives up to" what it perceives to be right. The divine, which is man's ideal highest and best, is realized in Buddha, and to be with him where he is, is the aspiration of life with his disciples. "To realize the unseen is the goal of the student of Buddha's teachings, and such a one has to lead an absolutely pure life. Buddha says:

"'Let him fulfill all righteousness; let him be devoted to that quietude of heart which springs from within; let him not drive back the ecstasy of contemplation; let him look through things; let him be much alone. Fulfill all righteousness for the sake of the living, and for the sake of the blessed ones that are dead and gone.'"

If we turn to the Christian presentation of the idea of God, we travel for the most part through a dreary waste of philosophy. It may be confessed, indeed, that the design of these learned disquisitions is to show the defensibility of God's self-revelation in the sacred Scriptures, and to justify it to reason; but the amount and preponderance of such reasoning is an indication of failing faith in revelation, and of the aspiring assumption of human intelligence in Christendom. But even here we find something new; a reconstruction of the old theistic arguments into harmony with the accepted importance of the idea of the divine immanence in nature and man, and a certain revolt of reason against unthinkable dogma. Perhaps it is because dogmatic theology has obscured the simple majesty of God's self-revelation in the Scriptures as the self-subsisting lover and thinker and doer, who is immanent by his Spirit in nature and in man, whose providence is the operation of his love and wisdom, according to their own law impressed upon the universe, who speaks to man by his Word and reveals himself and his love and redeeming power in Jesus Christ; perhaps it is because the mind seeks for this truth in the nature of things, which dogmatic theology has overlaid and obscured in Scripture, that we find in these presentations so little argument from revelation to faith, and so much argument from the necessities of the case, with critical examination of the processes by which we know that we know that God is. Certain it is, that in a careful review of all these declarations concerning God Christian scholars will be found in the attitude, not of apostles teaching the nations out of the church, but of apologists trying to extract from the nature of things reasons in defense of the idea of a heavenly Father. The effort is legitimate if necessary for any reason, and the arguments are an improvement on the old; but what does it come to? We may give the answer in the closing words of Doctor Momerie's paper on "The Moral Evidences of a Divine Existence":

"To sum up in one sentence — all knowledge, whether practical or scientific, nay, the commonest experience of every-day life, implies the existence of a mind which is omnipresent and eternal, while the tendency toward righteousness, which is so unmistakably manifest in the course of history, together with the response which this tendency awakens in our own hearts, combine to prove that the infinite thinker is just and kind and good. It must be because he is always with us that we sometimes imagine that he is nowhere to be found."

If any look for an exposition of the doctrine of one God in three coequal and coeternal persons, the prevalence of this faith may be found incidentally in forms of speech founded on it, and ideas of divine government derived from it, but in exposition it is greatly modified. In a paper on "Christ the Reason of the Universe," the Rev. James W. Lee presents the doctrine of the trinity in God in a way that shows the effort of reason to reconcile it with the absolute oneness of the Divine Being, and at the same time illustrates the intricacy of the processes of thought in the new intellectual activity of Christendom. He says: "What man seeks, and has always sought, is such a philosophy or synthesis of the facts of nature, of man, and of God as harmonizes him with himself, with his world, and with the being he calls God. We call Christ the reason of the universe because he brings to thought such a synthesis of nature, man, and God as harmonizes human life with itself, and with the facts of nature and God."

In the elucidation of this theme he seeks to show that a "self-causative, self-active, omnipotent energy is the deepest thing, and the first thing in the universe;" and again that self-consciousness, which is the "complete form of self-activity, self-causation, and self-relation," contains within itself "the subject that thinks, and the object that is thought, and also the identity of subject and object in a living, intelligent personality." He then proceeds as follows:

"In the absolute self-consciousness of God there is subject and object and the identity of subject and object in one divine personality. But it is necessary that what the absolute subject thinks must be, and must also be as perfect as the absolute subject. It is necessary also that the absolute object must be one. So in the divine self-consciousness the absolute subject is Father, and the thought of the Father, or the absolute object, is the Son. But as the Son is as perfect as the Father it is necessary that what he thinks must be also.

"Here it is that Christian philosophy and theology gets the imperfect world. The Son thinks himself first as eternally derived, as eternally begotten. In the fact that the Son differs from the first person in that he is eternally derived from him is found the thought of limitation, which is expressed in the imperfect world in all stages and grades of existence, from pure passivity up through space and atoms, and force and compounds, and plants and animals to man, who is in the image of God and at the top of creation. In God as Father the idea of transcendence is met, and thus we have the truth of monotheism; in God the Son the idea of an indwelling God is met, and we have the truth of polytheism. In God the Spirit the idea of God pervading the world is reached, and we have the truth of pantheism. Here we have a trinity not such as would be constituted by three judges in a court, or by three things imagined under sensible forms. The relations between three such judges or three such sensible things would be mechanical and accidental and not absolute and essential. The trinity of the Christian church is not simply the aggregation of three individuals or the unity of three mathematical points. The trinity revealed in the Christian Scriptures is such as makes a concrete unity through and by means of difference. This trinity makes a unity, the distinguishing feature of which is 'fullness' and not emptiness. It is a trinity constitutive of a real, experimental, and knowable unity. God is revealed in the Scriptures as intelligence, life, and love, and the living process of each is triune. The terms of a self, whose living function is intelligence, are three, subject, object, and the organic identity of the two. The terms of such a self are necessarily three, and yet its nature is necessarily one.

"If God is intelligent he is triune, because the process of intelligence is triune. There can not be mind without self-consciousness, and the object of the eternal self-consciousness is the eternal Logos, who is the full and complete expression of the eternal mind. Time or space is not necessary to the complete act of self-consciousness.

"The movement of the eternal mind passing through the Son into the Holy Spirit, and then through the finite world and the Christian church back to himself, has been called a procession. A procession, because infinite, eternally complete. Thus, while God eternally goes from himself he eternally returns to himself with spirits redeemed by the Son, and regenerated by the Spirit, capable of sharing the love and joy and life of himself.

"This view makes it necessary that God through the Son create the world. At this doctrine some people will stagger. One thing is sure, God has created the world, and if the necessity for creating it was not in his nature, then creation is an accident. There is no reason where there is no necessity. The necessity for a thing is the reason for it. If there was no necessity for creation, the creative act becomes wholly irrational. God is represented in the very first chapter of the Bible as Creator. It is necessary that a creator create.

"It is to be remembered, however, while it is necessary that God create, this is a necessity that falls within his own nature. This means that God is essentially a creative being. There is no necessity outside of God by which he is compelled to do anything. This would be the establishment of a fate greater than God. All necessity relating to God falls within his own being and is that which defines what he rationally and essentially is.

"But while the doctrine makes the creation of the finite world necessary, it does not make sin, or the self-assertion of a finite spirit necessary. But man is free, with a body made of the earth at the bottom of himself, and with a spirit the direct gift of God at the top of himself. Between man as body and man as spirit there is the realm of choice. If he acts with reference to himself as body simply, he sins. The possibility of sin in the case of man is found in that in his personality there come together a limited and an unlimited self, a carnal and a spiritual self, a self in time and space and a self under the form of eternity.

"This doctrine helps us again to account for the two poles of man's moral and intellectual consciousness. Human nature has a dual constitution. It is the unity of two principles, a principle of thought and will and a principle of truth and right. As a physical being he is dual. The subjective side of his physical self is hunger, the objective side of his physical nature is food. Now, before he can live as a physical being the hunger and the food must come together. On his subjective side man feels he is free, but on his objective side he feels he must obey. How is he to be free and obedient at the same time? When we remember that the nature of man is a reproduction of the nature of the Son of God, and that the Holy Spirit, proceeding from the Father and the Son, flows out into humanity to enlighten, to quicken, to convince of sin, and then to renew, to regenerate and to organize into the Christian church, we will see that the truth the Spirit presents to man's intellect is adapted to it as food is to his hunger, and that the law the Spirit stimulates and urges man to obey is the law of his own nature.

"This doctrine gives us the meaning of the struggle, conflict, pain, which are apparent throughout the realm of nature and human life. Liebnitz, looking at the top of things, at health, at joy, sunshine, laughter, and prosperity, said this was the best possible world. Schopenhauer, looking at the bottom, at storms, thorns, disease, poverty, death, said this was the worst possible world. The entrance of the divine procession into the limitations of time and space is advertised by the storm and stress, the ceaseless clash and strife which begin among the atoms. This struggle is kept up through all stages of organization until when we reach the plane of human life it is expressed in cries and wails, in tragedies, epics, litanies, which become the most interesting part of human literature. Into this struggle comes the Son of Man and the Son of God. He meets it, endures it, and conquers it, and is crucified, and his crucifixion is the culmination of the process of trial and storm and strife which begun with the atoms and continued through the whole course of nature. When Christ comes up from the dead then the truth of the ages gets defined, that through suffering and denial and crucifixion is the way to holiness and everlasting life. From thenceforth a redeemed humanity becomes the working hypothesis and the ideal of the race. Then it comes to be seen that the whole movement of God looks to the organization of the human race in Jesus Christ, the reason, the logos, the plan and the ideal framework of the universe."

It needs to be borne in mind, however, when seeking help of philosophy, that the very ideas with which it concerns itself are derived from revelation. As Bishop Keane said, in preparing the way for his discussion of the "incarnation idea in all history": "The sublime conception of the existence of God and of the existence of revelation is not a spontaneous generation from the brain of man. Tyndal and Pasteur have demonstrated that there is no spontaneous generation from the inorganic to the organic. Just as little is there, or could there be, a spontaneous generation of the idea of the infinite from the brain of the finite. The fact, in each case, is the result of a touch from above. All humanity points back to a golden age, when man was taught of the divine by the divine, that in that knowledge he might know why he himself existed, and how his life was to be shaped."

The necessity for a revealing God to be in continual revelation, and to a fallen race, in continual adaptation to its necessities, inevitably links the idea of incarnation with the Christian conception of the divine, and its fullest statement that which accounts for the appearance of Jesus Christ.

INCARNATION.

Bishop Keane, in tracing the history of the idea, shows it to be universal. The "primitive teaching of man by his creator has been transformed in the lapse of ages, in the vicissitudes of distant wanderings, of varying fortunes, and of changing culture; still, the comparative study of ancient religions shows that in them all there has existed one central, pivotal concept, dressed, indeed, in various garbs of myth and legend and philosophy, yet ever recognizably the same — the concept of the fallen race of man and of a future restorer, deliverer, redeemer, who, being human, should yet be different from and above the merely human."

Pointing out, then, the difference in the Eastern and Western concepts of man, leading to different ideas of the indwelling of the divine, and tracing the voice of the prophets pointing forward to him that is to come, and showing in its fulfillment the divine answer to a universal expectation and a universal need, he presents the reasonableness of the incarnation as follows:

"Reason sees that the finite could not thus mount to the infinite any more than matter of itself could mount to spirit. But could not the infinite stoop to the finite and lift it to his bosom and unite it with himself, with no confounding of the finite with the infinite nor of the infinite with the finite, yet so that they shall be linked in one? Here reason can discern no contradiction of ideas, nothing beyond the power of the infinite. But could the infinite stoop to this? Reason sees that to do so would cost the infinite nothing, since he is ever his unchanging self; it sees, moreover, that since creation is the offspring not of his need but of his bounty, of his love, it would be most worthy of infinite love to thus perfect the creative act, to thus lift up the creature and bring all things into unity and harmony. Then must reason declare it is not only possible but it is most fitting that it should be so.

"Moreover, we see that it is this very thing that all humanity has been craving for, whether intelligently or not. This very thing all religions have been looking forward to or have been groping for in the dark. Turn we then to himself and ask: 'Art thou he who is to come, or look we for another?' To that question he must answer, for the world needs and must have the truth. Meek and humble of heart though he be, the world has a right to know whether he be indeed 'the Expected of the Nations, the Immanuel, Lord with us.' Therefore does he answer clearly and unmistakably:

"Abraham rejoiced that he should see my day. He saw it and was glad.

"Art thou then older than Abraham?

"Before Abraham was I am.

"Who art thou, then?

"I am the beginning, who also speak to you.

"Whosoever seeth me seeth the Father; I and the Father are one.

"No one cometh to the Father but by me."

The appeal of Bishop Keane to Jesus Christ as the revealed God, in whom is the fulfillment of divine promise and the substance of things longed for by the sages of the Gentiles, was fitly followed by the address of the Rev. J. K. Smyth, of the New Jerusalem church in Boston Highlands, on "The Incarnation of God in Christ," from which we may quote at length:

"Christianity, in its broadest as well as its deepest sense, means the presence of God in humanity. It is the revelation of God in his world; the opening up of a straight, sure way to that God; and a new tidal flow of divine life to all the sons of men. The hope of this has, in some measure, been in every age and in every religion, stirring them with expectation. Evil might be strong; but a day would come when the seed of a woman would bruise the serpent's head, even though it should bruise the conqueror's heel. God in his world to champion and redeem it! This is what the religions of the ages have, in some form and with various degrees of certainty, looked for. This is what sang itself into the songs and prophecies of Israel. 'And the glory of Jehovah shall be revealed:

and all flesh shall see it together; for the mouth of Jehovah hath spoken it.

"'Behold, the Lord Jehovah will come in strength, and his arm shall rule for him. Behold his reward is with him and his work before him. He shall feed his flock like a shepherd. He shall gather the lambs with his arms, and carry them in his bosom, and shall gently lead those that are with young.'

"Christianity is in the world to utter her belief that he who revealed himself as the Good Shepherd realizes these expectations and fulfills these promises, and that in the Word made flesh the glory of Jehovah has been revealed and all flesh may see it together. Even in childhood he bears the name Immanuel, which, being interpreted, is 'God with us.' He explains his work and his presence by declaring that it is the coming of the kingdom — not of law, nor of earthly government, nor of ecclesiasticism, but of God. His purpose, to manifest and bring forth the love and the wisdom of God; his miracles, simply the attestations of the divine immanence; his supreme end, the culmination of all his labors; his sufferings, his victories, to become the open and glorified medium of divine life to the world. It is not another Moses, nor another Elias, but God in the world — God with us — this, the supreme announcement of Christianity, asserting his immanence, revealing God and man as intended for each other, and rousing in man slumbering wants and capacities to realize the new vision of manhood that dawns upon him from this luminous Figure.

"Christianity affirms as a fundamental fact of the God it worships that he is a God who does not hide or withhold himself, but who is ever going forth to man in the effort to reveal himself, and to be known and felt according to the degree of man's capacity and need. This self-manifestation or 'forthgoing of all that is known or knowable of the divine perfections' is the Logos, or Word; and it is the very center of Christian revelation. This Word is God, not withdrawn in dreary solitude, but coming into intelligible and personal manifestation. From the beginning — for so we may now read the 'Golden Proem' of St. John's Gospel, with its wonderful spiritual history of the Logos — from the beginning God has this desire to go forth to something outside of himself and be known by it. 'In the beginning was the Word.' Hence the creation. 'All things were made by him.' Hence, too, out of this divine desire to reveal and accommodate himself to man, his presence in various forms of religion. 'He was in the world.' Even in man's sin and spiritual blindness the eternal Logos seeks to bring itself to his consciousness.

"'The light shineth in the darkness.' But gradually through the ages, through man's sinfulness, his spiritual perceptions become dim and he sees as in a state of open-eyed blindness only the forms through which the divine mind has sought to manifest himself. 'He was in the world and the world knew him not.' What more can be done? Type, symbol, religious ceremonials, scriptures — all have been employed Has not man slipped beyond the reach of the divine endeavors? But the Christian history of the Logos moves on to its supreme announcement: 'And the Word was made flesh and dwelt among us, and we beheld his glory, the glory as of the only begotten of the Father, full of grace and truth.' Not some angel come from heaven to deliver some further message; not another prophet sprung from our bewildered race to chide, to warn, or to exhort; but the Logos, which in the beginning was with God and which was God; the Jehovah of the old prophecies, whose glory, it had been promised, would be revealed that all flesh might see it together. And so in the Christian view of it the history of the Logos completes itself in the story of the manger. And so, too, the incarnation, instead of being exceptional, is exactly in line with what the Logos has from the beginning been doing. God, as the Word, has ever been coming to man in a form accommodated to his need, keeping step with his steps until, in the completeness of this desire to bring himself to man where he is, he appears to the natural senses and in a form suitable to our natural life.

"In the Christian conception of God, as one who seeks to reveal himself to man, it simply is inevitable that the Word should manifest himself on the very lowest plane of man's life if at any time it would be true to say of the spiritual condition: 'This people's heart is waxed gross, and their ears are dull of hearing and their eyes they have closed.' It is not extraordinary in the sense of its being a hard or an unnatural thing for God to do. He has

SWAMI VIVEKANANDA,
Hindu Monk, India.

always been approaching man, always adapting his revelations to human conditions and needs. It is this constant accommodation and manifestation that has kept man's power of spiritual thought alive. The history of religions, together with their remains, is a proof of it. The testimony of the historic faiths presented in this parliament has confirmed it as the most self-evident thing of the divine nature in his dealings with the children of men, and the incarnation as its natural and completest outcome.

"And when we begin to follow the life of him whose footprints, in the light of Christian history and experience, are still looked upon as the very footprints of the Incarnate Word, the gospel story is a story of toil, of suffering, of storm, and tempest; a story of sacrifice, of love so pure and holy that even now it has the power to touch, to thrill, to re-create man's selfish nature. There is an undoubted actuality in the human side of this life, but just as surely there is a certain divine something forever speaking through those human tones and reaching out through those kindly hands. The character of the Logos is never lost, sacrificed, or lowered. It is always this divine something trying to manifest itself, trying to make itself understood, trying to redeem man from his slavery to evil and draw to itself his spiritual attachment.

"Here, plain to human sight, is part of that agelong effort of the Word to reveal itself to man only now through a nature formed and born for the purpose. We are reminded of it when we hear him say: 'Before Abraham was, I am.' We are assured of it when he declares that he came forth from the Father. And we know that he has triumphed when, at the last, we hear his promise, 'Lo, I am with you always.' It is the Logos speaking. The divine purpose has been fulfilled. The Word has come forth on this plane of human life, manifested himself and established a relationship with man nearer and dearer than ever before. He has made himself available and indispensable to every need or effort. 'Without me ye can do nothing.' In his divine humanity he has established a perfect medium whereby we may have free and immediate access to God's fatherly help. 'I am the Door of the sheep.' 'I am the Way, the Truth, and the Life.' In this thought of the divine character of the Son of Man the early Christians found strength and comfort. For a time they did not attempt to define this faith theologically. It was a simple, direct, earnest faith in the goodness and redeeming power of the God-man, whose perfect nature had inspired them to believe in the reality of his heavenly reign. They felt that the risen Lord was near them; that he was the Saviour so long promised; the world's hope, 'in whom dwelleth all the fullness of the Godhead bodily.' But to-day man claims his right to enter understandingly into the mysteries of faith, and reason asks, How could God or the divine Logos be made flesh?

"Yet, in seeking for an answer to such an inquiry, we are at the same time seeking to know of the origin of human life. The conception and birth of Jesus Christ, as related in the gospels, is, declares the reason, a strange fact. So, too, is the conception and birth of every human being. Neither can be explained by any principle of naturalism, which regards the external as first and the internal as second and of comparative unimportance. Neither can be understood unless it be recognized that spiritual forces and substances are related to natural forces and substances as cause and effect; and that they, the former, are prior and the active, formative agents playing upon, and received by, the latter. We do not articulate words and then try to pack them with ideas and intentions. The process is the reverse. First the intention, then that intention coming forth as a thought, and then the thought incarnating itself by means of articulated sounds or written characters.

"By this same law man is primarily, essentially, a spiritual being. In the very form of his creation that which essentially is the man, and which in time loves, thinks, makes plans and efforts for useful life, is spiritual. In his conception, then, the human seed must not only be acted upon but be derived from invisible, spiritual substances which are clothed with natural substances for the sake of conveyance. That which is slowly developed into a human being or soul must be a living organism composed of spiritual substances. Gradually that primitive form becomes enveloped and protected within successive clothings, while the mother, from the substances of the natural world, silently weaves the swathings and coverings which are to serve as a natural or physical body and make possible its entrance into this outer court of life.

"We do not concede, then, that there is anything impossible or contrary to order in the declaration of the gospel, but 'that which is conceived in her is of the Holy Spirit.' It is still in line with the general law of the conception and birth of all human beings. The primitive form or nature, as in the case of man, is spiritual. But in this instance it is not derived from a human father, but is especially formed or molded by the divine creative spirit; formed as with us, of spiritual substances; formed with a perfection and with infinite possibilities of development unknown to us; formed, too, for the special purpose of being the perfect instrument or medium upon and through which the divine might act as its very soul. Because that primitive form is divinely molded or begotten instead of being derived from a finite paternity, it is unique. It is divine in first principles. In the outer clothings of the natural mind and in the successive wrappings furnished by the woman nature it shares our weakness. But primarily, essentially, it is born with the capacity of becoming divine through the removal of whatever is imperfect or limiting, and through complete union with the divine which formed it for himself.

"Very like our humanity in all that pertains to the growth of the natural body and natural mind would be this humanity of the Son of Man. The same tenderness and helplessness of its infantile body; the same possibility of weariness, hunger, thirst, pain: the same exposure, too, in the lower planes of the mind, to the assaults of evil resulting in internal struggle, temptation, and anguish of spirit. And yet there is always an unlikeness, a difference, in that the very primitive, determining forms and possibilities of that humanity are divinely begotten. And so we think of this humanity of Jesus Christ as so formed and born as to be able to serve as a perfect instrument whereby the eternal Logos might come and dwell among us; might so express and pour forth his love; might so accommodate and reveal his truth; might, in a word, so set himself on all the planes of angelic and human existence as to be forever after immediately present in them, and so become literally, actually God-with-us.

"Gradually this was done. Gradually the divine life of love and wisdom came into the several planes which, by incarnation, existed in this humanity, removing from them whatever was limiting or imperfect, substituting what was divine, filling them, glorifying them, and in the end making them a very part of himself.

"This brings into harmony the two elements which we are apt to look upon and keep distinct, the human and the divine. For he himself tells us of a process, a distinct change which his humanity underwent, and which is the key to his real nature. 'The Holy Spirit,' says the record, 'was not yet given, because that Jesus was not yet glorified.' Some divine operation was going on within that humanity which was not fully accomplished. But on the eve of his crucifixion he exclaimed: 'Now is the Son of Man glorified and God is glorified in him.' It is this process of putting off what was finite and infirm in the human, and the substitution of the divine from within, resulting in the formation of a divine humanity. So long as that is going on the human as the Son feels a separation from the divine as the Father, and speaks of it and turns to it as though it were another person. But when the glorification is accomplished, when the divine has entirely filled the human and they act 'reciprocally and unanimously as soul and body,' then the declaration is: 'I and the Father are one.' Divine in origin, human in birth, divinely human through glorification. As to his soul, or inmost being, the Father; as to his human, the Son; as to the life and saving power that go forth from his glorified nature, the Holy Spirit.

"This story of the divine life in its descent to man, this coming or incarnation of the Logos through the humanity of Jesus Christ, it is the sweet and serious privilege of Christianity to carry into the world. I try to state it; I try from a new theological standpoint to show reasons for its rational acceptance. But I know that however true and necessary explanations may be, the fact itself transcends them all. No one in this free assembly is required or expected to hide his denominationalism. And yet I love to stand with my fellow Christians and unite with them in that simplest, most comprehensive creed that was ever uttered, *Credo Domino*. Denominationalism, dogmatism, aside! Aside, too, all prejudices and practices. What is the simplest, the fundamental idea of the being of Jesus Christ?

Brother men, are we not ready to unite in saying it is, and saying it to the whole round world: that the Lord Jesus Christ is the life or the love of God, manifesting itself to man, going out into the world, awakening the capacity which is in every man for spiritual, yes, for divine life? Is not that the very heart of the gospel, or rather is not that the gospel? And is it not equally true that up to this hour there is no fact so real, no fact so powerful, no fact that is working such spiritual wonders as the fact, the influence, the being of Jesus Christ?

"We are sitting here as the first great parliament of the religions of the world. We rightly believe, we boldly say, that from this time on the fatherhood of God and the brotherhood of man must mean more to us than ever before, and none can be so timid but would dare to stand here and say that in this hall the death-knell of bigotry has sounded. Yet it were a sacrilege to suppose that the large tolerance which has been shown here, and which has secured for the representatives of every faith such a hospitable reception, is the evolution of mere good nature. It is the Spirit of him whose utterance of those simple words, which have been inscribed as the text of the Columbian Liberty Bell, are already ringing in 'the Christ that is to be'—'A new commandment I give unto you, That ye love one another.'"

SIN AND RECONCILIATION.

If we turn now to the subject of Sin and Reconciliation, it is of interest to note the following testimony from the Rev. T. E. Slater of Bangalore, India. Having pointed out that the speculative problem before the Hindu philosopher and the struggle of the religious man have been how to break the dream, get rid of the impostures of sense and time, emancipate self from the bondage of a fleeting world, and attain the one reality, the divine, he shows that idolatry itself, degrading as it is, is an effort to realize to the senses what otherwise is only an idea.

"Idolatry" he says, "is a strong human protest against pantheism, which denies the personality of God, and atheism, which denies God altogether; it testifies to the natural craving of the heart to have before it some manifestation of the unseen — to behold a humanized God. It is not, at bottom, an effort to get away from God, but to bring God near.

"Once more. The idea of the need of sacrificial acts, 'the first and primary rites' — eucharistic, sacramental, and propitiary — bearing the closest parallelism to the provisions of the Mosaic economy, and prompted by a sense of personal unworthiness, guilt, and misery — that life is to be forfeited to the Divine Proprietor — is ingrained in the whole system of Vedic Hinduism. A sense of original corruption has been felt by all classes of Hindus, as indicated in the prayer: 'I am sinful, I commit sin, my nature is sinful. Save me, O thou lotus-eyed Hari, the remover of sin.'

"No literature," he continues, "not even the Jewish, contains so many words relating to sacrifice as Sanskrit. The land has been saturated with blood. The secret of this great importance attached to sacrifice is to be found in the remarkable fact that the authorship of the institution is attributed to 'Creation's Lord' himself and its date is reckoned as coeval with the creation. The idea exists in the three chief Vedas, and in the Brahmanas and Upanishads that Prajapati, 'the lord and supporter of his creatures'—the Purusha (primeval male)—begotten before the world, becoming half immortal and half mortal in a body fit for sacrifice, offered himself for the devas (emancipated mortals) and for the benefit of the world; thereby making all subsequent sacrifice a reflection or figure of himself. The ideal of the Vedic Prajapati, mortal and yet divine, himself both priest and victim, who by death overcame death, has long since been lost in India. Among the many gods of the Hindu pantheon none has ever come forward to claim the vacant throne once reverenced by Indian rishis. No other than the Jesus of the Gospels—'the Lamb slain from the foundation of the world'—has ever appeared to fulfill this primitive idea of redemption by the efficacy of sacrifice; and when this Christian truth is preached it ought not to sound strange to Indian ears. An eminent Hindu preacher has said that no one can be a true Hindu without being a true Christian. But one of the saddest and most disastrous facts of the India of to-day is that modern Brahmanism, like modern Parseeism, is fast losing its old ideas, relaxing its hold on the more spiritual portions, the distinctive tenets of the ancient faith. Happily, however, a reaction has set in, mainly through the exertions of these scholars, and the more thoughtful minds are earnestly seeking to recover from their sacred books some of the buried treasures of the past."

The reference here to Parseeism recalls what J. J. Modi says in his paper on the religion of Zoroaster about the Parsee doctrine of purification. Man to be perfect before God must shun evil, and work righteousness; and the sacred fire is the symbol of the purifying temptation by which he is perfected.

"Now what does a fire so prepared signify to a Parsee? He thinks to himself: 'When this fire on this vase before me, though pure in itself, though the noblest of the creations of God, and though the best symbol of the divinity, had to undergo certain processes of purification, had to draw out, as it were, its essence — nay, its quintessence — of purity to enable itself to be worthy of occupying this exalted position; how much more necessary, more essential, and more important it is for me — a a poor mortal who is liable to commit sins and crimes, and who comes into contact with hundreds of evils, both physical and mental — to undergo the process of purity and piety by making my thoughts, words, and actions pass, as it were, through a sieve of piety and purity, virtue and morality, and to separate by that means my good thoughts, good words, and good actions from bad thoughts, bad words, and bad actions, so that I may in my turn be enabled to acquire an exalted position in the next world.' Again, the fires put together as above are collected from the houses of men of different grades in society. This reminds a Parsee that, as all these fires from the houses of men of different grades have all, by the process of purification, equally acquired the exalted place in the vase, so before God all men — no matter to what grades of society they belong — are equal, provided they pass through the process of purification, *i. e.*, provided they preserve purity of thoughts, purity of words, and purity of deeds.

"Again, when a Parsee goes before the sacred fire, which is kept all day and night burning in the fire temple, the officiating priest presents before him the ashes of a part of the consumed fire. The Parsee applies it to his forehead just as a Christian applies the consecrated water in his church, and thinks to himself: 'Dust to dust. The fire, all brilliant, shining, and resplendent, has spread the fragrance of the sweet-smelling sandal and frankincense round about, but is at last reduced to dust. So it is destined for me. After all I am to be reduced to dust and have to depart from this transient life. Let me do my best to spread, like this fire, before my death, the fragrance of charity and good deeds and lead the light of righteousness and knowledge before others.' In short, the sacred fire burning in a fire temple serves as a perpetual monitor to a Parsee standing before it to preserve piety, purity, humility, and brotherhood."

And in evidence that there is no thought of a substitutional righteousness in connection with the symbol, but a real and living righteousness to be adopted and established in the worshiper, he says:

"All Parsee prayers begin with an assurance to do acts that would please the Almighty God. The assurance is followed by an expression of regret for past evil thoughts, words, or deeds, if any. Man is liable to err, and so, if during the interval any errors of commission or omission are comitted, a Parsee in the beginning of his prayers repents for those errors. He says:

"'O Omniscient Lord! I repent of all my sins. I repent of all evil thoughts that I might have entertained in my mind, of all the evil words that I have spoken, of all the evil actions that I might have committed. O Omniscient Lord! I repent of all the faults that might have originated with me, whether they refer to thoughts, words, or deeds, whether they appertain to my body or soul, whether they be in connection with the material world or spiritual.'"

This does not greatly differ in its ideal from what is known among us as liberal Christianity, which holds that moral conduct when performed by man in acknowledgment of God, and in harmony with his divine and all-pervading life, has a spiritual value. Thus Prof. C. H. Toy of Harvard University, in a paper on "Religion and Conduct," says:

"In the sphere of religion the two sorts of sanction are what we call natural and supernatural. The laws of nature may be considered to be laws of God, and the natural penalties and rewards of life to be divine sanctions. Obedience to these laws is a moral act, because it involves control of self in the interest of organic development; but supernatural sanctions are inorganic and non-moral, since they do not appeal to a rational self-control. He who is honest merely to escape punishment or receive reward fixed by external law is not honest at all; but he who observes the laws of health or of honesty because he perceives that they are necessary to the well-being of the world is also religious if he recognizes these laws as the ordination of God.

"When religious sanctions are spoken of it is commonly the supernatural sort that is meant. It is an interesting question how far the belief in these is now morally effective. That it has at various times been influential can not be doubted. In the ancient world and in medieval Europe the deity was believed to intervene supernaturally in this life for the protection of innocence and the punishment of wickedness; but this belief appears to be vanishing and can not be called an effective moral force at the present day. Men think of reward and punishment as belonging to the future, and this conception is probably of some weight; yet its practical importance is much diminished by the distance and the dimness of the day of reckoning. The average man has too little imagination to realize the remote future. At the critical moment it is usually passion or the present advantage that controls action.

"It is also true that the supernatural side of the belief in future retribution is passing away; it is becoming more and more the conviction of the religious world that the future life must be morally the continuation and consequence of the present. This must be esteemed a great gain — it tends to banish the mechanical and emphasize the ethical element in life and to raise religion to the plane of rationality. Rational religious morality is obedience to the laws of nature as laws of God.

"We are thus led to the other side of religion, communion with God as the effective source of religious influence on conduct. It is this, in the first place, that gives eternal validity to the laws of right. Resting on conscience and the constitution of society, these laws may be in themselves obligatory on the world of men, but they acquire a universal character only when we remember that human nature itself is an effluence of the divine, and that human experience is the divine self-revelation.

"Further, the consciousness of the divine presence should be the most potent factor in man's moral life. The thought of the ultimate basis of life, incomprehensible in his essence yet known through his self-outputting in the world as the ideal of right, as a comrade of man in moral life, should be, if received into the soul as a living every-day fact, such a purifying and uplifting influence as no merely human relationship has ever engendered.

"The true power of religion," he concludes, "lies in the contact between the divine soul and the soul of man. It must be admitted that to attain this is no easy thing. To feel the reality of a divine personality in the universe, to value this personality as the ideal of justice and love, to keep the image of it fresh and living in the mind day by day in the midst of the throng of petty and serious cares of life, demands an imaginative power and a force of will rarely found among men. It is in this power that the great creative religious minds have excelled. The mass of religious people are controlled by lower considerations, and never reach the plane of pure religious feeling. Most men look to God as their helper in physical things, or as an outside law-giver, rather than as their comrade in moral struggle. Thus religion has not come to its rights in the world; it still occupies, as a rule, the low plane of early non-moral thought; but is there any reason why it should continue in this inferior plane? Is there anything to prevent our living in moral contact with the soul of the world, and thence deriving the inspiration and strength we need? What has been done by some may be done in a measure by all. Inadequate conceptions of God and of the moral life must be swept away, the free activity of the human soul must be recognized and relied on, the habit of contemplation of the ideal must be cultivated; we must feel ourselves to be literally and truly co-workers with God. In the presence of such a communion would not moral evil be powerless over man? Finally, we here have a conception of religion in which almost all, perhaps all, the systems of the world may agree. It is our hope of unity."

Still, on the other hand, it is contended that all the systems of the world show man's need of a divine reconciliation. The old doctrine of a substitutional sacrifice and vicarious atonement was set forth by Rev. Dr. Kennedy, in a paper on "The Redemption of Sinful Man through Jesus Christ,' with great frankness. Of the fall, and its effects, he says: "Adam of his own free will upset the first order of God's providence, and he now came under another order; he had been innocent and just, he was now a guilty and fallen man; he could not enter into heaven, and he was doomed to suffer the other miseries brought on by his own sin until God saw fit to send him a Redeemer. He no doubt soon repented of his sin; and if he returned to God with a sincerely contrite heart the guilt would be remitted and he would not be punished eternally for it. But he was powerless to repair the injury done, because the gifts and graces he had lost were gratuitous favors, not due to his nature, but granted through pure love and goodness by God; hence their restoration was subject to his good pleasure.

"Unfortunately for us this fall of the father of the human race affected his posterity. The perfections of original justice would have passed to his descendants had he remained faithful, but he failed to comply with the conditions on which they had been granted, and, having lost them himself, he could not transmit them to his children. In consequence of his sin we too were deprived of the supernatural perfections that he possessed. Though not guilty of any actual personal sins, the children of Adam are, as St. Paul says (Eph. ii, 3), 'by nature children of wrath '; they are displeasing in the sight of God, because he does not see in their souls the graces, virtues, and perfections he had intended for all, and of which they were deprived through the fault of Adam by an act in which he was morally the representative of the human race. This is what is meant by original sin; at least this is the explanation of its essence given by the majority of theologians; and if any one tries to see in original sin as taught by the church a personal act by which men offend God, he will not succeed, because it is not a personal sin; it is the habitual state displeasing to God in which the souls of men are left since the father of the human race offended God by an act of proud disobedience.

"With the supernatural grace the preternatural gifts were also lost. We became subject to death, not only as to a law of nature but also as a penalty, for 'by one man sin entered into this world, and by sin death, and so death passed upon all men, in whom all have sinned.' (Rom. v, 12.) We also experience the stings of conscience, the war of the flesh against the spirit, which would, in the benevolent designs of providence, have been prevented by the subjection of the mind to grace. Our nature, also, was wounded, like the nature of Adam, with the three wounds of ignorance, weakness, and passion. Then began the rule of him who had the empire of death, that is to say, the devil (Heb. ii, 14), which was to last until Christ came to destroy that empire by his death. St. Augustine, in one of his sermons, calls this unhappy condition a sickness of human nature that had spread over the face of the earth, '*Magnus per orbem jacebat ægrotus.*' And in another place he says that in consequence of sin, the nature of man, which should have been a beautiful olive tree planted and watered and nurtured by the hand of God, and bearing fruits for eternity, became a miserable oleaster, contemptible and disagreeable by the ugliness of its appearance and the bitterness of its false fruits. The work of the gardener had been interfered with and man was condemned to taste the bitter fruits of his own planting. He was displeasing to God and he needed some one who could reconcile him with the heavenly Father by atoning for his sins; he had lost the grace of God, and of himself could not recover it; he was a slave under the power of Satan, and stood in need of a redeemer."

Expounding the plan of redemption, he continues: "In the first place, it must be borne in mind that God could, if he willed, have chosen another method of redemption. Being Lord of all things, he might have condoned Adam's offense and restored to man his lost prerogatives without demanding any atonement. He might, if he willed, have accepted in satisfaction for sin the salutary penances of Adam or of some of his descendants. But, says St. Athanasius, in this we must consider not what God could have done, but what was best for man, for that was chosen. Away then with all thoughts of excessive rigor on the part of God. He willed to redeem and save us through the sufferings and merits of Christ, because it was better for us; and at the same time he gave to the world the greatest manifestation ever known of his own goodness, power, wisdom, and justice, as we are told by St. John Damascene and St. Thomas Aquinas — two princes of theology. This plan of redemption was freely and lovingly accepted by the second person of the trinity, and the Son came into the world in the form of man that he might be our Saviour; and as a Saviour he manifested himself from the first moment of his incarnation until the day of his ascension; a Saviour he is still, for as St. Paul tells us (Rom. viii, 34), sitting now at the right hand of God he continually intercedes for us, offering to the Father in our behalf his superabundant merits. He was a Saviour by his teaching, by his example, and by his death. The prophet Isaiah had foretold, 800 years before his birth: 'Behold, I have given him for a witness before the people, for a leader and for a master to the Gentiles' (lv, 4); and when he came, after he had been baptized by St. John, the Father's voice from the clouds announced that he was the divinely appointed teacher of mankind: 'This is my beloved Son, in whom I am well pleased; hear ye him' (Matt. xvii, 5), and St. Peter afterward proposed that his Master's doctrine was heavenly and salutary: 'Thou, O Lord, hath the words of eternal life' (John vi, 69).''

Then, of the efficacy of Christ's death, he says: "Then it was that our Saviour consented to be a voluntary victim offered up in expiation for the sins of the world. 'The Word was made flesh and dwelt amongst us' (John i, 14); Christ came into the world, true God and true man. Being man, he could suffer; being God, any one of his actions would have infinite value both for merit and for atonement. 'God laid on him the iniquity of us all,' says Isaiah (liii, 6); by his death God's justice was satisfied and man was redeemed; for, says St. Peter (I Ep. i, 18), we were 'not redeemed with corruptible things, as gold and silver, but with the precious blood of Christ, as of a lamb unspotted and undefiled.' Thus was blotted out the handwriting of the decree that was against us (Col. ii, 14). By his death Christ not only freed us from evil, he also merited for us the graces we need in order that we may do good, performing actions meritorious of eternal life. Without Christ we can do nothing (John xv, 5). All those who were saved under the old law were saved through faith in the Redeemer to come; grace was granted to them owing to his foreseen merits. In the new law all our sufficiency is from him (II Cor. ii, 3); all graces are granted, as we ask them, 'through the merits of our Lord and Saviour Jesus Christ.' He merited these graces for us by all the acts of his life, but principally by dying for us; the precious blood shed on Calvary flows through the church; it vivifies the sacraments, the channels of grace, by partaking of which we drink from that 'fountain of water springing into life everlasting' (John iv, 14).''

Equally orthodox, but carrying the discussion into the realm of the effect in man of the acceptance of Christ's sacrifice, was the address of Walter Elliott, of the Paulist Convent, New York, from which we cite the following as showing the orthodox ideal of the atonement, arbitrary though the means may seem, is with some, at least, conceived as a real and living union of the soul with God:

"'The justification of a wicked man is his translation from the state in which man is born as a son of the first Adam into the state of grace and adoption of the sons of God by the second Adam, Jesus Christ, our Saviour.' These words of the Council of Trent affirm that the boon of God's favor is not merely restoration to humanity's natural innocence. God's friendship for man is elevation to a state higher than nature's highest, and infinitely so, and yet a dignity toward which all men are drawn by the unseen attraction of divine grace and toward which in their better moments they consciously strive, however feebly and blindly. Religion, as understood by Christianity, means new life for man, different life, additional life. The Christian mind is thus to be discovered and tested by comparison with the highest standard: 'Be ye perfect, as your heavenly Father is perfect.'

"Before coming to the ways and means and processes of acquiring this divine life we must consider atonement for sin. It may be asked, Why does Christ elevate us to union with his Father through suffering? The answer is that God is dealing with a race which has degraded itself with rebellion and with crime, which naturally involves suffering. God's purpose is now just what it was in the beginning, to communicate himself to each human being, and to do it personally, elevating men to brotherhood with his own divine Son, making them partakers of the same grace which dwells in the soul of Christ, and sharers hereafter in the same blessedness which he possesses with the Father. To accomplish this purpose God originally constituted man in a supernatural condition of divine favor. That lost by sin, God, by an act of grace yet more signal, places his Son in the circumstances of humiliation and suffering due to sin. This is the order of atonement, a word which has come to signify a mediation through suffering, although the etymological meaning of it is bringing together into one. Mediation is now, as ever before, the constant and final purpose of God's loving dealing with us.

"Religion is positive. It makes me good with Christ's goodness. Religion does essentially more than rid me of evil. In the mansions of the Father, sorrow opens the outer door of the atrium in which I am pardoned, and love leads to the throne room. If forgiveness and union be distinct, it is only as we think of them, for to God they are one. And this is to be noted: all infants who pass into heaven through the laver of regeneration have had no conscious experience of any kind, and yet will enjoy the union of filiation forever. Nor can it be denied that there are multitudes of adults whose sanctification has had no conscious process of the remission of grave sin, for many such have never been guilty of it. To excite them to a fictitious sense of sinfulness is untruthful, unjust, and unchristian. Hounding innocent souls into the company of demons is false zeal and is cruel. The expiation of sin is the removal of an obstacle to our union with God. Nothing hinders the progress of guileless or repentant souls, even their peace of mind, more than prevalent misconceptions on this point. Freed from sin many fall under the delusion that all is done; not to commit sin is assumed to be the end of religion. In reality pardon is but the initial work of grace, and even pardon is not possible without the gift of love. The sufferings of Christ as well as whatever is of a penitential influence in his religion are not in the nature of merely paying a penalty, but is chiefly an offering of love. Atonement is related to mediation as its condition and not as its essence. We are washed in the Redeemer's blood, but that blood does not remain on the surface; it penetrates us and sanctifies our own blood, mingling with it. We are not ransomed only, but ennobled. The process on man's part of union with God is free and loving acceptance of all his invitations, inner and outer, natural and revealed, organic and personal. Loving God is the practical element in our reception of the Holy Spirit. The fruition of love is union with the beloved. If to be regenerated means to be born of God, then what is to be sought after is newness of life by the immediate contact with life's source and center in love. The perfection of any finite being is the closest possible identity with its ideal. The supreme end and office of religion is to cause men by love personally to approximate to the ideal, not merely of humanity, but of humanity made one with the Deity."

The objection to this idea of the divine government and plan of atonement has always been its ideal of God. It presupposes that he needs to be reconciled and appeased and his government vindicated; whereas the apostle declares, "God was in Christ reconciling the world unto himself." The problem with most minds is, How did God in Christ redeem mankind from the great weight and bondage of evil, and how does he carry over to man the power of his life and work so as to be in man a real and vital reconciliation and union with God?

On this point the paper of the Rev. Theodore F. Wright, Ph. D., of Cambridge will be read with interest, and by many with satisfaction, as presenting a view of the subject distinctive from the orthodox and from the moral influence theory of atonement, and one which makes the statement of his subject significant. His subject was "Reconciliation Vital, not Vicarious."

"There are certain dicta of Scripture," he said, "which are universal because fundamental and fundamental because universal. One of these is that saying of the Apostle John, 'God is love; and he that dwelleth in love dwelleth in God, and God in him.' Once of sympathies so narrow that he was for bringing fire from heaven down upon a village which would not receive his Lord as he journeyed, he was now so tenderly conscious of the infinite love which had sought him out and gathered him that he could say: 'He that loveth not knoweth not God, for God is love; beloved, if

God so love us, we also ought to love one another.' John had attained to this conviction by the process of religious experience. Others have seen the same infinite fact written in vernal fields and ripening harvests. Others find it in the intricate harmony of natural forces. They all see that there is as the center and source of life a fountain of fatherliness which is ever begetting and nurturing, so that, indeed, we can not conceive of the idle God, the neglectful God, or the God of limited interests. Our minds will not work until we place before them the ever-creating God, who neither slumbers nor sleeps; the ever present help. 'Peradventure he sleepeth' might be said of Baal, for there was no answer; but when Elijah called on the God of Abraham, of Isaac, and of Israel, 'the fire of the Lord fell.' It is in the light of this fact of the universal divine love that the fallen condition of man finds its remedy disclosed. There may have been a time when this light was so dim that Judaism fancied its God a partisan, and a regressive Christianity thought that it had ascertained the limits of the divine care, but now we know that God is one, and that 'his tender mercies are over all his work.' This being so, it is true to say that fallen man was succored by the same love that created him. The father of the prodigal does not sulk in his tent while some elder brother is left to search out the wanderer and bring him in, pointing to the wounds he got in rescuing him as a means of softening the heart of the father; nay, the father watches the pathway with longings, and sends his love after the boy, and when the wayward one is yet a great way off, he sees, he hath compassion, he runs, he falls on his neck, he kisses him; he bids them bring the robe, the ring, the shoes, the fatted calf; he reproves the cold vindictiveness of the elder brother; he is all shepherd-like.

"We need not dogmatize as to the fallen state of man. Intellectually man has not fallen. He is as bright as he ever was. He is growing brighter. The evolution of the intellect is indisputable. But as to the will, what is man? Is he the worshiping child that he once was? Does he eagerly do the truth he learns or does he find it necessary to compel himself to do it? There is a degree of ignorance, of illiteracy, but it is easy to find a remedy for it in the common school. There is on every side a spectacle of lust, and greed, and indolence, and selfishness, and our schools touch it not. We are making men shrewd, but we are not making them good. The human mind wants reaching in its depths. The motives behind our thinking want renewal, else mind-life is like John Randolph's mackerel in the moonlight, which stank as it shone. So was man in the sad days of Roman sensuality and Jewish hypocrisy, and so do our daily chronicles testify to-day. The cure for the lost sheep is to seek for it till it is found. 'All we like sheep have gone astray; we have turned every one to his own way.' (Is. liii, 6.) The question is, How should the divine love accomplish the purpose with which it must be teeming — the recovery of the lost state? Our answer is in general to say that the remedy was within the keeping of the infinite love and wisdom which had so far made and conducted man, or we must hold some view which limits the Holy One of Israel. If God would come with any mercy he must descend to the place of the fallen. If he would conquer the evil without destroying them, he must contend with them on their own plane. To take upon himself the nature born of woman would be his means of redemption. He must take on the office of Joshua, who led the people out of the wilderness into their inheritance. And a virgin conceived and bore a son, and called his name Jesus — that is, Joshua. The Wisdom or Word of God was made flesh, so that we behold the glory of the Father. It was the Father in the Son who did the works. How marvelously clear are the prophetic songs of Mary and Zacharias. She said: 'My spirit hath rejoiced in God, my Saviour. He hath showed strength with his arm. He hath holpen his servant, Israel, in remembrance of his mercy, as he spake to our fathers.' And the father of the forerunner said: 'Blessed be the Lord God of Israel, for he hath visited and redeemed his people; that we, being delivered out of the hands of our enemies, might serve him without fear all the days of our life; the day-spring from on high hath visited us, to give light to them that sit in darkness and the shadow of death, to guide our feet in the way of peace.' Therefore John the Baptist proclaimed him as 'the Lamb of God that taketh away the sin of the world,' and therefore he bade his hearers prepare the way of Jehovah, and make straight his path.

"Born of woman, and so open to every temptation, he was early led to find the written word, his light of life. He went about his father's business by expounding it. Tried in the wilderness, he made no other answer than the law. Going about doing good, he healed the sick and gave sight to the blind, and brought good tidings to the meek. At Jerusalem he cleansed the temple of its corruption, even as he was daily rendering his own nature the temple of God. The inevitable conflict was not shunned. The perceived unfaithfulness of many did not provoke a word of resentment. The attempts of habitual sinners of this world and the other to overthrow him failed again and again, but it was inevitable that there must be a last and most direful assault. He foresaw it; but behold the conduct of infinite love! He bathed his disciples' feet in order to teach them the new commandment of love to one another. He bade them be not troubled, and spoke of the peace he had to give to them. He chastened himself in the garden. On his way to the cross he asked them to weep rather for themselves than for him. He gave the mother a son to care for her old age. To perjured Peter his answer had been but a look. To the false accusations he had been dumb. For his love they were his adversaries, but he gave himself unto prayer. Rising again, he came with indescribable gentleness to the recognition of Mary Magdalene. To the two discouraged disciples he was all patience. To doubting Thomas he was infinitely condescending. As he stood there, for the time made visible to their spiritual sight, having entered where the doors were shut, he was the embodiment of prophecy fulfilled, of divine love triumphant. He was, he is, 'Our Lord and our God,' 'the brightness of his glory, the express image of his person.'

"This is no merely vicarious act of a subordinate or additional person of God. It was the act of God himself to restore the vital union between man and himself, that union which man had severed by increasing self-assertion, waywardness, and wickedness, and which could only be renewed by contrition and return and reconciliation. In the case of the man healed of his blindness, in the ninth chapter of John, we have first the evil condition, then the remedy offered, next the remedy accepted, at once the cure effected, and finally a vital union of safety for him established with the Lord, as shown by his saying, 'Lord, I believe,' and by his worshiping him. In more difficult cases, as we know by some experience, the knowledge of the remedy may be cold and unfruitful in the memory until in seeking to lead a less selfish life, to be worthy of a loving wife or a trusting child, or to consecrate our lives in full to the Lord's service, we begin to form new motives with the divine aid; to hate what we once wickedly loved, and to love what we once wickedly hated; and so, little by little, born from above, a new heart is formed within us, and we come to act as faithful rather than as unfaithful servants of the Lord, as friends rather than as enemies. So do we cease to do evil and learn to do well, if we will. Thus we may see that the will and the power to rescue and to reconcile wayward souls sprang from the infinite love; that the method is that of the divine order, and that the result in the individual redeemed through repentance and regeneration is just what man's fallen state required and requires. It is precisely as Paul said: 'God was in Christ reconciling of the world unto himself.' (II Cor. v, 19.) And again he said: 'In him dwelleth all the fullness of the Godhead bodily.' (Col. xi, 9.) 'We dwell in him,' said John once more, 'and he in us; we loved him because he first loved us.' 'This is the true God and eternal life.'

> "'That uncreated beauty, which has gained
> My raptured heart, has all my glory stained;
> His loveliness my soul has prepossessed,
> And left no room for any other guest.'"

REVELATION AND THE SCRIPTURES.

If we turn to the subject of revelation we find abundant testimony to the universality of belief in revelation of some sort from God to man. An interesting descriptive and illustrative paper on "The Sacred Books of the World as Literature" was furnished by Prof. Milton S. Terry, D. D., who said in appeal for a larger study of all sacred literatures: "I am a Christian, and must needs look at things from a Christian point of view; but that fact should not hinder the broadest observation. Christian scholars have for centuries admired the poems of Homer, and will never lose interest in the story of Odysseus, the myriad-minded Greek, who traversed the roaring seas, touched many a foreign shore, and observed the habitations and customs of many men. Will they be likely to discard the recently deciphered Accadian hymns and Assyrian penitential psalms? Is it probable that men who can devote studious years to the philosophy of Plato and Aristotle will care nothing about the invocations of the old Persian Avesta, the Vedic hymns, the doctrines of Buddha, and the maxims of Confucius? Nay, I repeat it, I am a Christian; therefore I think there is nothing human or divine in any literature of the world that I can afford to ignore."

Beginning with a quotation from the Chinese on creation and setting in comparison with citations from the Vedas, and referring to the Scandinavian Edda, and the Chaldean account of creation, he says: "As theologians we naturally study these theosophic poems with reference to their origin and relationship. But we now call attention to the place they hold in the sacred literatures of the world. Each composition bears the marks of an individual genius. He may, and probably does, in every case express the current belief or tradition of his nation, but his description reveals a human mind wrestling with the mysterious problems of the world, and suggesting, if not announcing, some solution. As specimens of literature the various poems of creation exhibit a world-wide taste and tendency to cast in poetic form the profoundest thoughts which busy the human soul."

Speaking of the scriptures of Buddhism he gives some interesting facts: "The sacred scriptures of Buddhism comprise three immense collections known as the Tripitaka, or 'three baskets.' One of these contains the discourses of Buddha, another treats of doctrines and metaphysics, and another is devoted to ethics and discipline. In bulk these writings rival all that was ever included under the title of Veda, and contain more than seven times the amount of matter in the Scriptures of the Old and New Testaments. The greater portion of this extensive literature, in the most ancient texts, exists as yet only in manuscript. But as Buddhism spread and triumphed mightily in Southern and Eastern Asia, its sacred books have been translated into Pali, Burmese, Siamese, Tibetan, Chinese, and other Asiatic tongues. The Tibetan edition of the Tripitaka fills about 325 folio volumes. Every important tribe or nation which has adopted Buddhism appears to have a more or less complete Buddhist literature of its own. But all this literature, so vast that one lifetime seems insufficient to explore it thoroughly, revolves about a comparatively few and simple doctrines. First we have the four sublime Verities: (1) All existence, being subject to change and decay, is evil. (2) The source of all this evil is desire. (3) Desire and the evil which follows it may be made to cease. (4) There is a fixed and certain way by which to attain exemption from all evil. Next after these Verities are the doctrines of the Eightfold Path: (1) Right belief, (2) right judgment, (3) right utterance, (4) right motives, (5) right occupation, (6) right obedience, (7) right memory, and (8) right meditation. Then we have further, five commandments: (1) Do not kill; (2) do not steal; (3) do not

MISS JEANNE SORABJI,
Christian Convert, Bombay, India.

lie; (4) do not become intoxicated; (5) do not commit adultery."

Advancing to the sacred literature of China, he speaks as follows of the "books of Confucianism, which is par excellence the religion of the Chinese Empire. But Confucius was not the founder of the religion which is associated with his name. He claimed merely to have studied deeply into antiquity and to be a teacher of the records and worship of the past. The Chinese classics comprise the five King and the four Shu. The latter, however, are the works of Confucius' disciples, and hold not the rank and authority of the five King. The word King means a web of cloth (or the warp which keeps the thread in place), and is applied to the most ancient books of the nation, as works possessed of a sort of a canonical authority. Of these ancient books the Shu King and the Shih King are of chief importance. One is a book of history and the other of poetry. The Shu King relates to a period extending over seventeen centuries, from about 2357 B. C. to 627 B. C., and is believed to be the oldest of all the Chinese Bible, and consists of ballads relating to events of the national history and songs and hymns to be sung on great state occasions. They exhibit a primitive simplicity and serve to picture forth the manners of the ancient time."

"In passing now from sacred literatures of the far East to those of the West I linger for a moment over the religious writings of the ancient Babylonians and the Persians. Who has not heard of Zoroaster and the Zend-Avesta? But the monuments of the great valley of the Tigris and Euphrates have in recent years disclosed a still more ancient literature. The old Accadian and Assyrian hymns might be collected into a volume which would perhaps rival the Veda in interest if not in value."

"As for the sacred scriptures of the Parsees, the Avesta, it may be said that few remains of antiquity are of much greater interest to the student of history and religion. But these records of the old Iranian faith have suffered sadly by time and the revolutions of the empire. One who had made them a special life study observes: 'As the Parsees are the ruins of a people, so are their sacred books the ruin of a religion. There has been no other great belief that ever left such poor and meager monuments of its past splendor.' The oldest portions of the Avesta consist of praises to the holy powers of heaven and invocations for them to be present at the ceremonial worship. The entire collection taken together is mainly of the nature of a prayer-book or ritual."

As for these and other sacred scriptures, the people among whom they are received regard them as in some way the revelation of the divine wisdom for man. What recognition have Christians to give to them, how do they explain their origin, and value them in comparison with our own sacred Scriptures? On this point Professor Carpenter of Oxford, in his plea for "a wider conception of revelation," says: "The early Christians were confronted with the fact that Greek poets and philosophers had reached truths about the being of God not at all unlike those of Moses and the prophets. Their solution was worthy of the freedom and universality of the spirit of Jesus. They were for recognizing and welcoming truth wherever they found it, and they referred it without hesitation to the ultimate source of wisdom and knowledge, the Logos, at once the inner thought and the uttered word of God. The martyr Justin affirmed that the Logos had worked through Socrates, as it had been present in Jesus; nay, with a wider outlook he spoke of the seed of the Logos implanted in every race of man. In virtue of this fellowship, therefore, all truth was revelation and akin to Christ himself. 'Whatsoever things were said among all men are the property of us Christians.' The Alexandrian teachers shared the same conception. The divine intelligence pervaded human life and history and showed itself in all that was best in beauty, goodness, truth. The way of truth was like a mighty river, ever flowing, and as it passed it was ever receiving fresh streams on this side and that. Nay, so clear in Clement's view was the work of Greek philosophy that he not only regarded it like law and gospel as a gift of God, it was an actual covenant as much as that of Sinai, possessed of its own justifying power, or following the great generalization of St. Paul, the law was a tutor to bring the Jews to Christ. Clement added that philosophy wrought the same heaven-appointed service for the Greeks. May we not use the same great conception over other fields of the history of religion? 'In all ages,' affirmed the author of the wisdom of Solomon, 'wisdom entering into holy souls maketh them friends of God and prophets.' So we may claim in its widest application the saying of Mohammed: 'Every nation has a creator of the heavens, to which they turn in prayer; it is God who turneth them toward it. Hasten, then, emulously after good wheresoever ye be. God will one day bring you all together.'"

It is interesting in this connection to recall the theory of Maurice Phillips of Madras, quoted above, that the Vedic Hinduism was derived from primitive revelation, and to raise the question whether all these sacred Scriptures are not the more or less perverted streams of such primitive revelation. They all show an antecedent history, which is not the history of savage man. They not only show interior relation and striking family resemblance, but they issue at full head out of the gateway of an unapproachable past. They are colored by the washing of the channels through which they run; but what is essential to each is common to all, and testifies to a divine fountain of the water of life. They use the same symbols and imagery, and suggest a mystical meaning. "The idea of a divine revelation," says the author of the paper on "Concessions to Native Ideas," "the idea of a 'word of God' communicated directly to inspired sages or rishis, according to a theory of inspiration higher than that of any other religion in the world, is perfectly familiar to Hindus, and is, indeed, universally entertained. Yet the conclusion reached is this, that a careful comparison of religions brings out this striking contrast between the Bible and all other scriptures; it establishes its satisfying character in distinction from the seeking spirit of other faiths. The Bible shows God in quest of man rather than man in quest of God. It meets the questions raised in the philosophies of the East, and supplies their only true solution."

Is this because the Bible contains a verbal revelation, given as at the first by inspiration, and maintained in purity by divine providence, while all other scriptures are derived from traditions of a primitive word of God? In confirmation of this faith, it may be recalled that Rawlinson says, "The facts appear on the whole to point to the existence of a primitive religion communicated to man from without, and the gradual clouding over of this primitive revelation everywhere, unless it were among the Hebrews."

The origin of religion in revelation will be admitted by those who incline to the theory of natural development as well as those who think of it as the voice of God from above; but what is the idea of revelation? It would appear from the deliverances before the congress that there are essentially two, and only two, ideas of revelation in the world to-day. One almost universally accepted in some form or other is that it is the voice of God in human consciousness. The other, accepted probably by a very few, that it is the involution of the divine in human speech, through human instruments, but by a divine act; and that it is through the inspiration in men of such verbal communication from God that spiritual and divine ideas can be communicated to man's conscious recognition.

The first theory, the revelation of the divine in consciousness, appears in declarations from the Orient and from Christendom. Mr. Mozoomdar, in his eloquent address on "The World's Debt to Asia," voiced this thought of revelation in his poetic way: "In the high realms of that undying wisdom the Hebrew, the Hindu, the Mongolian, the Christian are ever at one, for that wisdom is no part of themselves, but the self-revelation of God. The Hindu books have not plagiarized the Bible, Christianity has not plundered Buddhism, but universal wisdom is like unto itself everywhere. Similarly love, when it is unselfish and incarnal, has its counterpart in all lands and all times. The deepest poetry, whether in Dante, Shakespeare, or Kalidasa, is universal. The love of God repeats itself century after century in the pious of every race; the love of man makes all mankind its kindred. True holiness is the universal idea, however much personal prejudices or passions stand in the way of the light. Hence Asia, seeking the universal God in her soul, has discovered God to all the world. This process of seeking and finding God within is an intense spiritual culture, known by various names in various countries; in India we call it Yoga. The self-concentrated devotee finds an immersion in the depths of the indwelling deity. God's reason becomes man's reason, God's love becomes man's love. God and man become one. Introspection finds the universal soul — the over-soul of your Emerson — beating in all humanity, and a human and divine are thus reconciled."

This doctrine in its more definite statement by western thinkers, is substantially this: That God is immanent in nature and man, and by his operation in the human soul draws man to seek him, and enables man to find him, and more or less truly to record what he has found. All sacred Scriptures are such record. Scripture and interpretation alike are the voice of God in the unfolding consciousness of man. It is this which gives coördinate authority for Doctor Briggs to Scripture and reason and the church. Scripture is the record of what God has taught in gifted souls; reason separates the essential from the non-essential and corrects the record in fuller light; the church perserves the record and keeps pure the witness to essential truths by a consensus of the voice of the divine Spirit in many through long time; each is serviceable to correct the other, and God works through all for the perfecting of each. The same theory lies at the root of the doctrine of the Catholic church concerning the Bible, only in its claim the superior authority is with the church, which by its Catholic decision establishes the written word, and by its Catholic consensus interprets it. It is probable, also, that the same theory underlies Joseph Cook's emphatic and characteristic declaration that "the worth of the Bible results from the fact that it contains a revelation of religious truth not elsewhere communicated to man." For he says this is true "irrespective of any question as to the method of inspiration," and rests its religious infallibility upon "the literal infallibility of the strictly self-evident truths of Scripture." Dr. Briggs can say as much, as follows:

"We may now say confidently to all men: 'All the sacred books of the world are now accessible to you; study them, compare them, recognize all that is good and noble and true in them all and tabulate results, and you will be convinced that the holy Scriptures of the Old and New Testaments are true, holy, and divine.' When we have gone searchingly through all the books of other religions we will find that they are as torches of various sizes and brilliance lighting up the darkness of the night, but the holy Scriptures of the Old and New Testaments are like the sun shining in the heavens and lighting up the whole world."

But the sacred Scriptures are not the word of God, they are records of the Word as it was revealed in holy men, and the records are not without error, nor have they any magical or peculiar divine power which makes them authoritative over reason which is God's voice now in men. Thus he says of the writers:

"They were guided by the divine Spirit in their comprehension and expression of the divine instruction, but, judging also from their work, it seems most probable that they were not guided by the divine Spirit in grammar, rhetoric, logic, expression, arrangement of material, or general editorial work.

They were left to those errors which even the most faithful and scrupulous of writers will sometimes make. The science which approaches the Bible from without and the science which studies it from within agree as to the essential facts of the case. Now, can the truthfulness of Scripture be maintained by those who recognize these errors? There is no reason why the substantial truthfulness of the Bible shall not be consistent with circumstantial errors. God did not speak himself in the Bible except a few words recorded here and there; he spoke in much greater portions of the Old Testament through the voices and pens of the human authors of the Scriptures. Did the human minds and pens always deliver the inerrant word?

"All that we can claim is inspiration and accuracy for that which suggests the religious lessons to be imparted. God is true. He is the truth. He can not lie; he can not mislead or deceive his creatures. But the question arises, when the infinite God speaks to finite man must he speak words which are not error? This depends not only upon God's speaking, but on man's hearing, and also of the means of communication between God and man. It is necessary to show the capacity of man to receive the word before we can be sure that he transmitted it correctly. The inspiration of the holy Scriptures does not carry with it inerrancy in every particular; it was sufficient if the divine truth was given with such clearness as to guide men aright in religious life.

"The errors of holy Scripture are not errors of

falsehood or deceit, but of ignorance, inadvertence, partial and inadequate knowledge, and of incapacity to express the whole truth of God which belonged to man as man. Just as light is seen not in its pure and unclouded state, but in the beautiful colors of the spectrum, so it is that the truth of God, its revelation and communication to man, met with such obstacles in human nature. Men are capable of receiving it only in its diverse operations, and diverse manners as it comes to them through the diverse temperaments and points of view of the Biblical writers. The religion of the Old Testament is a religion which includes some things hard to reconcile in an inerrant revelation. The sacrifice of Jephthah's daughter, the divine command to Abraham to offer up his son as a burnt offering, and other incidents seem unsuited to divine revelation. The New Testament taught that sacrifices must be of broken, contrite hearts and humble and cheerful spirits. What pleasure would God take in smoking altars? How could the true God prescribe such puerilities?"

With more confidence, because established in the supreme authority of the church, through which, acting in its Catholic capacity as an organized body, it is claimed, the divine Spirit reveals itself infallibly, the Rt.-Rev. Mgr. Seton declared the Catholic doctrine of the Bible:

"The church is a living society commissioned by Jesus Christ to preserve the Word of God pure and unchanged. This revealed Word of God is contained partly in the holy Scripture and partly in tradition. The former is called the written Word of God, writing — not necessarily, indeed, on paper, but as often found on more durable materials, such as clay or brick tablets, stone slabs and cylinders, and metal plates — being the art of fixing thoughts in an intelligible and lasting shape, so as to hand them down to other generations and thus perpetuate historical records. There is a special congruity that the Almighty, from whose instructions, not only original spoken, but probably also written, language was derived, should have put his divine revelations in writing through the instrumentality of chosen men; and as the human race is originally one, we think that the fact that scriptures of some sort claiming to be inspired are found in all the civilized nations of the past shows that such conceptions, although outside of the orthodox line of tradition, are derived from the primitive unity and religion of the human family. The church teaches that the sacred Scriptures are the written Word of God and that he is their author, and consequently she receives them with piety and reverence. This gives a distinct character to the Bible which no other book possesses, for of no mere human composition, however excellent, can it ever be said that it comes directly from God. The church also maintains that it belongs to her, and to her alone, to determine the true sense of the Scriptures, and that they can not be rightly interpreted contrary to her decision; because she claims to be and is the living, unerring authority to whom, and not to those who expound the Scripture by the light of private judgment, infallibility was promised and given."

The second theory of revelation was set forth by the Rev. Frank Sewall, with an appeal to the testimony of the Scriptures themselves, so full and frank as to challenge that "criticism" of which Doctor Briggs thinks so highly that he says the faith which shrinks from it is a faith so weak and uncertain that it excites suspicion as to its life and vitality. When, in preparing for the parliament, it was observed that the programme provided for no presentation of the plenary inspiration of the Scriptures, I asked that the Rev. Mr. Sewall be assigned "The Character and Degree of the Inspiration of the Christian Scriptures." The paper, because it stands alone in the doctrine advocated both as to the canon and as to nature of inspiration, and presents its argument from the Scriptures themselves, will interest even those committed to the prevailing theories.

"There is a common consent among Christians that the Scriptures known as the Holy Bible are divinely inspired; that they constitute a book unlike all other books in that they contain a direct communication from the divine Spirit to the mind and heart of man. The nature and the degree of the inspiration which thus characterizes the Bible can only be learned from the declaration of the holy Scriptures themselves, since only the divine can truly reveal the divine or afford to human minds the means of judging truly regarding what is divine.

"The Christian Scripture, or the Holy Bible, is

written in two parts, the Old and the New Testament. In the interval of time that transpired between the writing of these two parts, the divine truth and essential Word, which in the beginning was with God and was God, became incarnate on our earth in the person of our Lord Jesus Christ. He, as the Word made flesh and dwelling among men, being himself 'the true Light that lighteth every man that cometh into the world,' placed the seal of divine authority upon certain of the then existing sacred Scriptures. He thus forever fixed the divine canon of that portion of the written Word; and from that portion we are enabled to derive a criterion of judgment regarding the degree of divine inspiration and authority to be attributed to those other Scriptures which were to follow after our Lord's ascension and which constitute the New Testament.

"The divine canon of the Word in the Old Testament Scriptures is declared by our Lord in Luke, twenty-fourth chapter, forty-fourth verse, where he says: 'All things must be fulfilled which were written in the law of Moses, and in the Prophets, and in the Psalms concerning me.' And in verses twenty-five to twenty-seven: 'O fools, and slow of heart to believe all that the prophets have spoken' — 'and beginning at Moses and all the prophets, he expounded unto them in all the Scriptures things concerning himself.' The Scriptures of the Old Testament thus enumerated as testifying of him and as being fulfilled in him embrace two of the three divisions into which the Jews at that time divided their sacred books. These two are the Law (Torah), or the five books of Moses, so called, and the Prophets (Nebiim). Of the books contained in the third division of the Jewish canon, known as the Kethubim or 'other writings,' our Lord recognizes but two: he names by title 'the Psalms;' and in Matthew, twenty-fourth chapter, fifteenth verse, when predicting the consummation of the age and his own second coming, our Lord cites the prophecy of Daniel. It is evident that our Lord was not governed by Jewish tradition in naming these three classes of the ancient books which were henceforth to be regarded as essentially 'the Word,' because of having their fulfillment in himself. In the very words of Jesus Christ the canon of the Word is established in a twofold manner: First, intrinsically, as including those books which interiorly testify of him and were all to be fulfilled in him. Secondly, the canon is fixed specifically by our Lord's naming the books which compose it under the three divisions: 'The Law, the Prophets, and the Psalms.' The canon in this sense comprises consequently the five books of Moses, or the 'Law,' so-called; the books of Joshua, the Judges, First and Second Samuel, First and Second Kings, or the so-called earlier prophets; the later prophets, including the four 'great' and the twelve 'minor' prophets, and finally the Book of Psalms. The other books of the Old Testament, namely: Ezra, Nehemiah, Job, Proverbs, First and Second Chronicles, Ruth, Esther, the Songs of Solomon, and Ecclesiastes, are as well as the so-called, 'Apocrypha.'

Of those books, which compose the divine canon itself, it may be said that they constitute the inexhaustible source of revelation and inspiration. We may regard, therefore, as established that the source of the divinity of the Bible, of its unity, and its authority as divine revelation lies in having the Christ, as the eternal Word within it, at once its source, its inspiration, its prophecy, its fulfillment, its power to illuminate the minds of men with a knowledge of divine and spiritual things, to 'convert the soul,' to 'make wise the simple.'

"We next observe regarding these divine books that, besides being thus set apart by Christ, they declare themselves to be the word of the Lord in the sense of being actually spoken by the Lord, and so as constituting a divine language. This shows that not only do these books claim to be of God's revealing, but that the manner of the revelation was that of direct dictation by means of a voice actually heard, as one hears another talking, although by the internal organs of hearing. The same is also true throughout the prophetical books above enumerated. Here we are met with the constant declaration of the 'Word of the Lord coming,' as the 'voice of the Lord speaking,' to the writers of these books, showing that the writers wrote not of themselves, but from the 'voice of the Lord through them.'

"We now turn to the New Testament, and applying to those books which in the time of Christ were yet unwritten criteria derived from those books which had received from him the seal of divine authority, namely, that they are words spoken by the Lord or given by his Spirit, and that they testify of him and so have in them eternal life, we find in the four Gospels either—

"1. The words 'spoken unto' us by our Lord himself when among men as the Word, and of which he says: 'The words which I speak unto you they are spirit and they are life.' 2. The acts done by him or to him 'that the Scriptures might be fulfilled,' or finally the words 'called to the remembrance' of the apostles and the evangelists by the Holy Spirit according to his promise to them in John xiv, 26. Besides the four Gospels we have the testimony of John the Revelator that the visions recorded in the Apocalypse were vouchsafed to him by the Lord himself, thus showing that the Book of Revelation is no mere personal communication from the man John, but is the actual revelation of the Divine Spirit of Truth itself.

"No such claims of direct divine inspiration or dictation are made in any other part of the New Testament. Only to the four Gospels and to the Book of Revelation could one presume to apply these words, written at the close of the Apocalypse and applying immediately to it: 'If any man shall take away from the words of the prophecy of this book, God shall take away his part out of the book of life, and out of the holy city, and from the things which are written in this book.' In the portion of the Bible which we may thus distinguish preëminently as the 'Word of the Lord' it is therefore the words themselves that are inspired, and not the men that transmitted them. This is what our Lord declares.

Moreover, the very words which the apostles and the evangelists themselves heard, and the acts which they beheld and recorded, had a meaning and content of which they were partially and in some cases totally ignorant. Thus when our Lord speaks of the 'eating of his flesh' the disciples murmur, 'This is an hard saying; who can bear it?' And when he speaks of 'going away to the Father and coming again,' the disciples say among themselves, 'What is this that he saith? We can not tell what he saith.' If we look at the Apocalypse, with its strange visions, its mysterious numbers and signs; if we read the prophets of the Old Testament, with their commingling of times and nations, and lands and seas, and things animate and inanimate in a manner discordant with any conceivable earthly history or chronology; if we read the details of the ceremonial law dictated to Moses in the mount by the 'voice of Jehovah'; if we read in Genesis the account of creation and of the origins of human history -- we are compelled to admit that the penmen recording these things were writing that of which they knew not the meaning; that what they wrote did not represent their intelligence or counsel, but was the faithful record of what was delivered to them by the voice of the Spirit speaking inwardly to them. Here, then, we see the manner of divine revelation in human language, again definitely declared and exemplified in Jesus the Word incarnate, in that not only in his acts did he employ signs and miracles, but in teaching his disciples he 'spake in parables,' and 'without a parable spake he not to them, that it might be fulfilled which was spoken by the prophet, saying, I will open my mouth in parables; I will utter things which have been kept sacred from the foundation of the world.' We learn, therefore, that the divine language is that of parable, wherein things of the kingdom of heaven are clothed in the familiar figures of earthly speech and action. If the Bible is divine, the law of its revelation must be coincident with that of divine creation. Both are the involution of the divine and infinite in a series of veils or symbols, which become more and more gross as they recede from their source. In revelation the veilings of the divine truth of the essential Word follow in accordance with the receding and more and more sensualized states of mankind upon earth. Hence the successive dispensations, or church eras, which mark off the whole field of human history. After the Eden days of open vision, when 'heaven lay about us in our infancy,' followed the Noetic era of a sacred language, full of heavenly meanings, traces of which occur in the hieroglyphic writings and the great world-myths of most ancient tradition; then came the visible and localized Theocracy of a chosen nation, with laws and ritual, and a long history of its war and struggle, and victory and decline, and the promise of a final renewal and perpetuation; all being at the same time a revelation of God's providence and government over man, and a picture of the process of the regeneration of the human soul and its preparation for an eternal inheritance in heaven. But even the law of God thus revealed in the form of a national constitution, hierarchy, and ritual was at length made of non-effect through the traditions of men, and men 'seeing saw not, and hearing heard not, neither did they understand.' Then for the redemption of man in this extremity 'the Word itself was made flesh and dwelt among us,' and now, in the veil of a humanity subject to human temptation and suffering, even to the death upon the cross.

"Thus the process of the evolution of the Spirit out of the veil or of the letter of the Scripture, begun in our Lord's own interpretation of the 'Law for those of ancient time,' is a process to whose further continuance the Lord himself testifies. The letter of Scripture is the cloud which everywhere proclaims the presence of the infinite God with his creature man. The cloud of the Lord's presence is the infinitely merciful adaptation of divine truth to the spiritual needs of humanity. The cloud of the literal gospel and of the apostolic traditions of our Lord is truly typified by that cloud which received the ascending Christ out of the immediate sight of men. The same letter of the Word is the cloud in which he makes known his second coming in power and great glory, in revealing to the church the inner and spiritual meanings of both the Old and New Testament of his Word. For ages the Christian church has stood gazing up into heaven in adoration of him whom the cloud has hidden from their sight, and with the traditions of human dogma and the warring of schools and critics more and more dense has the cloud become. In the thickness of the cloud it behooves the church to hold the more fast its faith in the glory within the cloud.

"The view of the Bible and its inspiration thus presented is the only one compatible with a belief in it as a divine in contradistinction from a human production. Were the Bible a work of human art, embodying human genius and human wisdom, then the question of the writers' individuality and their personal inspiration, and even of the time and circumstances amid which they wrote, would be of the first importance. Not so if the divine inspiration and wisdom is treasured up in the very words themselves as divinely chosen symbols and parables of eternal truth. Far from placing a human limitation upon the divine Spirit, such a verbal inspiration as this opens in the Bible vistas of heavenly and divine meanings such as they could never possess were its inspirations confined to the degree of intelligence possessed by the human writers, even under a special illumination of their minds. The difference between inspired words of God and inspired men writing their own words is like that between an eternal fact of nature and the scientific theories which men have formulated upon or about it. The fact remains forever a source of new discovery and a means of ever new revelation of the divine; the scientific theories may come and go with the changing minds of men.

"It is not, then, from man, from the intelligence

of any Moses, or Daniel, or Isaiah, or John, that the Word of God contains its authority as divine. The authority must be in the words themselves. If they are unlike all other words ever written; if they have a meaning, yea, worlds and worlds of meaning, one within or above another, while human words have all their meaning on the surface; if they have a message whose truth is dependent upon no single time or circumstance, but speaks to man at all times and under all circumstances; if they have a validity and an authority self-dictated to human souls which survives the passing of earthly monuments and powers, which speaks in all languages, to all minds, wise to the learned, simple to the simple; if, in a word, these are words that experience shows no man could have written from the intelligence belonging to his time, or from the experience of any single human soul, then may we feel sure that we have in the words of our Bible that which is diviner than any penman that wrote them. Here is that which 'speaks with authority and not as the scribes.' The words that God speaks to man are 'spirit and are life.' The authorship of the Bible, and all that this implies of divine authority to the conscience of man, is contained, like the flame of the Urim and Thummim on the breastplate of the high priest, in the bosom of its own language, to reveal itself by the Spirit to all who will 'have an ear to hear.' So shall it continue to utter the 'dark parables of old which we have known and our fathers have told us,' and 'to show forth to all generations the praises of the

Lord,' becoming ever more and more translucent with the glory that shines within the cloud of the letter; and so shall the church rest, amid all the contentions that engage those who study the surface of revelation, whether in nature or in Scripture, in the undisturbed assurance that the 'Word of the Lord abideth forever.'"

IMMORTALITY.

The doctrine of personal immortality received general acknowledgment and confirmation, as based on considerations of man's place in nature, the incompleteness of the present life, and the universal aspiration and intuition of the soul. Even the argument of scientific evolutionists led them to the inference of immortality. Professor Bruce of Glasgow closed the paper on "Man's Place in Nature," contributed by him, as follows:

"Does the view of man as the crown of the evolutionary process throw any light on his eternal destiny? Does it contain any promise of immortality? Here one feels inclined to speak with bated breath. A hope so august, so inconceivably great, makes the grasping hand of faith tremble. We are tempted to exclaim, behold, we know not anything. Yet it is worthy of note that leading advocates of evolutionism are among the most pronounced upholders of immortality. Mr. Fisk says: 'For my own part I believe in the immortality of the soul, not in the sense in which I accept the demonstrable proofs of a science, but as a supreme act of faith in the reasonableness of God's work.' He can not believe that God made the world, and especially its highest creature, simply to destroy it, like a child who builds houses out of rocks just for the pleasure of knocking them down. Not less strongly Le Conte writes: 'Without spirit-immortality this beautiful cosmos, which has been developing into increasing beauty for so many millions of years, when its evolution has run its course and all is over, would be precisely as if it had never been — an idle dream, an idle tale, signifying nothing.' These utterances of course do not settle the question; but, considering whence they emanate, they may be taken at least as an authoritative indication that the tenet of human immortality is congruous to, if it be not a necessary deduction from, the demonstrable truth that man is the consummation of the great world-process by which the universe has been brought into being."

This of course teaches nothing that man wants to know. It simply asserts what all men refuse to disbelieve. What most men would like to know, is something about the mode of man's immortality. Even the Buddhist acknowledges so much as is asserted by Professor Bruce, and he carries on the evolutionary process, through the working of cause and effect in character, by means of repeated incarnations, until the process reaches perfection, when he loses sight of it in the divine, and can affirm nothing more of the soul's state and mode of being. His whole doctrine of transmigration is a doctrine of evolution, elaborated in the effort to solve the apparent inequality of opportunity, and manifest incompleteness of every mortal life. Back of it lies a tradition, which his doctrine seeks to interpret; but what he would ask of Christianity is some better explanation of the soul's longings and the necessity of self-conquest, and the obvious incompleteness of most lives, consistent with a benevolent conception of the divine order of the universe. One wonders that this is all that Buddhism has to say; that it makes no claim to Gautama's seership and introduction into an inner and higher world at the time of his illumination, which others have claimed for him. But its representatives before the parliament showed no such thought, nor any idea of Nirvana which could be described as a state of rest in conscious love and thought and activity in harmony with "the spirits of just men made perfect," in a spiritual world, in conscious reciprocal union with God. Nor can it be said that Christians were forward with assured and helpful explanations, with two exceptions to be noted presently.

The paper on "The Religious System of the Parsees" showed that "Zoroastrianism teaches the immortality of the soul," and that the Parsees "believe in heaven and hell." Heaven is called by a word which literally means "the best life." Heaven is represented as a place of radiance, splendor, and glory, and hell as that of gloom, darkness, and stench. And the state of the soul and trend of life determines man's place in the hereafter.

"According to the Parsee Scriptures, for three days after a man's death his soul remains within the limits of the world under the guidance of the angel Serosh. If the deceased be a pious man or a man who led a virtuous life, his soul utters the words signifying, 'Well is he by whom that which is his benefit becomes the benefit of any one else.' If he be a wicked man or one who led an evil life, his soul utters the plaintive words which signify, 'To which land shall I turn? Whither shall I go?'

"On the dawn of the third night the departed souls appear at the 'Chinvat Bridge.' This bridge is guarded by the angel Meher the judge. He presides there as a judge, assisted by the angels Rashne and Astad, the former representing justice and the latter truth. At this bridge, and before this angel Meher, the soul of every man has to give an account of its doings in the past life. The judge weighs a man's actions by a scale-pan. If a man's good actions outweigh his evil ones, even by a small particle, he is allowed to pass from the bridge to the other end, to heaven. If his evil actions outweigh his good ones, even by a small weight, he is not allowed to pass over the bridge, but is hurled down into the deep abyss of hell. If his meritorious and evil deeds counterbalance each other, he is sent to a place corresponding to the Christian 'purgatory' and the Mohammedan 'aeraf.' His meritorious deeds done in the past life would prevent him from going to hell, and his evil actions would not let him go to heaven.

"Again Zoroastrian books say that the meritoriousness of good deeds and the sin of evil ones increase with the growth of time. As capital increases with interest, so good and bad actions done by a man in his life increase, as it were, with interest in their effects. Thus a meritorious deed done in young age is more effective than that very deed done in advanced age. A man must begin practicing virtue from his very young age. As in the case of good deeds and their meritoriousness so in the case of evil actions and their sins. The burden of the sin of an evil action increases, as it were, with interest. A young man has a long time to repent of his evil deeds and to do good deeds that could counteract the effect of his evil deeds. If he does not take advantage of these opportunities the burden of those evil deeds increases with time."

The expositions of Mohammedanism had little to say of the soul's future life; and Christian references to the subject were confined to the usual general assumption of continued existence in a state of happiness and peace in union with God, or of unhappiness in separation from God and the good. One noble paper on "The Argument for Immortality," and one on "The Soul and Its Future Life," constitute the only exceptions to these general references to the subject; and these, taken together, were so excellent as to make one almost glad that they stand alone.

Doctor Moxom's treatment of "The Argument for Immortality" was eloquent and exhaustive, as showing the rational necessity for the conception of continued personal existence under spiritual conditions. As to the nature of evidence, he said:

"None of the highest, the essentially spiritual facts of man's knowledge and experience fall within the scope of what is known as scientific proof. God, the soul, truth, love, righteousness, repentance, faith, beauty, the good — all these are unapproachable by scientific tests; yet these, and not salts and acids, and laws of cohesion, and chemical affinity, and gravitation, are the supreme realities of man's life, even in this world of matter and force. When one demands scientific proof of immortality, then, it is as if he demanded the linear measurement of a principle, or the troy weight of an emotion, or the color of an affection, or as if he should insist upon finding the human soul with his scalpel or microscope."

He made a strong plea for the doctrine of continuity of existence, and for the personal consciousness and individuality which it implies; referred with feeling to the Saviour's comforting promise, "I go to prepare a place for you," which he said infects one's heart with happy confidence; and ended with the statement that hope grows into an assurance of immortality, and serene faith deepens into a conscious experience as the soul knows God and strives toward the ideals of culture and character which rise in divine beckonings before us. If it could have been followed by a paper on the evidence from the sacred Scriptures showing that to opened vision of prophets and seers the spiritual world was displayed, and the demands of reason and the expectation of hope justified in fact, the showing would have been a complete and fitting preparation for the paper which followed, and constituted the only attempt to set forth the mode of man's immortality.

This paper, by the Rev. Samuel M. Warren of Roxbury, on "The Soul and Its Future Life," assuming immortality, considered in what form and body and under what conditions man lives again. Starting with the propositions "That the soul is substantial, though not of earthly substance, and is the very man, and that the body is merely the earthly form and instrument of the soul, and that every part of the body is produced from the soul according to its likeness, in order that it may perform its functions in the world during the brief but important time that this is the place of man's conscious abode," the argument proceeds as follows:

"If, as all Christians believe, man is an immortal being, created to live on through the endless ages of eternity, then the longest life in this world is, comparatively, but as a point, an infinitesimal part of his existence.. In this view, it is not rational to believe that that part of man which is for his brief use in this world only, and is left behind when he passes out of this world, is the most real and substantial part of him; every rational mind perceives that it can not be so. That is more substantial which is more enduring, and that is the more real part of a man in which his characteristics and his qualities are. All the facts and phenomena of life confirm the doctrine that the soul is the real man. What makes the quality of a man? What gives him character as good or bad, small or great, lovable or detestable? Do these qualities pertain to the body? Every one knows that they do not. But they are the qualities of the man. Then the real man is not the body, but is 'the living soul.' The body has absolutely no human quality but what it derives from the soul, not even its human form; and all that is human about it departs when the soul leaves the body — even its human form quickly vanishes. But the man endures. If there is immortal life he has not vanished, except from mortal and material sight. As between the soul and the body, then, there can be no rational question as to which is the substantial and which the evanescent thing.

"Again, if the immortal soul is the real man, and is substantial, what must be its form? It can not be a formless, vaporous thing and be a man. Can it have other than the human form? Reason clearly sees that if formless or in any other form he would not be a man. The soul of man, or the real man, is a marvelous assemblage of powers and faculties of will and understanding; and the human form is such as it is because it is perfectly adapted to the exercise of these various powers and faculties. In other words, the soul forms itself, under the divine Maker's hand, into an organism by which it can adequately and perfectly put forth its wondrous and wonderfully varied powers, and bring its purposes into acts.

"The human form is thus an assemblage of organs that exactly correspond to and embody and are the express image of the various faculties of the soul. And there is no organ of the human form the absence of which would not hinder and impede the free and efficient action and putting forth of the soul's powers. And by the human form is not meant merely, nor primarily, the organic forms of the material body. The faculties are of the soul, and if the soul is the man, and endures when the body decays and vanishes, it must itself be in a form which is an assemblage of organs perfectly adapted and adequate to the exercise of its powers; that is, in the human form. The human form is then primarily and especially the form of the soul — which is the perfection of all forms, as man at his highest is the consummation and fullness of all loving and intelligent attributes.

"But when does the soul itself take on its human form? Is it not until the death of the body? Manifestly, if it is the very form of the soul, the soul can not exist without it, and it is put on in and by the fact of its creation and the gradual development of its powers. It could have no other form and be a human soul. Its organs are the necessary organs of its faculties and powers, and these are clothed with their similitudes in dead material forms animated by the soul for temporary use in the material world. The soul is omnipresent in the material body, not by diffusion, formlessly, but each organ of the soul is within and is the soul of the corresponding organ of the body; so that every organic form of the body, inward and outward, is the material embodiment and counterpart of a corresponding organ of the soul, by which the soul manifests and puts forth its affections and its powers. Thus the saying of the Apostle Paul is literally and exactly true, that, 'If there is a natural body there is also a spiritual body' (I Cor. xv, 44), and that, 'If the earthly house of our tabernacle be dissolved, we have a building of God, a house not made with hands, eternal in the heavens' (II Cor. v, 1).

"That the immortal soul is the very man involves the eternal preservation of his identity; for in the soul are the distinguishing qualities that constitute the individuality of a man — all those certain characteristics, affectional and intellectual, which make him such or such a man, and distinguish and differentiate him from all other men. He remains, therefore, the same man to all eternity. He may become more and more, to endless ages, an angel of light — even as here a man may advance greatly in wisdom and intelligence, and yet is always the same man. This doctrine of the soul involves also the permanency of established character. The life in this world is the period of character building. It has been very truthfully said that a man is a bundle of habits. What manner of man he is depends on what his manner of life has been. This is meant by the words of the Scriptures, 'Their works do follow them' (Rev. xiv, 13), and 'He shall render unto every man according to his deeds' (Mark xvi, 27).

"If evil and vicious habits are continued through life they are fixed and confirmed and become of the very life, so that the man loves and desires no other life, and does not wish to, will not be led out of them, because he loves the practice of them. On the other hand, if from childhood a man has been inured to virtuous habits, these habits become fixed and established and of his very soul and life. In either case the habits thus fixed and confirmed are of the immortal soul and constitute its permanent character. The body, as to its part, has been but the pliant instrument of the soul.

"With respect to the soul's future life the first important consideration is what sort of a world it will inhabit. If we have shown good reasons for believing the doctrine that the soul is not a something formless, vague, and shadowy, but is itself an organic human form, substantial, and the very man, then it must inhabit a substantial and very real world. It is a gross fallacy of the senses that there is no substance but matter, and nothing substantial but what is material. Is not God, the divine, omnipotent Creator of all things, substantial? Can Omnipotence be an attribute of that which has no substance and no form? Is such an existence conceivable? But he is not material and not visible or cognizable by any mortal sense. Yet we know that he is substantial; for it is manifest in his wondrous and mighty works. There is, then, other substance than that which is cognizable to the senses, there is even divine substance; and if, as we have clearly shown, the soul is substantial, there is spiritual substance. And of such substance must be the world wherein the soul is eternally to dwell. That the spiritual world and the things of it are not visible, and not cognizable by any earthly sense, is no evidence that they are unsubstantial and unreal. The interior and most potent things of this natural world are not themselves tangible or visible or cog-

PRINCE MOMOLU MASSAQUOI,
Of the Veys, West Africa.

nizable by any sense. It is proverbial that nature works unseen. What, for example, do we know of electricity except by its wonderful phenomena? Its phenomena, its wondrous power in and upon things visible and tangible, give proof of it. But what are these to the stupendous and varied powers of the spiritual within the natural universe which we see about us in all the phenomena of vegetable life, and even in the inorganic things of nature, which as servants of the divine Creator, himself invisible, inspire and effect the numberless and marvelous activities which make an otherwise inert and dead material world to be quick and living, and filled with all things beautiful and desirable by man. It is the reality of the spiritual world that makes this world real, just as it is the reality of the soul that makes the human body a reality and a possibility. As there could be no body without the soul, there could be no natural world without the spiritual. Moreover, as it is not rational to believe that the body which the soul briefly inhabits is more substantial than the soul itself, which endures forever, so it does not satisfy enlightened reason to think that this world which is the place of man's temporary sojourn is more substantial than that which the soul inhabits forever — that the temporal is substantial, and the eternal world spectral and unreal. Indeed every rational consideration, however viewed, goes to confirm the doctrine that the spiritual world is a substantial and real world.

"Not only is that world substantial, but it must be a world of surpassing loveliness and beauty. It has justly been considered one of the most beneficent manifestations of the divine love and wisdom that this beautiful world that we briefly inhabit is so wondrously adapted to all man's wants and to call into exercise and gratify his every faculty and good desire. And when he leaves this temporary abode, a man with all his faculties and refined by freedom from the incumbrance of the flesh, an incumbrance which we are often very conscious of, will he not enter a world of beauty exceeding the loveliest aspects of this? The soul is human, and the world in which it is to dwell is adapted to human life; and it would not be adapted to human life if it did not adequately meet and answer to the soul's desires. Is it reasonable that this material world should be so full of life and loveliness and beauty, where 'Nature spreads for every sense a feast,' to gratify every exalted faculty of the soul, and not the spiritual world wherein the soul is to abide forever? Can it be there is no loveliness of sight and sound, no springing, joyful life, nothing to excite to noble contemplation and fill the mind with gratitude and joy? It is not so; but rather as it is written: 'Eye hath not seen, nor ear heard, neither have entered into the heart of man the things which God hath prepared for them that love him' (I Cor. ii, 9).

"And the life of that world is human life. The same laws of life and happiness obtain there that govern here, because they are grounded in human nature. Man is a social being, and everywhere, in that world as in this, desires and seeks the companionship of those that are congenial to him — that is, who are of similar quality to himself. Men are thus mutually drawn together by spiritual affinity. This is the law of association here, but it is less perfectly operative in this world, because there is much dissimulation among men, so that they often do not appear to be what they really are, and thus by false and deceptive appearances the good and the evil are often associated together.

"And so it is for a time and in a measure in the first state and region into which men come when they enter the spiritual world. They go into that world as they are, and are at first in a mixed state, as in this world. This continues until the real character is clearly manifest, and good and evil are separated, and they are thus prepared for their final and permanent association and abode. They who in the world have made some real effort and beginning to live a good life, but have evil habits not yet overcome, remain there until they are entirely purified of evil, and are fitted for some society of heaven; and those who inwardly are evil and have outwardly assumed a virtuous garb remain until their dissembled goodness is cast off and their inward character becomes outwardly manifest. When this state of separation is complete there can be no successful dissimulation — the good and the evil are seen and known as such, and the law of spiritual affinity becomes perfectly operative by their own free volition and choice. Then the evil and the good become entirely separated into their congenial societies. The various societies and communities of the good thus associated constitute heaven and those of the evil constitute hell — not by any arbitrary judgment of an angry God, but of voluntary choice, by the perfect and unhindered operation of the law of human nature that leads men to prefer and seek the companionship of those most congenial to themselves.

"As regards the permanency of the state of those who by established evil habit are fixed and determined in their love of evil life, it is not of the Lord's will, but of their own. We are taught in his holy Word that he is ever 'gracious and full of compassion.' He would that they should turn from their evil ways and live, but they will not.

"There is no moment, in this or in the future life, when the infinite mercy of the Lord would not that an evil man should turn from his evil course and live a virtuous and upright and happy life; but they will not in that world for the same reason that they would not in this, because when evil habits are once fixed and confirmed they love them and will not turn from them. 'Can the Ethiopian change his skin or the leopard his spots? Then may they also do good that are accustomed to do evil.' Heaven is a heaven of men and the life of heaven is human life. The conditions of life in that exalted state are greatly different from the conditions here, but it is human life adapted to such transcendent conditions, and the laws of life in that world, as we have seen, are the same as in this. Man was created to be a free and willing agent of the Lord to bless his kind. His true happiness comes, not in seeking happiness for himself, but seeking to promote the happiness of others. Where all are animated by this desire, all are mutually and reciprocally blest.

"Such a state is heaven, whether measurably in this world or fully and perfectly in the next. Then must there be useful ways in heaven by which they can contribute to each other's happiness. And of such kind will be the employments of heaven, for there must be useful employments. There could be no happiness without to beings who are designed and formed for usefulness to others. What the employments are in that exalted condition we can not well know except as some of them are revealed to us, and of them we have faint and feeble conception. But undoubtedly one of them is attendance upon men in this world. It is written, and the words apply to every man: 'He shall give his angels charge over thee, to keep thee in all thy ways' (Ps. xci, 11); and, 'Are they not all ministering spirits, sent forth to minister for them who shall be heirs of salvation?' (Heb. i, 14)."

SOCIOLOGY.

If the deliverances before the parliament on theological subjects are not all that could be wished, if Christian as well as non-Christian speakers seemed less clear and less confident than we had hoped on the great subjects of revelation, and reconciliation and union with God, and man's future life and ultimate destiny, it must be admitted that on practical subjects, and in the realm of the motive and method of man's helpfulness to man, a positive and, so far as it goes, a clear doctrine was set forth. Here we meet religion in a new aspect and girded for a new experiment. If theology is becoming less exact and confident and more speculative, practical religion, at least, is becoming more scientific. There has sprung up within the memory of this generation a new science, with its systematic study of the whole structure of society, to discover its laws and remove the hindrances, political, economical, or customary, which are in the way of its welfare. It has given new emphasis to the doctrine that society is a man; that "the social fabric is in its structure and intent a unit," that "the interdependence of its parts is as a body with its many members unified by a common vitality." The Lord had declared it; Paul had expounded it; the church had once and again asserted it as the bond of fellowship and care among its own members; but in later times it has come to the front as a doctrine of social science independent of religion — that the law "Thou shalt love thy neighbor as thyself" is a "law incorporated in the nature of man;" that "men are so made that if they would secure for themselves, or for the society in which they live, perfection and blessedness, they must obey this law;" that "a rational self-love must at least be made the measure of the love and service of others;" and that this is a law of nature and necessity, and when violated man comes under its penalties.

It is a notable fact that in the Parliament of Religions this doctrine of social science was taken up in the name of religion, and treated with more fullness than any other subject, and that, moreover, as the one practical religious consideration. And it was here that Christian thought showed its unmistakable preëminence, in defining ethical doctrines, to which the non-Christian peoples are strangers, and in which they are to find their social regeneration. Papers were presented on "Christ and the Social Question," by Prof. F. G. Peabody of Harvard University; on "Religion and Wealth," by Rev. Washington Gladden, D.D.; on "Individual Efforts at Reform not Sufficient," by Prof. R. C. Henderson, D.D., of the University of Chicago; on "The Church and Labor," by Rev. James M. Cleary; on "Christianity as a Social Force," by Prof. Richard T. Ely of the University of Wisconsin; "Religion and the Erring and Criminal Classes," by Rev. Anna G. Spencer, and on other allied subjects.

This remarkable series of papers was introduced by a brief speech from Thomas Wentworth Higginson, who called attention to the fact that the subject of the day marked "a natural turning-point in the history of the Parliament of Religions." Up to this time, he said, attention had been given almost wholly to speculative and abstract ideas; now it was to be turned to the actual facts of life and the social questions which press upon us so tremendously. He told a characteristic story of "the Scotch candidate for the ministry who was being examined by some of the sternest of the presbyters, or whatever they call them. Every one of his examiners stood firm in favor of justification by faith, and each one had fifteen minutes of questions, all bearing upon faith, to put to him. By and by, when the candidate was in an exhausted condition, one indiscreet examiner said, 'Well, what do you think of good works?' 'Oh,' said the exhausted candidate, looking around at his persecutors, "I'll not say that it might not be well enough to have a few of them.'" Every oriental that comes to us, he said, concedes to us the power of organization, the power of labor, the method in actual life, which they lack. We could test the real worth of these conceded virtues by examining how far they have been brought to bear on works for the moral and social welfare of men.

In the paper on "Religion and the Erring and Criminal Classes," Anna G. Spencer sought to show that "not only does religion give ethics its root, but it has also played an enormous part in the variations of the moral standards of the world;" and after tracing the history of some of these variations, she said:

"There is a new form of religion dawning upon the Western world, and I believe also upon the Eastern. Christianity was and is a composite faith, compounded of Jewish religious ideals, of Greek thought, Roman organization, and of Germanic racial influences of domestic and social habit. The new religious ideal which is shaping the reform movements of Christianity, and of other great historic faiths as well, is the outgrowth on its thought side of that new conception of the universe and man's relation to it, that new conception which is cosmical and universal rather than racial or special. The new religious philosophy finds the synthesis of all religions in the universal and eternal elements of human aspiration toward the everlasting truth, the absolute right, the boundless love, and the perfect beauty! This conception, in brief, puts at the center of all things perceived or experienced 'one law, one light, one element, and one far-off divine event toward which the whole creation moves.' This new and scientific thought conception makes of morals, not a series of obligatory commands given by one God or many gods to one race or many races, but a turning of the will of man by the force of moral gravitation toward that central law which reveals itself in the human conscience and is developed through social influences, and in obedience to which alone mankind finds his true orbit of action. This view of morals, which is fast becoming common to all enlightened men of all historic faiths, has already started the newest tendencies in the treatment of vice and crime. Those newest tendencies we set down as reformatory, those which aim to make over the criminal and erring into law-abiding and respectable members of society."

"The new scientific element in religion," she said, "has given us social science of which enlightened penology is a part. The old word of religion said to the soul: 'Be ye perfect here and now, no matter how ye were born or trained, or in what depths of social degradation ye find yourself.' The new religion says that also — such forever must be the clarion call to the will to work out a personal salvation or it will cease to be religion. The religion of the future, however, which is already born, has taken counsel of facts as well as of faith, and it has added the social ideal to the personal. It has learned that evil heredity, and poor physique, and degraded home influences, and bad social surroundings, and too severe toil, and too little happiness and education make for millions of mankind walled barriers of circumstance, behind which the dull and torpid soul catches but faint echoes of the divine summons. The relation of this new religion to the criminal and erring classes is not only the tenderness of human sympathy which would not that any should perish; it is the consecration of human wisdom to social betterment which shall yet forbid that any shall perish. In this new ideal of religion the call is not only to justice for the criminal and erring after they come within the scope of social control, but it is the call also to a study of those conditions in the individual and in society which make for crime and vice; and above all it is the call for the social lifting of all the weaker souls of our common humanity upon the winged strength of its wisest and best. The new social ideal in religion calls upon us to make this world so helpful a place to live in 'for the least of these our brethren' that it shall yet be as easy for the will to follow goodness 'and the heart to be true, as for grass to be green or skies to be blue,' in the 'natural way of living.'"

What she calls the new religion, Prof. F. G. Peabody contends is the religion of the gospels, but with care to balance the importance of the individual and social factors as objects of Christian love. Pointing out that the theological seminaries are adding the new field of sociology, he asks, Is there danger that the new humanitarianism may crowd out the old religion?

"When the Christian turns to the social questions is he, on the one hand, turning away from the themes of a Christian church, or is he, on the other hand, sacrificing Christ to society, or is there, lastly, any law laid down by Christ himself which directs a Christian in his study of such affairs? That is the question with which we turn to Christ, and he gives us a clear and often-reiterated reply. One of the first things which strikes one as he reads the gospels is that Jesus Christ was a great individualist. His appeal is always to the single life; his central doctrine of humanity is that of the infinite worth of each single soul.

"Nothing can make up for the loss of the individual. The shepherd goes out after the one lost sheep; the woman sweeps the house to find the one bit of money; the gain of the world is nothing if a man loses his own soul. Thus Christ and his teachings stand forever over against the schemes which are going to redeem the world by any impersonal mechanical plan. He seeks to save men one at a time; his kingdom is within; he calls his disciples singly; he calleth his own sheep by name and leadeth them out. It is a personal relation, an individual work."

This personal method of Jesus, he shows, has

given the idea of individual worth, and influenced largely the effort of the churches to benefit men. And then he turns to consider "one whole side of the teaching of Jesus which such a view entirely ignores. Suppose one goes on to ask humbly: 'Why does Christ thus appeal to the individual? Why is the single soul of such infinite worth to him? Is it for its own sake? Is there this tremendous significance about my little being and doing that it has its own isolated worth?' Not at all. A man's life, taken by itself, is just what it seems — a very insignificant affair. What is it that gives significance to such a single life? It is its relation to the whole of which it is a part. Just as each minutest wheel is essential in some great machine, just as the health of each slighted limb or organ in your body affects the vitality and health of the whole, so stands the individual in the organic life of the social world. 'We are members of one another.' 'We are one body in Christ;' 'no man liveth or dieth to himself'—so runs the Christian conception of the common life; and in this organic relationship the individual finds the meaning and worth of his own isolated self. What is this conception in Christ's own language? It is his marvelous ideal of what he calls 'the kingdom of God,' that perfected world of humanity in which, as in a perfect body, each part should be sound and whole, and thus the body be complete. How Jesus looked and prayed for this coming of a better world! The kingdom of heaven is the one thing to desire. It is the good seed of the future; it is the leaven dropped into the mass of the world; it is the hidden treasure, the pearl of great price. It may come slowly, as servants look for a reckoning after years of duty done; it may come suddenly, as virgins wake and meet the bridegroom.

"However and wherever this Christian commonwealth, this kingdom of God, arrives, then and there only will the hopes of Jesus be fulfilled. 'Thy kingdom come' is the central prayer of the disciple of Christ. What does this mean, then, as to Christ's thought of society? It means that a completed social order was his highest dream. We have seen that he was the great individualist of history. We now see that he was the great socialist as well. His hope for man was a universal hope. What he prophesied was just that enlarged and consolidated life of man which many modern dreams repeat, where all the conflicts of selfishness should be outgrown, and there should be one kingdom and one king; one motive — that of love; one unity — that of the spirit; one law — that of liberty. Was ever socialistic prophet of a revolutionary society more daring, or sanguine, or, to practical minds, more impracticable than this visionary Jesus with his assurance of a coming kingdom of God?

"But how can it be, we go on to ask once more, that the same teacher can teach such opposite truths? How can Christ appeal thus to the single soul and yet hope thus for the kingdom? How can he be at once the great individualist and the great socialist of history? Are we confronted with an inconsistency in Christ's doctrine of human life?

On the contrary, we reach here the very essence of the gospel in its relation to human needs. The two teachings, that of the individual and that of the social order, that of the part and that of the whole, are not exclusive of each other or opposed to each other, but are essential parts of the one law of Christ. Why is the individual soul of such inestimable value? Because of its essential part in the organic social life. And why is the kingdom of God set before each individual? To free him from all narrowness and selfishness of aim. Think of those great words of Jesus, spoken as he looked back on his completed work: 'For their sakes I sanctify myself.' 'For their sakes'—that is the sense of the common life working as a motive beyond all personal desire, even for holiness itself. 'I sanctify myself'—that is the way in which the common life is to be saved. The individual is the means; the kingdom of God is the end.

"The way to make a better world is first of all to make your own soul better, and the way to make your own soul better is to stir it with the sense of the common life. And so the same master of the problem of life becomes at once the most positive of individualists and the most visionary of socialists. His first appeal is personal: 'Sanctify thyself.' His second call is to the common life: 'For their sakes'; and the end and the means together make the motto of a Christian life—'For their sakes I sanctify myself.' Such is Christ in his dealing with the social question. He does not ignore the social problems of any age, but he approaches them always at their personal ends. With unfailing sagacity he declines to be drawn into special questions of legislation or programmes of reform. Changes of government are not for him to make. 'Render unto Cæsar the things that are Cæsar's.' The precise form of the coming kingdom is not for him to define. 'To sit on my right hand is not mine to give.' It is in vain to claim Jesus Christ as the expounder of any social panacea. He simply brings all such schemes and dreams to the test of a universal principle, the principle of sanctifying one's self for others' sakes, the two-fold principle of the infinite worth of the individual and the infinite hope of a kingdom of God, and of every plan and work which is proposed for social welfare, Christ says: 'Let it begin with the individual — his character, his liberty, his enlargement of life — and then out of this individual sanctification will grow the better social world.'"

Professor Peabody admits that we have not advanced far in the solution of these problems; panaceas have not worked, and individual reformation does not seem to issue in works that have much social value. He turns to ask Christ's method toward poverty, and shows that what he wants is man's soul "trained into personal power, individual capacity, self-help," and concludes there is more "Christian charity in teaching a trade than in alms, in finding work than in relieving want." He turns on the other hand to ask Christ's attitude toward the rich, and concludes that his condemnation "was directed, not against the fact of wealth, but against the abuses and perils of wealth." He would have us warned of the same dangers to-day. "We might as well face the fact that one of the severest tests of character which our time affords has to be borne by the rich. The person who proposes to maintain simplicity and sympathy, responsibility and high-mindedness in the midst of the wealth and luxury of the modern times is undertaking that which he had better at once understand to be very hard. The rich have some advantages, but they unmistakably have also many disadvantages, and the Christianization of wealth is beyond question the most serious of modern problems. But this is not saying that rich men should be abolished. Wealth only provides a severer school for the higher virtues of life, and the man or woman who can really learn the lesson of that school has gained one of the hardest, but also one of the most fruitful, experiences of modern times."

He concludes that in the complications of modern society wealth has a new function, and in its administration the Christian has a new mission. "Christ comes into the business world of to-day and, seeking the man who wants to be his disciple, says to him, 'This world of affairs is not to be abandoned, nor yet to be feared; it is to be redeemed. Enter into it. Be as sagacious, far-sighted, intelligent, judicious as the children of this world. Be a thoughtful, good man of business. And then add to this self-culture the larger motive, the bringing in of my kingdom. Ask yourself this question of your business: 'Am I in it hindering or helping the better life of men? Am I in any degree responsible for the ends of the present industrial system, or am I lessening them by the methods of my own? Is my success at the cost of my employés' degradation, or do they share the satisfaction of my own prosperity? In short, am I helping to make this world God's world, or would it, if all dealt as I do, soon be the devil's world?' Then, having answered this question in your soul, realize still further how many of the first signs of the coming kingdom wait for business men to show.'

"The Christian in business to-day is looking for every stable relation between employer and employed. Coöperation is to him better than competition. He sees his own life in the light of the common good. The Christian in business discovers that good lodgings for the working classes are both wise charity and good business. The Christian in business holds his sagacity and insight at the service of public affairs. He is not ensnared in the meshes of his own prosperity. He owns his wealth; it does not own him. The community leans on him instead of his being a dead weight on the community. He teaches us the higher use of wealth instead of warning us of its fearful perils. And when the Christian business man dies the properties he has controlled do not rise in the market because the risk of his management is gone, but the business world says of him, 'This man was a consistent Christian. He did not fear or flee from the world, but he made it the instrument of the higher life of man. In this world's battles he was a good soldier of Jesus Christ.'"

Prof. Richard T. Ely spoke in more emphatic and positive terms of "Christianity as a Social Force," to show that individualism, as commonly understood, is non-Christian. Wealth, and talent, and position, and powers are in trust for the common good, and individual salvation which ignores this is not, within the true Christian idea, possible. Offering some severe criticism of the social condition of Christendom, Professor Ely concludes as follows:

"We may thus say that Christianity as a social force stands for the conservation of energy. It seeks the utilization of all human power for the advancement of the welfare of man, and it tends to preserve the achievements of the past because it means peaceful progress. It may be thus said that Christianity stands for progress emphatically, but for conservative progress. Christianity means a mighty transformation and turning of things upside down, and while it seeks to bring about the most radical changes in peace, it has forces within it which nothing can withstand and resistance to which is sure to result in revolutionary violence. It is true that Christ said he came to bring not peace, but a sword — signifying the opposition of malevolence to social progress; yet a fruitless opposition, for in the end the peace of Christ must triumph. We can imagine Christ among us to-day, pointing, as of old, to our great temples and warning us that the time will come when one stone of them shall not rest upon another. We can imagine Christ pointing to our grade crossings and to our link and pin couplers, covered with the blood of mutilated brakemen, and crying out to us: 'Woe unto you, hypocrites! Ye do these things, and for a pretense make long prayers.' We can also imagine him summoning before our vision the thousands who have lost their limbs in needless industrial accidents, and pointing to the hospitals to relieve them, and the charities to furnish them with artificial limbs, and again uttering one of his terrible maledictions: 'Woe unto you, hypocrites!' We can also imagine him in his scathing denunciations and heart-searching sermons opening our eyes to our social iniquities and shortcomings, and calling to mind the judgment to come in which reward or penalty shall be visited upon us, either as we have or have not ministered to those who needed our ministrations — the hungry, the naked, the prisoner, and the captive. The reward: 'Come, ye blessed of my Father, inasmuch as ye have done it unto the least of these ye have done it unto me;' the penalty: 'Inasmuch as ye have not done it unto the least of these — depart from me.'"

Discussing "Religion and Riches," the Rev. Washington Gladden, so well and widely known in this field of research, declared "poverty and perfection incompatible," and held that "the religious man must be a co-worker with God, not only in the production of wealth, but also in the distribution of wealth." In answering the question, "Can we discover God's plan for this distribution?" he says:

"It is pretty clear that the world has not as yet discovered God's plan. The existing distribution is far from being ideal. While tens of thousands are rioting in superfluity, hundreds of thousands are suffering for the lack of the necessaries of life; some are even starving. That the suffering is often due to indolence and improvidence and vice — a natural penalty which ought to be set aside — may be freely admitted, but when that is all taken account of there is a great deal of penury left which it is hard to justify in view of the opulence everywhere visible. What is the rule by which the wealth of the world is now distributed? Fundamentally, I think, it is the rule of the strongest. The rule has been greatly modified in the progress of civilization; a great many kinds of violence are now prohibited; in many ways the weak are protected by law against the encroachments of the strong; human rapacity is confined within certain metes and bounds; nevertheless, the wealth of the world is still, in the main, the prize of strength and skill. Our laws furnish the rules of the game, but the game is essentially as Rob Roy describes it. To every one according to his power is the underlying principle of the present system of distribution. It is evident that under such a system, in spite of legal restraints, the strong will trample upon the weak. We can not believe that such a system can be in accordance with the will of a Father to whom the poor and needy are the especial objects of care.".

Discussing the three socialistic principles which have been by one and another suggested, "to every one alike; to every one according to his needs; to every one according to his work," he thinks it evident "that none of these methods, taken by itself, would furnish a rule in perfect harmony with divine justice and benignity. The communistic rule is clearly unjust and impracticable. To give to all an equal portion would be wasteful in the extreme, for some could by no possibility use their portion; much of it would be squandered and lost. Some could use productively and beneficently ten times, or even a thousand times more than others. The divine wisdom must follow somewhat closely the rule of the man in the parable who distributed his goods among his servants, giving 'to every man according to his several ability.' But ability here is not ability to take, but ability to use beneficently and productively, which is a very different matter." And he concludes that "the divine plan must, therefore, be that wealth shall be so distributed as to secure the greatest results. And religion, which seeks to discern and follow the divine plan, must teach that the wealth of the world will be rightly distributed only when every man shall have as much as he can wisely use to make himself a better man and the community in which he lives a better community — so much and no more."

In a paper on "Churches and City Problems," Prof. A. W. Small, Ph. D., of the University of Chicago, declared that "churches as such do not think the thoughts, nor talk the language, nor share the burdens which, for the masses in cities, contain the real problems in life." "The churches," he says again, "have no explicit policy toward city problems; lack intelligent interest in them; they are even suspicious of every endeavor to commit the churches to coöperation in solutions." He concludes that the churches must choose between the only alternatives: "First, they may confine themselves to the functions of spiritual edification, of indoctrinating the children of their members, of defending their denominational orthodoxy, and of evangelizing at home and abroad;" or "second, they may accept the full responsibility of revealers and realizers of right relations of men to each other as well as of men to God." In choosing the first alternative the function might be logically fundamental, but it must prove practically partial and self-limiting. In choosing the other alternative, there must be interdenominational organization and coöperation, on the basis of brotherhood, without sinking doctrinal differences.

Professor Small notes that recent papal deliverances upon the attitude of the Roman church toward "labor problems" are perhaps the nearest approach to a settlement of denominational policy with reference to any of these problems. A paper by Charles F. Donnelly, on "The Relations of the Roman Catholic Church to the Poor and Destitute," traced the history of her St. Vincent de Paul and other societies based on the principle of charity which would lift men into conditions of integrity and self-help, both morally and materially.

Another by the Rev. James M. Cleary defined the position of the church with reference to "Labor Problems" as follows:

"The church having taught every child of Adam who earned his bread by laborious toil to assert his own dignity and to understand his own worth, and having hitherto led a hopeless multitude from the dismal gloom of slavery to the cheering brightness of the liberty of the children of God, bravely defended the rights and the privileges of her emancipated children. 'The church has regarded with religious care the inheritance of the poor.' The poor are the special charge of the church. Every living soul is in God's immediate care, the rich as well as the poor; there is no distinction of class or privilege with him. Every soul, whether refined or rude, is in his keeping. But with an especial care he watches over those who 'eat bread in the sweat of their brow.' None need the Divine Comforter more than the weary children of toil, and none need and have received the sympathy of the church as they do. In his exhaustive encyclical on the condition of labor Leo XIII. lays down the principle that the workman's wages is not a problem to be solved by the pitiless arithmetic of avaricious greed. The wage-earner has rights which he can not surrender, and which no man can take from him, for he is an intelligent, responsible being owing homage to God and duties to human society. His recompense, then, for his daily toil can not be measured by a heartless standard of supply and demand, or a cruel code of inhuman economics, for man is not a money-making machine, but a citizen of earth and an heir to the kingdom of heaven. He has a right, of which no man has the power to deprive him, 'to the pursuit of life, liberty, and happiness.' Every man has a God-given right to live in decency and comfort. Labor has a right to freedom; labor has also a right to protect its own independence and liberty. Hence labor unions are lawful and have enjoyed the sanction and protection of the church in all ages. Our times have witnessed no more edifying spectacle than the noble, unselfish pleading of our own Cardinal Gibbons for the cause of organized labor at the See of Peter. In organization there is strength, but labor must use its power for its own protection, not for invading the rights of others. The strike, or refusal of united labor to work, is a declaration of war, for it seriously disturbs many human activities. It is justifiable only and should be resorted to only when all other means have failed, when every other expedient has been exhausted, and can be defended only on the plea that the workman is treated unjustly by organized capital. That form of strike, however, by which labor unions use unlawful means to prevent willing men who are anxious to earn a livelihood for their families from engaging in honest work can in no way be defended, and must surely fall under the unqualified censure of religion. Labor has a right, it is true, to prevent its own degradation, and is justified in insisting that wages shall not be so reduced as to prevent Christian men from living like civilized beings, but religion, which is the guardian angel of social order and just law, must insist that when such evils threaten society they are remedied by legislation and not by appeals to force.

"Our Christian civilization must not be endangered by false maxims and harsh methods of social economy. Our civilization is a failure if it aims only at the protection of wealth and the guardianship of property.

> "Ill fares the land, to hastening ills a prey,
> Where wealth accumulates and men decay.

"Men are more precious than money. The contented Christian homes of an intelligent people, happy in the opportunity of earning a decent competence for present and future needs, are the safest and most hopeful support of a nation and encouraging evidences of national prosperity. Religion's duty is to teach the rich the responsibilities of wealth and the poor respect for order and law. The security of capital against the discontent and envy of labor is the best security also for the workingman. When capital becomes timid and shrinks from the hazard of investment, labor soon feels the pangs of hunger, and the dread specter of want casts its dismal shadow over many a humble home.

"Religion is the only influence that has been able to subdue the pride and the passions of men, to refine the manners and guide the conduct of human society, so that rich and poor alike, mindful of their common destiny, respect each other's rights, their mutual dependence, and the rights of their common Father in heaven. The religious teachers and guides who apply the principles of the 'Sermon on the

Mount' to the every-day affairs of men, and lead humanity upward to a better and nobler realization of God's compassion for the weary ones of earth, will merit the undying gratitude of men and heaven's choicest rewards."

Space will not admit of further analysis of this valuable series of papers. If the result in outline of methods of social reform is not wholly satisfactory, it is at least evident that the religious motive for the study and solution of social problems has received eminent consideration, and is asserted with a unanimity which demonstrates great progress in Christendom along these lines. If the study of sociology and efforts in social reform have to be carried on for the most part independent of Christian ecclesiastical organizations, it is evident that its advocates intend to claim the sanction and authority of Christ and the gospels in the adjustment of the inherent and necessary rights and responsibilities of the individual and the social body, under the ideal of the voluntary contribution of each to the common good and of all to the good of each.

WOMAN.

"The place which woman has taken in the Parliament of Religions and in the denominational congresses," said the remarkably efficient and ever-gracious president of the woman's branch, Mrs. Charles Henrotin, in her concluding address, "is one of such great importance that it is entitled to your careful attention."

It will interest many to know what place exactly woman occupied to her own highest honor, and as indicating the field of her most permanent achievements, in the judgment of this executive woman, who had such exceptional opportunities for estimating the value of the work of her sister co-laborers. The series of auxiliary congresses was opened in May with a congress of representative women, which was one of the most largely attended and popular in the whole series. This, with the active part taken by women in all the succeeding congresses, led many to wonder if the order of the world might not be changing, and woman be destined to take the lead in the forensic work which has heretofore been assumed to belong to man. The men and women who worked together on committees, in the laborious and varied preparations which were necessary to the success of the congresses, knew well that if the field of her endeavor is enlarging, her power is just what it has always been — the power of patient, persistent, gracious, and humanizing work. It is interesting in this connection to have the following testimony from such a representative of her sex as Mrs. Henrotin:

"As day by day the parliament has presented the result of the preliminary work of two years, it may have appeared to you an easy thing to put into motion the forces of which this evening is the crowning achievement, but to bring about this result hundreds of men and women have labored. There are sixteen committees of women in the various departments represented in the Parliament of

Religions and denominational congresses, with a total membership of 228. In many cases the men's and the women's committee have elected to work as one and in others the women have held separate congresses. Sixteen women have spoken in the Parliament of Religions, and that more did not appear is due to the fact that the denominational committee had secured the most prominent women for their presentation. Doctor Barrows treated the woman's branch with that courtesy and consideration, and I may add justice, which he has extended to the representatives of every creed. In the denominational congresses the first in order was that of the Jewish women, and here is the key-note to woman's position in the modern religious world. It is that of the worker, for it is not in the Parliament of Religions, as able as have been the women representing her in the parliament, that you can judge of the tremendous power which she wields. It is in the denominational congress that her work is best illustrated.

"In the Roman Catholic congress the work of the women for their church was most ably presented. His Eminence Cardinal Gibbons, in his paper, 'The Needs of Humanity Supplied by the Catholic Religion,' demonstrated that the needs of humanity were ministered unto by women, laity as well as sisters, in the Catholic church. His paper could fitly have been named, 'What Woman Has Accomplished for the Catholic Church.' The congress of the Jewish women was a memorable occasion, as it was the first time in the world's history that the Jewish women met together as a religious power. Eighty-five delegates from the different Jewish communities from all parts of the United States were present, and before this congress adjourned an international association of Jewish women was formed, and if it brings into the religious world the same zeal which has animated that historic race, it is easy to conceive what a tremendous force has here been put into motion. The committee of Congregational women held an interesting session treating of practical questions connected with church work. The women of the Lutheran church succeeded in uniting the Lutheran women all over the United States in one congress, and held four sessions in which Lutheran women spoke on the work of women in their church. Before this congress closed an international league of Lutheran women was formed. The King's Daughters presented their work on Monday, October 2d. In all the other denominational congresses women have presented their work in the general congress. Two hundred and twelve women have taken part in the denominational and mission congresses. Now the question presents itself, along what line of thought have most of these women presented papers? And I may truly answer *that they have treated of practical efforts* for the bettering of social conditions."

In the many excellent papers presented by women on the theory of woman's place and work in the world, many suggestions were set forth, but the one assured conviction and purpose running through them all is perhaps most adequately voiced by the following passages from Miss Willard's address:

"We are then beginning to train those with each other who were formed for each other, and the English-speaking home, with its Christian method of a twofold headship, based on laws natural and divine, is steadily rooting out all that remains of the medieval, continental, and harem philosophies concerning this greatest problem of all time. The true relations of that complex being whom God created by uttering the mystic thought that had in it the potency of paradise, 'In our own image let us make man, and let him have dominion over all the earth,' will ere long be ascertained by means of the new correlation and attuning each to other of a more complete humanity upon the Christ-like basis that 'there shall be no more curse.'"

"She is the embodiment of what shall be. In an age of force woman's greatest grace was to cling; in this age of peace she doesn't cling much, but is every bit as tender and as sweet as if she did. She has strength and individuality, a gentle seriousness; there is more of a sister, less of the siren; more of the duchess and less of the doll. Woman is becoming what God meant her to be, and Christ's gospel necessitates her being, the companion and counselor, not the incumbrance and toy, of men. To meet this new creation how grandly men themselves are growing, how considerate and brotherly, how pure in word and deed! The world has never yet known half the aptitude of character and life to which men will attain when they and women live in the same world. It doth not yet appear what they shall be, or we either, for that matter, but in many a home presided over by a temperance voter and a white-ribbon worker I have thought the heavenly vision was really coming down to terra firma. With all my heart I believe, as do the best men of the nation, that woman will bless and brighten every place she enters, and that she will enter every place. Its welcome of her presence and her power will be the final test of any institution's fitness to survive."

As Mrs. Henrotin said: "It is too soon to prognosticate woman's future in the churches. Hitherto she has been not the thinker, the formulator of creeds, but the silent worker. That day has passed; it remains for her to take her rightful position in the active government of the church, and to the question, if men will accord that position to her, my experience and that of the chairmen of the woman's committees warrants us in answering an emphatic yes. Her future in the western churches is in her own hands, and the men of the eastern churches will be emboldened by the example of the western to return to their country and bid our sisters of those distant lands to go and do likewise. Woman has taken very literally Christ's command to feed the hungry, clothe the naked, heal the sick, and to minister unto those who are in need of such ministrations; as her influence and power increase, so also will her zeal for good works. That the experiment of an equal presentation of men and women in a parliament of religions has not been a failure I think can be proved by the part taken by the women who have had the honor of being called to participate in this great gathering. I must now bear witness to the devotion, the unselfishness, and the zeal of the chairman of every committee who has assisted in arranging these programmes. I would that I had the time to name them one by one. Their generous coöperation and unselfish endeavor are of those good things the memory of which is in this life a foreshadowing of how divine is the principle of loyal coöperation in working for righteousness."

These generous words, in which she pays tribute to her earnest, modest, and as a rule notably prudent and intelligent co-workers, set the text upon which every man intimately associated in the preparations for the congresses, and in their conduct, would like to enlarge. Regretting that the limits of this review will not permit detailed notice of the manifold ways in which the women of the several committees contributed to their success, I wish to record the conviction, founded in observation and experience, that without the self-sacrificing and wise work of these women, continued from the beginning throughout the organization, neither the parliament nor the denominational congresses could have been carried out with such breadth, and in such a spirit of charity and coöperation, as was achieved, and which constitutes their chief value.

B. B. NAGARKAR.
Brahmo-Somaj, Bombay, India.

CHAPTER V.

THE DENOMINATIONAL CONGRESSES.

THE Parliament of Religions was but a part of the series of religious congresses, and though it was in itself an event so notable and of such popular interest as to overshadow the others at the time, it will be found when the contributions to the several denominational congresses are published that the highest and most valuable work of Christian thinkers was put into the preparation for them. Over thirty congresses of different denominations and religious societies were held concurrently with and in the weeks preceding and following the parliament, each one of which was of sufficient dignity and importance to have attracted international attention at any other time. There was among the committees some disappointment that the programmes, so carefully matured, and commanding the best thought of representative men and women in preparation, should have been so completely overshadowed; but upon second thought it has appeared to most of those interested that the great success of that event, as a signal demonstration of both the need and the possibility of fraternal frankness and comparison, will give to the proceedings of the special congresses, when published, an importance and value entirely worthy of the labor spent upon them. Without any attempt to represent the matter of over thirty elaborately prepared programmes, we can only here glance at a few characteristic features of them.

The Jewish Congress, beginning August 27th, showed how completely modern Judaism is organizing for the ethical education of its people, and displayed more zeal of propagandism than it has been usually credited with. Subjects ranging from the fundamental doctrines of Judaism through ethics and the influence of Judaism upon civilization down to the organization and methods of charitable relief were treated, presenting the whole scope of Jewish thought, organization, and work; and to this was added the congress of Jewish women, treating of women, home, charity, and mission work among the uneducated — a thoroughly practical series of papers, of value mainly to their own people as imparting to them the inspiration of history, and a larger conception of educational, ethical, and charitable work.

The Columbian Catholic Congress, which was held the week preceding the parliament, presented a programme notable for the attention given to the relation of the church to government and social questions. Assured of its position, only eager to define the harmony of its spiritual interests with the civil order and institutions among which it works, it addressed itself largely to the "social question" in its various phases, the rights of labor, the duties of capital, poverty, public and private charities, labor unions, strikes and arbitration, women and their work, and education. Both the papers, and the discussions in the sections to which they were assigned, showed the completeness and elasticity of the organization, which has been built up to cover all ranges of life, and carry help to the lowest in the name of religion.

The Congregational, Methodist, Lutheran, and other evangelical Protestant bodies ran much to the history of the denomination, less to the origin and development of doctrine; giving full attention to missionary motive and machinery, and, where the women took a distinctive part, to education, the home, missionary appeal to the erring, and help to the helpless.

Universalism argued the goodness of God, the essential holiness of man, the destructibility of sin, the self-perpetuating power of goodness, with pardonable rejoicing at the "Renaissance of Universalism" in the various sects of Christendom. Unitarianism presented its theological method, its place in the development of Christianity, its influence in literature, philanthropy, and in the growth of democracy, its history, doctrines, and organized working forces. Even the Congress of Evolutionists gave much time to ethics and religion, setting forth the bearing of the doctrine of evolution upon belief in immortality and the development of Christianity.

In the New Jerusalem Church Congress an elaborate series of papers set forth the Swedenborgian doctrine on the unity of God's ways to man in the successive dispensations or churches, on the history of revelation and the opening of the spiritual sense of the sacred Scriptures, revealing the one Lord, and one church with its successive ages, and the doctrines which constitute the basis of a universal faith and charity. In another series the mission of its doctrines to the Gentiles, to the Christian denominations, to biblical criticism, to science, to philosophy, to the historian, to literature and art, to sociology and government, and in education. In still another series the relation of woman's work to man's, in the church, the home, and the religious world.

Congresses were held by the Young Men's and Young Women's Christian associations, by the Evangelical Alliance, and a world's congress of missions, covering the needs, problems, and provisions for city, home, and foreign evangelization — all serious, generous in plan, and striking in the ability of the contributions offered to the advancement of the causes represented. Indeed, the only criticism to be offered is upon the appalling breadth of subject, amount of detail, and wealth of thought brought under review. This difficulty can only be overcome when the several committees publish their papers for the use of those whose interest and fitness lead them into one or another of these interesting fields of inquiry. But if the complete library stood before us, no single mind could fully appreciate the amount and worth of original, honest, and painstaking thought in this Columbian exhibit of the mind and work of the world in morals and religion.

CHAPTER VI.

FAREWELL MEETINGS IN COLUMBUS AND WASHINGTON HALLS.

THE closing scene of the Parliament of Religions fulfilled the promise of its opening, and will live forever in the memory of those who were fortunate enough to participate in it or to witness it. If the 8,000 people who assembled to hear the words of farewell could have been gathered into one great assembly, with suitable surroundings, the impression would have been intensified. That this immense body of people could be separated into two audiences, uncomfortably seated in bare and uninviting halls, to listen half of them to speeches already once delivered to the other half, without any diminution of enthusiasm, witnesses the greatness of the occasion.

It was early apparent that Columbus Hall would not accommodate half the people who desired to attend the closing exercises, and tickets were accordingly issued for an overflow meeting in Washington Hall, which the writer of this review and the Rev. Jenkins L. Jones were asked to conduct. Both halls were filled to their utmost capacity. In the president's reception-room were assembled the representatives of the oriental religions and the creeds of Christendom, Buddhist and Baptist, Mohammedan and Methodist, Catholic and Confucian, Monotheist, Polytheist, and Pantheist, Episcopalian, Evangelical, and Evolutionist, Orthodox and Heterodox, the New Dispensation in India, and the New Dispensation in Christendom — all forms and colors of faith, and varied cut and color of vestment, mingling together in happy fellowship. It was manifest that the interest expectant in both the halls was only to be satisfied by both seeing and hearing; and we who were to be responsible for the overflow meeting confronted a problem of no small difficulty.

It was arranged that the procession of guests and speakers should form and march first to the platform of Washington Hall, there to group and stand while introduced by Doctor Barrows, with the promise that when each had spoken in Columbus Hall he should be escorted to that platform and repeat his words to that audience. And it was agreed between Mr. Jones and myself that we would alternately escort the speakers in the order of their presentation to the other audience, and introduce them to the assembly in Washington Hall. This programme was fully carried out, with the happiest results.

As the company of guests arranged themselves on the platform of Columbus Hall the Apollo Club, under the leadership of Professor Tomlins, opened with "Lift up your heads, O ye gates!" Then at the invitation of President Bonney the assembly stood in silent prayer. After which Cardinal Newman's hymn, "Lead, Kindly Light!" was sung by the chorus.

"The demands of the occasion," said President Bonney. "require the utmost possible economy of our time. We shall endeavor to present during the evening a large number of brief speeches rather than a few long ones. Doctor Barrows will now present some of the distinguished guests whom we have entertained during the past three weeks, and who have taken such an active part in the World's Parliament of Religions."

Meanwhile in Washington Hall the audience was entertained by a brief catholic and inspiring paper on the "Future of Religion" by Merwin Marie Snell, who had rendered valuable service in the conduct of the scientific section during the sessions of the parliament. At the close of his address, and while Doctor Momerie was speaking in the Hall of Columbus, it fell to my lot to say the few words I had been appointed to say. The audience was put into the best of spirits by the evident purpose to compensate them for the disappointment in being barred from the first table, as it were, and received with evident approval the suggestion that the results of this parliament would be not less religion but more, not vagueness as to origins but greater definiteness of faith.

"One of the lessons of the parliament is that not doctrine alone but life according to doctrine constitutes and qualifies religion. Wherever there is any religion there are two parties to constitute it, God and man; for there must be conjunction between them. And there are two means to this conjunction: the life of divine love which flows in inwardly with all men, and the truths of faith which are provided in some form, in more or less fullness, with every nation that has a religion. So far as any one in any religion yields his heart to live according to the truths of faith taught in his religion, the Lord, the true and only God, conjoins the good of life. And as good and truth, faith and life are united in man, he comes into harmony with the stream of God's providence, and is capable of enlightenment and development of life under favoring conditions in this world and the next.

"Every religion teaches that there is a God, and that evils are to be shunned as sins against him; and in almost every religion there is witness in some form to the life after death, with its conditions that flow from the life here, as lived in acknowledgment of God and obedience to his precepts. The vitality of religion everywhere is in the fidelity of life to belief. And the supreme good of this parliament is the emphasis it has given to that one truth. The fatherhood of God and the brotherhood of man without that truth would mean nothing, for brotherhood in religion flows from that common fountain, fidelity to what one believes from God. That is my best, and that in every other man is brother to that best in me. It is this recognition which exalts the importance of the scriptures and traditions in which the non-Christian religions are founded, and constitutes the appeal of the Christian Scriptures to them, as lighting up their own origins, and giving expansion and validity to their conception of God and righteousness. He is in the way of eternal life who lives up to his belief in God and his law; not by this or that doctrine, but by 'what is written in the law? How readest thou? This do and thou shalt live.' The emphasis and illustration which has been given to this fundamental truth in the Parliament of Religions can not but issue in permanent and happy results " And as Doctor Momerie entered at this point, reminding me of Frederick Robertson of Brighton, I could call him to witness to that great preacher's prophecy of the recognition sometime of the importance of this truth — not that it makes no difference what we believe, but, as Robertson said, "Obedience is the organ of spiritual enlightenment."

Doctor Momerie was introduced by the Rev. Mr. Jones, with happy reference to our satisfaction in his visit and contribution to the work of the congress, almost leading us to forget the disappointment at the unfortunate failure of the Anglican church to be officially represented.

Doctor Momerie responded that he wished to say three things. "First of all, I want to tender my warmest congratulations to Doctor Barrows. I do not believe there is another man living who could have carried this congress through and made it such a gigantic success. It needed a head, a heart, an energy, a common sense, and a pluck such as I have never known to be united before in a single individual.

"Secondly, I should like to offer my congratulations to the American people. This Parliament of Religions has been held in the New World. I confess

I wish it had been held in the Old World, in my own country, and that it had had its origin in my own church. It is the greatest event so far in the history of the world, and it has been held on American soil. I congratulate the people of America. Their example will be followed in time to come in other countries and by other peoples, but there is one honor which will always be America's — the honor of having led the way. And certainly I should like to offer my congratulations to you, the citizens of Chicago. While our minds are full of the parliament I can not forget the Fair. I have seen all the expositions of Europe during the last ten or twelve years, and I am sure I do not exaggerate when I say that your exposition is greater than all the rest put together. But your Parliament of Religions is far greater than your exposition. There have been plenty of expositions before. Yours is the best, but it is a comparatively common thing. The Parliament of Religions is a new thing in the world. Most people, even those who regarded the idea with pleasure, thought that it was an impossibility; but it has been achieved. Here in this Hall of Columbus vast audiences have assembled day after day, the members of which came from all churches and from all sects, and sometimes from no church at all. Here they sat side by side during the long hours of the day, listening to doctrines which they had been taught to regard with contempt; listening with respect, with sympathy, with an earnest desire to learn something which would improve their own doctrines." And with a reference to the harmony among the representatives of churches and sects which once hated and cursed one another, he closed with congratulation and benediction for Chicago.

Returning from Columbus Hall with Mr. Mozoomdar, where his speech had been received with the enthusiasm he never fails to arouse, it was evident that the second audience was not likely to prove a burden to the speakers. There was such a good-humored cordiality and informal sphere pervading Washington Hall that the speakers seemed to feel a certain lightness of spirit and freedom of address which made the repetition of the speech just delivered to the other audience a gracious pleasure. In presenting Mr. Mozoomdar, I could not but refer again to the phrase descriptive of the mission Brahmo-Somaj, namely, "The New Dispensation in India," to which his quotation from their great leader, Chunder Senn, in the address which follows, gives peculiar significance. He said:

"This Parliament of Religions, this concourse of spirits, is to break up before to-morrow's sun. What lessons have we learned from our incessant labors? Firstly, the charge of materialism, laid against the age in general, and against America in particular, is refuted forever. Could these myriads have spent their time, their energy, neglected their business, their pleasures, to be present with us if their spirit had not risen above their material needs or carnal desires? The spirit dominates still over matter and over mankind. Secondly, the unity of purpose and feeling unmistakably shown in the harmonious proceedings of these seventeen days teaches that men with opposite views, denominations with contradictory principles and histories, can form one congregation, one household, one body, for however short a time, when animated by one Spirit. Who is or what is that Spirit? It is the Spirit of God himself. This unity of man with man is the unity of man with God, and the unity of man with man in God is the kingdom of heaven. When I came here by the invitation of your President, I came with the hope of seeing the object of my lifelong faith and labors, viz., the harmony of religions, effected. The last public utterance of my leader, Cheshub Chunder Senn, made in 1883, in his lecture called 'Asia's Message to Europe,' was this:

"'Here will meet the world's representatives, the foremost spirits, the most living hearts, the leading thinkers and devotees of each church, and offer united homage to the King of kings and the Lord of lords. This central union church is no utopian fancy, but a veritable reality, whose beginning we see already among the nations of the earth. Already the right wing of each church is pressing forward, and the advanced liberals are drawing near each other under the central banner of the new dispensation. Believe me, the time is coming when the more liberal of the Catholic and Protestant branches of Christ's church will advance and meet upon a common platform and form a broad Christian community, in which all shall be identified, in spite of all diversities and differences in non-essential matters of faith. So shall the Baptists and Methodists,

Trinitarians and Unitarians, the Ritualists and the Evangelical, all unite in a broad and universal church organization, loving, honoring, serving the common body while retaining the peculiarities of each sect. Only the broad of each sect shall for the present come forward, and others shall follow in time. The base remains where it is; the vast masses at the foot of each church will yet remain, perhaps for centuries, where they now are. But as you look to the lofty heights above you will see all the bolder spirits and broad souls of each church pressing forward, onward, heavenward. Come, then, my friends, ye broad-hearted of all the churches, advance and shake hands with each other and promote that spiritual fellowship, that kingdom of heaven which Christ predicted.'

"These words were said in 1883, and in 1893 every letter of the prophecy has been fulfilled. The kingdom of heaven is to my mind a vast concentric circle with various circumferences of doctrine, authorities, and organizations from outer to inner, from inner to inner still, until heaven and earth become one. The outermost circle is belief in God and the love of man. In the tolerance, kindliness, goodwill, patience, and wisdom which have distinguished the work of this parliament that outermost circle of the kingdom of heaven has been described. We have influenced vast numbers of men and women of all opinions and the influence will spread and spread. So many human unities drawn within the magnetic circle of spiritual sympathy can not but influence and widen the various denominations to which they belong. In the course of time those inner circles must widen also till the love of man and the love of God are perfected in one church, one God, one salvation. I conclude with acknowledging the singular cordiality and appreciation extended to us orientals. Where every one has done so well we did not deserve special honor, but undeserved as the honor may be, it shows the greatness of your leaders, and especially of your chairman, Doctor Barrows. Doctor Barrows, humanly speaking, has been the soul of this noble movement. The profoundest blessings of the present and future generations shall follow him. And now farewell. For once in history all religions have made their peace, all nations have called each other brothers, and their representatives have for seventeen days stood up morning after morning to pray Our Father, the universal father of all, in heaven. His will has been done so far, and in the great coming future may that blessed will be done further and further, forever and ever."

Without further attempt to describe two meetings, we may go on in the order of the second, with which the writer is most familiar. Prince Serge Wolkonsky, who endeared himself to everybody by his enthusiasm for humanity, was next felicitously introduced by Rev. Mr. Jones, and responded in the following characteristic speech:

"I hardly realize that it is for the last time in my life I have the honor, the pleasure, the fortune to speak to you. On this occasion I would like to tell you so many things that I am afraid that if I give free course to my sentiments I will feel the delicate but imperative touch of Mr. President's hand on my shoulder long before I reach the end of my speech. Therefore, I will say thanks to all of you ladies and gentlemen in the shortest possible words — thanks for your kind attention, for your kind applause, your kind laughter, for your hearty hand-shakes. You will believe how deeply I am obliged to you when I tell you that this was the first time in my life that I ever took an active part in a congress, and I wish any enterprise I might undertake later on might leave me such happy remembrances as this first experience.

"Before bidding you farewell, I want to express a wish; may the good feelings you have shown me so many times, may they, through my unworthy personality, spread to the people of my country, whom you know so little and whom I love so much. If I ask you that, it is because I know the prejudices which prevail among the people of your country. A compatriot said the other day that Russians thought all Americans were angels, and that Americans thought all Russians were brutes. Now once in awhile these angels and these brutes come together, and both are deceived in their expectations. You see that you certainly are not angels, and you see we are not quite as much brute as you thought we were. Now why this disappointment? Why this surprise? Why this astonishment? Because we won't remember that we are men, and nothing else and nothing more. We can not be anything more, for to be a man is the highest thing we can pretend to be on this earth. I do not know whether many have learned in the sessions of this parliament what respect of God is, but I know that no one will leave the congress without having learned what respect of man is. And should the Parliament of Religions of 1893 have no other result but this, it is enough to make the names of Doctor Barrows and those who have helped him imperishable in the history of humanity.

"Should this congress have no other result than to teach us to judge our fellow-man by his individual value, and not by the political opinion he may have of his country, I will express my gratitude to the congress, not only in the name of those your brothers who are my countrymen, but in the name of those our brothers whom we so often revile because the political traditions of their country refuse the recognition of home rule; in the name of those our fellow-men whose mother-land stands on the neck of India, in the name of those our brothers whom we so often blame only because the governments of their countries send rapacious armies on the western, southern, and eastern coasts of Africa; I will express my gratitude to the congress in the name of those my brothers whom we often judge so wrongly because of the cruel treatment their government inflicts upon the Chinese. I will congratulate the congress in the name of the whole world if those who have been here have learned that as long as politics and politicians exist there is no happiness possible on earth. I will congratulate the congress in the name of the whole humanity if those who have attended its sessions have realized that it is a crime to be astonished when we see that another human being is a man like ourselves." And in concluding he paid a tribute of respect and praise to Mr. Bonney for his unfailing courtesy and charity.

Mr. Hirai of Japan, who was one of the first to tell Christians some things they ought to know about the wrongs of so-called Christian civilization, had only words of good-will in farewell.

"We can not but admire the tolerant forbearance and compassion of the people of the civilized west. You are the pioneers in human history. You have achieved an assembly of the world's religions, and we believe your next step will be toward the ideal goal of this parliament, the realization of international justice. We ourselves desire to witness its fulfillment in our lifetime and to greet you again with our deepest admiration. By your kind hospitality we have forgotten that we are strangers, and we are very much attached to this city. To leave here makes us feel as if we were leaving our native country. To part with you makes us feel as if we were parting from our own sisters and brothers. When we think of our homeward journey we can not help shedding tears. Farewell. The cold winter is coming, and we earnestly wish that you may be in good health. Farewell."

The kindly and gentle appeal in the speech of the

Chinese ambassador Pung Quang Yu is also something of a reproach to Christian America. After formal thanks, he said:

"It is unnecessary for me to touch upon the existing relations between the government of China and that of the United States. There is no doubt that the Chinese minister at Washington and the honorable Secretary of State are well able to deal with every question rising between the two countries in a manner satisfactory and honorable to both. As I am a delegate to the religious congresses, I can not but feel that all religious people are my friends. I have a favor to ask of all the religious people of America, and that is that they will treat, hereafter, all my countrymen just as they have treated me. I shall be a hundred times more grateful to them for the kind treatment of my countrymen than of myself. I am sure that the Americans in China receive just such considerate treatment from the cultured people of China as I have received from you. The majority of my countrymen in this country are honest and law-abiding. Christ teaches us that it is not enough to love one's brethren only. I am sure that all religious people will not think this request too extravagant. It is my sincere hope that no national differences will ever interrupt the friendly relations between the two governments and that the two peoples will equally enjoy the protection and blessings of heaven. I intend to leave this country shortly. I shall take great pleasure in reporting to my government the proceedings of this parliament upon my return. With this I desire to bid all my friends farewell."

The high priest of the Shinto sect, of Japan, while invoking eight million deities, expressed the spirit of brotherhood which carries with it the acknowledgment of a supreme Father.

"I am here in the pulpit again to express my thanks for the kindness, hearty welcome, and applause I have been enjoying at your hands ever since I came here to Chicago. You have shown great sympathy with my humble opinion, and your newspaper men have talked of me in high terms. I am happy that I have had the honor of listening to so many famous scholars and preaching the same opinion of the necessity of universal brotherhood and humanity. I am deeply impressed with the peace, politeness, and education which characterize your audiences. But is it not too sad that such pleasures are always short-lived? I, who made acquaintance with you only yesterday, have to part with you to-day, though reluctantly. This Parliament of Religions is the most remarkable event in history, and it is the first honor in my life to have the privilege of appearing before you to pour out my humble idea, which was so well accepted by you all. You like me, but I think it is not the mortal Shibata that you like, but you like the immortal idea of universal brotherhood. What I wish to do is to assist you in carrying out the plan of forming universal brotherhood under the one roof of truth. You know unity is power. I, who can speak no language but Japanese, may help you in crowning that grand project with success. To come here I had many obstacles to overcome, many struggles to make. You must not think I represent all Shintoism. I only represent my own Shinto sect. But who dares to destroy universal fraternity? So long as the sun and moon continue to shine all friends of truth must be willing to fight courageously for this great principle. I do not know as I shall ever see you again in this life, but our souls have been so pleasantly united here that I hope they may be again united in the life hereafter. Now I pray that 8,000,000 deities protecting the beautiful cherry-tree country of Japan may protect you and your government forever, and with this I bid you good-by."

The Rev. Dr. George T. Candlin, who is a Christian missionary to China, who showed his faith on several occasions that God has not left himself without a witness in any nation, and that the mission of Christianity is to educate rather than subdue, said:

"It is with deepest joy that I take my part in the congratulations of this closing day. The parliament has more than justified my most sanguine expectations. As a missionary I anticipate that it will make a new era of missionary enterprise and missionary hope. If it does not it will not be your fault, and let those take the blame who make it otherwise. Very sure I am that at least one missionary, who counts himself the humblest member of this noble assembly, will carry through every day of work, through every hour of effort on till the sun of life sets on the completion of his task, the strengthening memory and uplifting inspiration of this Pentecost. By this parliament the city of Chicago has placed herself far away above all the cities of the earth. In this school you have learned what no other town or city in the world yet knows. The conventional idea of religion which obtains among Christians the world over is that Christianity is true, all other religions false; that Christianity is of God, while other religions are of the devil; or else, with a little spice of moderation, that Christianity is a revelation from heaven, while other religions are manufactures of men. You know better, and with clear light and strong assurance can testify that there may be friendship instead of antagonism between religion and religion; that so surely as God is our common Father, our hearts alike have yearned for him and our souls in devoutest moods have caught whispers of grace dropped from his throne. Then this is Pentecost, and behind is the conversion of the world."

There is diversity of gifts, and one differs from another in fitness and function as well as in glory. This was sure to be realized in introducing him, by one who had become really acquainted with the loving, the lovable, and love-inspiring Dharmapala. He responded:

"Peace, blessings, and salutations, brethren. This congress of religions has achieved a stupendous work in bringing before you the representatives of the religions and philosophies of the East. The committee on religious congresses has realized the utopian idea of the poet and the visionary. By the wonderful genius of two men — Mr. Bonney and Doctor Barrows — a beacon-light has been erected on the platform of the Chicago Parliament of Religions to guide the yearning souls after truth.

"I, on behalf of the 475,000,000 of my co-religionists, followers of the gentle Lord Buddha Gautama, tender my affectionate regards to you and to Dr. John Henry Barrows, a man of noble tolerance, of sweet disposition, whose equal I could hardly find. And you, my brothers and sisters, born in this land of freedom, you have learned from your brothers of the far East their presentation of the respective religious systems they follow. You have listened with commendable patience to the teachings of the all-merciful Buddha through his humble followers. During his earthly career of forty-five years he labored in emancipating the human mind from religious prejudices, and teaching a doctrine which has made Asia mild. By the patient and laborious researches of the men of science you are given to enjoy the fruits of material civilization, but this civilization by itself finds no praise at the hands of the great naturalists of the day.

"Learn to think without prejudice, love all beings for love's sake, express your convictions fearlessly, lead a life of purity, and the sunlight of truth will illuminate you. If theology and dogma stand in your way in search of truth, put them aside. Be earnest and work out your own salvation with diligence, and the fruits of holiness will be yours."

The Vedas, they say, have no beginning and no

end, and that is because their streams flow from the eternal fountain of the water of life. "There is a river the streams whereof make glad the city of our God," and in every land waters of instruction and refreshment are provided and preserved for those who are there, by a providence which embraces them as truly as the most favored. Something of this faith, uttered in the introduction of Swami Vivekananda, was justified in his own words.

"The World's Parliament of Religions has become an accomplished fact, and the merciful Father has helped those who labored to bring it into existence and crowned with success their most unselfish labor. My thanks to those noble souls whose large hearts and love of truth first dreamed this wonderful dream and then realized it. My thanks to the shower of liberal sentiments that has overflowed this platform. My thanks to this enlightened audience for their uniform kindness to me and for their appreciation of every thought that tends to smooth the friction of religions. A few jarring notes were heard from time to time in this harmony. My special thanks to them, for they have by their striking contrast made the general harmony the sweeter. Much has been said of the common ground of religious unity. I am not going just now to venture my own theory; but if any one here hopes that this unity would come by the triumph of any one of these religions and the destruction of the others, to him I say: 'Brother, yours is an impossible hope.' Do I wish that the Christian would become Hindu? God forbid. Do I wish that the Hindu or Buddhist would become Christian? God forbid. The seed is put in the ground, and earth, and air, and water are placed around it. Does the seed become the earth, or the air, or the water? No. It becomes a plant, it develops after the law of its own growth, assimilates the air, the earth, and the water, converts them into plant substance and grows a plant. Similar is the case with religion. The Christian is not to become a Hindu or a Buddhist, nor a Hindu or a Buddhist to become a Christian. But each must assimilate the others and yet preserve its individuality and grow according to its own law of growth. If the Parliament of Religions has shown anything to the world it is this: It has proved to the world that holiness, purity, and charity are not the exclusive possessions of any church in the world and that every system has produced men and women of the most exalted character. In the face of this evidence if anybody dreams of the exclusive survival of his own and the destruction of the others I pity him from the bottom of my heart, and point out to him that upon the banner of every religion would soon be written, in spite of their resistance: 'Help and not fight,' 'Assimilation and not destruction,' 'Harmony and peace and not dissension.'"

A quiet lawyer of Bombay, secretary and representative of the Jain Association, a form of religion he declared older than Buddhism, Mr. Ghandi, won many friends, to whom he said in parting:

"Are we not all sorry that we are parting so

soon? Do we not wish that this parliament would last seventeen times seventeen days? Have we not heard with pleasure and interest the speeches of the learned representatives on this platform? Do we not see that the sublime dream of the organizers of this unique parliament have been more than realized? If you will only permit a heathen to deliver his message of peace and love I shall only ask you to look at the multifarious ideas presented to you in a liberal spirit, and not with superstition and bigotry. as the seven blind men did in the elephant story. Once upon a time in a great city an elephant was brought with a circus. The people had never seen an elephant before. There were seven blind men in the city who longed to know what kind of animal it was, so they went together to the place where the elephant was kept. One of them placed his hands on the ears, another on the legs, a third on the tail of the elephant, and so on. When they were asked by the people what kind of an animal the elephant was, one of the blind men said: 'Oh, to be sure, the elephant is like a big winnowing fan.' Another blind man said: 'No, my dear sir, you are wrong. The elephant is more like a big round post.' The third: 'You are quite mistaken, it is like a tapering stick.' The rest of them gave also their different opinions. The proprietor of the circus stepped forward and said: 'My friends, you are all mistaken. You have not examined the elephant from all sides. Had you done so you would not have taken one-sided views.' Brothers and sisters, I entreat you to hear the moral of this story, and learn to examine the various religious systems from all standpoints.

"I now thank you from the bottom of my heart for the kindness with which you have received us and for the liberal spirit and patience with which you have heard us."

Prince Momolu Massaquoi, of the Vey Nation, West Africa, is a Christian convert, educated in Liberia and in this country; but his heart is near his people, and on many occasions he testified to the reality of their religion and soundness of their morality, both the Mohammedans and pagans among them. He did not appear before the parliament in any formal address, though he spoke in the subordinate congresses, winning all with his dignified and simple bearing and unaffected grace of speech. Presented as a representative of Africa, he referred to the receptive and teachable character of the African, to his affectionate disposition and susceptibility to supernatural influences and guidance, and said:

"Permit me to express my hearty thanks to the chairman of this congress for the honor conferred upon me personally by the privilege of representing Africa in this World's Parliament of Religions. There is an important relationship which Africa sustains to this particular gathering. Nearly 1,900 years ago, at the great dawn of the Christian morning, the world saw benighted Africa opening her doors to the infant Saviour Jesus Christ, afterward the founder of one of the greatest religions man ever embraced, and the teacher of the highest and noblest sentiments ever taught, whose teaching has resulted in the presence of this magnificent audience. As I sat in this audience listening to the distinguished delegates and representatives in this assembly of learning, of philosophy, of systems of religions, I said to myself: 'What shall the harvest be?'

"The very atmosphere seems pregnant with an indefinable, inexpressible something—something too solemn for human utterance—something I dare not express. Previous to this gathering the greatest enmity existed among the world's religions. To-night—I dare not speak as one seeing visions or dreaming dreams—but this night it seems that the world's religions, instead of striking one against another, have come together in amicable deliberation and have created a lasting and congenial spirit among themselves. May the coming together of these wise men result in the full realization of the general parliament of God, the brotherhood of man, and the consecration of souls to the service of God."

At this point in the programme occurred a scene in Columbus Hall in which the audience in Washington Hall could not participate. Doctor Barrows referred to President Bonney as the one to whom the marvelous success of the parliament was due, whereupon the vast audience arose as by a single impulse and gave the Chautauqua salute with enthusiasm.

Mr. Bonney stood for a moment, after the enthusiasm subsided, almost overcome with emotion, and then said: "Not unto us, not unto us, but unto thy name give glory — to the God that inspired this movement and has guided and aided it by his blessing, through a multitude of the best men and women in the world under the leadership of Doctor Barrows." The Apollo Club then sang the Hallelujah Chorus. Its repetition was demanded, and President Bonney remarked that it was most fitting; it had never been given on a more appropriate occasion, though it probably never entered the thought of the gifted composer that such an occasion as the present could arise. While it was being sung the second time the Rev. Dr. George Dana Boardman of Philadelphia was introduced in Washington Hall, and delivered this remarkable and effective witness:

"Fathers of the contemplative East, sons of the executive West, behold how good and how pleasant it is for brethren to dwell together in unity. The New Jerusalem, the city of God, is descending, heaven and earth chanting the eternal hallelujah chorus."

Brief speeches from American representatives followed, from which we select passages as showing their estimate of the event.

Dr. Emil Hirsch said: "None could appreciate the deeper significance of this parliament more fully than we, the heirs of a past spanning the millenia, and the motive of whose achievements and fortitude was and is the confident hope of the ultimate break of the millennium. Millions of my co-religionists hoped that this convocation of this modern great synagogue would sound the death-knell of hatred and prejudice under which they have pined and are still suffering, and their hope has not been disappointed. Of old, Palestine's hills were every month aglow with fire-brands announcing the rise of a new month. So here were kindled the cheering fires telling the whole world that a new period of time had been consecrated. We Jews came hither to give and to receive. For what little we could bring we have been richly rewarded in the precious things we have received in turn. According to an old rabbinical practice, friends among us never part without first discussing some problem of religious life. Our whole parliament has been devoted to such discussion, and we take hence, with us in parting, the richest treasures of religious instruction ever laid before man. Thus the old Talmudic promise will be verified in us, that when even three come together to study God's law his Shekhinah abides with them."

Dr. Frank Bristol, beginning with a stanza from Burns' "Shall brithers be for a' that," said: "Good, and only good, will come from this parliament. To all who have come from afar we are profoundly and eternally indebted. Some of them represent civilization that was old when Romulus was founding Rome, whose philosophies and songs were ripe in wisdom and rich in rhythm before Homer sang his Iliad to the Greeks, and they have enlarged our ideas of our common humanity. They have brought to us fragrant flowers from the gardens of Eastern faiths, rich gems from the old mines of great philosophies, and we are richer to-night from their contributions of thought, and particularly from our contact with them in spirit. Never was there such a bright and hopeful day for our common humanity along the lines of tolerance and universal brotherhood. And we shall find that by the words that these visitors have brought to us, and by the influence they have exerted, they will be richly rewarded in the consciousness of having contributed to the mighty movement which holds in itself the promise of one faith, one Lord, one Father, one brotherhood. A distinguished writer has said it is always morn somewhere in the world. The time hastens when a greater thing will be said: 'Tis always morn everywhere in the world. The darkness has passed, the day is at hand, and with it will come the greater humanity, the universal brotherhood.'"

The Rev. Jenkin Lloyd Jones bade "the parting guests the godspeed that comes out of a soul that is glad to recognize its kinship with all lands and with all religions; and when you go, you go, not only leaving behind you in our hearts more hospitable thoughts for the faiths you represent, but also warm and loving ties that bind you into the union that will be our joy and our life forevermore." And referring to an intended motion for a second parliament of religions, he continued: "At first I thought that Bombay might be a good place, or Calcutta a better place, but I have concluded to move that the next parliament of religions be held on the sacred banks of the Ganges, in the ancient new city of

Benares, where we can visit these brethren at their noblest headquarters. And when we go there we will do as they have done, leaving our heavy baggage behind, going in light marching order, carrying only the working principles that are applicable in all lands."

Mrs. Henrotin, always working, never hurried, giving to every preparation that womanly touch needed to quiet anxiety and stimulate courage, bore her testimony to the earnest and harmonious work of the committees of women, and to its worth, especially in connection with the denominational congresses, quoted above. And Miss Chapin followed:

"We have heard," she said, "of the fatherhood of God, the brotherhood of man, and the solidarity of the human race, until these great words and truths have penetrated our minds and sunken into our hearts as never before. They will henceforth have larger meaning. No one of us all but has been intellectually strengthened and spiritually uplifted. We have been sitting together upon the mountain of the Lord. We shall never descend to the lower places where our feet have sometimes trod in times past. I have tried, as I have listened to these masterly addresses, to imagine what effect this comparative study of religions would have upon the religious world and upon individual souls that come directly under the sweep of its influence. It is not too much to hope that a great impulse has been given to the cause of religious unity, and to pure and undefiled religion in all lands."

Bishop Arnett, of the African Methodist Episcopal church, always popular, always frank and genial, said many good things, but nothing better than this: "The ten commandments, the sermon on the mount, and the golden rule have not been superseded by any that have been presented by the various teachers of religion and philosophy, but our mountai[n is] just as high and our doctrines are just as [true] before our meeting, and every man and wo[man has] been confirmed in the faith once delivered [to the] saints. Another good of this convention: [it has] taught us a lesson that while we have truth [on our] side we have not had all the truth; while w[e have] had theory we have not had all the prac[tice; and] the strongest criticism we have received wa[s not] to our doctrines or methods, but as to our pr[actice] not being in harmony with our own teachings and with our own doctrines."

Bishop Keane made a characteristic address, asserting the primitive unity of religion and appea[l]ing for a restored unity; and then Mr. Bonney said: "In the midst of all these representatives of the various faiths and churches sits a Presbyterian minister who has performed one of the greatest o[ffi]ces ever committed to the hand of man — the unification of the world in the things of religion. T[his] man now comes to say his closing words to [the] World's Parliament of Religions, and I have the

wome
Ou
t
us
t

HON. PUNG QUANG YU.
Secretary of Chinese Legation.

honor to present Rev. Dr. John Henry Barrows, chairman of the general committee." When the ovation which followed had subsided he spoke as follows:

"The closing hour of this parliament is one of congratulation, of tender sorrow, of triumphant hopefulness. God has been better to us by far than our fears, and no one has more occasion for gratitude than your chairman, that he has been upheld and comforted by your cordial coöperation, by the prayers of a great host of God's noblest men and women, and by the consciousness of divine favor. Our hopes have been more than realized. The sentiment which has inspired this parliament has held us together. The principles in accord with which this historic convention has proceeded have been put to the test, and even strained at times, but they have not been inadequate. Toleration, brotherly kindness, trust in each other's sincerity, a candid and earnest seeking after the unities of religion, the honest purpose of each to set forth his own faith without compromise and without unfriendly criticism — these principles, thanks to your loyalty and courage, have not been found wanting.

"I thank God for these friendships which we have knit with men and women beyond the sea, and I thank you for your sympathy and over-generous appreciation, and for the constant help which you have furnished in the midst of my multiplied duties. Christian America sends her greetings through you to all mankind. We cherish a broadened sympathy, a higher respect, a truer tenderness to the children of our common father in all lands, and, as the story of this parliament is read in the cloisters of Japan, by the rivers of Southern Asia, amid the universities of Europe, and in the isles of all the seas, it is my prayer that non-Christian readers may, in some measure, discover what has been the source and strength of that faith in divine fatherhood and human brotherhood which, embodied in an Asiatic peasant who was the Son of God, and made divinely potent through him, is clasping the globe with bands of heavenly light. Most that is in my heart of love, and gratitude, and happy memory must go unsaid. If any honor is due for this magnificent achievement, let it be given to the spirit of Christ, which is the spirit of love in the hearts of those of many lands and faiths who have toiled for the high ends of this great meeting. May the blessing of him who rules the storm and holds the ocean waves in his right hand follow you, with the prayers of all God's people, to your distant homes. And as Sir Joshua Reynolds closed his lectures on 'The Art of Painting' with the name of Michael Angelo, so, with a deeper reverence, I desire that the last words which I speak to this parliament shall be the name of him to whom I owe life, and truth, and hope, and all things, who reconciles all contradictions, pacifies all antagonisms, and who, from the throne of his heavenly kingdom, directs the serene and unwearied omnipotence of redeeming love — Jesus Christ, the Saviour of the world."

At the close of Doctor Barrows' address, Mr.

Bonney, who from first to last had shown such appreciation of everybody, and such felicitous sense of the fitting thing to be said in the opening, and encouragement of the parliament and every one of the diverse subordinate congresses, closed with an appropriate summing up and forecast of results, from which we select these characteristic passages:

"The influence which this congress of the religions of the world will exert on the peace and the prosperity of the world is beyond the power of human language to describe; for this influence, borne by those who have attended the sessions of the Parliament of Religions to all parts of the world, will affect in some important degree all races of men, all forms of religion, and even all governments and social institutions.

"The results of this influence will not soon be apparent in external changes, but will manifest themselves in thought, feeling, expression, and the deeds of charity. Creeds and institutions may long remain unchanged in form, but a new spirit of light and peace will pervade them, for this congress of the world's religions is the most marvelous evidence yet given of the approaching fulfillment of the apocalyptic prophecy, 'Behold! I make all things new.'

"And now farewell. A thousand congratulations and thanks for the coöperation and aid of all who have contributed to the glorious results which we celebrate this night. Henceforth the religions of the world will make war, not on each other, but on the giant evils that afflict mankind. Henceforth let all throughout the world who worship God and love their fellow-men join in the anthem of the angels:

>"Glory to God in the highest!
>Peace on earth, good will among men!"

CHAPTER VII.

WHAT WILL BE THE RESULT?

"THE world's congresses of 1893 have advanced the thought of the world fifty years."

"These congresses will exercise a powerful influence on mankind for centuries to come."

"The Parliament of Religions is the most wonderful event since the time of Christ."

"The results of these congresses seem likely to be too vast and far-reaching to be easily specified."

So have able and competent judges passed upon the merits of these meetings. It is to be hoped that the proceedings, from first to last of the whole exhibit of the thought of the times, of which it has been said, "It marks a new era in literature by its wealth of thought and felicity of expression gathered from all parts of the world," may be published by the United States Government and placed in the libraries of the world. Then results will take care of themselves.

But of this movement in the religious world especially, which has attracted such wide-spread attention, many are asking, "Whence comes it? What does it mean?" No one has given any better account of causes than its originator, who refers it to "the New Age." Speaking to the Columbian Catholic Congress, in an address grateful to earnest Catholics, and instructive to all fair-minded men, President Bonney said of the spirit of the age:

"Descended from the Sun of Righteousness this spirit of progress is filling the whole earth with its splendor and beauty, its warmth and vivifying power, and making the old things of truth and justice new in meaning, strength, and energy to execute God's will for the welfare of man."

After rehearsing some of the evidences of progress in Catholic deliverances and decisions, and among Protestants on the other hand, he says of the meaning of these changes: "Blind indeed must be the eyes that can not see in these events the quickened march of the ages of human progress toward the fulfillment of the divine prophecy of one fold and one shepherd, when all forms of government shall be one in liberty and justice, and all forms of faith and worship one in charity and human service."

There are many who will not see it so. There are some Catholics who can conceive of one fold only as Protestants and heathen are gathered into the allegiance of Rome, and there are some Protestants who would not enter a fold which should include Catholics without the most solemn subscription to their own catechism of faith and to their ecclesiastical polity. There are some, perhaps there are many, who, so far from rejoicing that the heathen give evidence of a real religion, are so little confident of Christian truth and triumph that they greatly fear the effect of this comparison and friendly interchange. The religious press reflects all these prejudices, doubts, and fears. It must be admitted that bigotry is not dead, and that one love-feast is not the millenium. The old-line theologians and ecclesiastical managers, who took little part in the congresses, look with distrust upon the movement. They recognize that an important event has occurred, but seem uncertain as to results, and hesitating as to the attitude they ought to assume toward it. On the other hand, it is obvious that the great body of worshiping and working Christian people are much impressed, and expectant of good results; though just what permanent results and healthful movements are to follow they have not clearly defined.

One thing is clear, namely, that there is a new spirit in Christendom, a spirit not very generally or generously adopted by religious leaders, perhaps, but strong enough to bring into conspicuous coöperation a few broad and able men, from among Catholics and Protestants, and representing both orthodox and liberal views, and to so far dominate opposition and quiet distrust and stimulate generous impulses as to issue in this universal conference. A few years ago, these men could not have worked together for three years to a common end; could not have issued the call in the name of Christendom without a clamor of protest that would have discounted its validity; could not have conducted a programme covering three sessions a day for seventeen days without getting into disgraceful conflicts and humiliating displays of bad feeling.

There is a new spirit in Christendom, not only of toleration and good feeling, but of faith in the divine care for all men, of respect for the 'liberty of willing and thinking' which belongs to all men of divine gift and must be regarded in all efforts to help and benefit one another. There is in this new spirit, moreover, less concern about the form of belief than about the fruit it bears; a disposition to judge its substance and quality by the life it confers rather than by the form of its statement; a conviction that the true principle of unity is love and not faith, fidelity in life to what a man understands to be the will of God and not uniformity of confession. Where this bond of charity, the common possession of an inward acknowledgment and living loyalty to what one believes to be of the divine, exists, matters of faith are subjects of reasonable conference and instruction among brethren, the wise helping the less wise and pointing out errors, not to compel, but to show a better way of life. The recognition of this true bond of brotherly love, the fellowship of those who are seeking to do the will of God, is not by any means an indifference to the comparative value of beliefs, or to the distinctions of truth and error, but a new estimate of the end of all right belief, which is to guide the life into harmony and union with God. It must be called a new spirit, rather than a defined doctrine, because it has come in like the vernal influences of sun and wind, and is operative rather as an impulse than as a definite purpose. But it has come into Christendom, and has been met and sweetly reciprocated by the representatives of the non-Christian faiths. It is new and it spreads. However few relatively to the whole body the representatives of Christian churches who participated in the parliament, it is manifest that in this spirit they feel the support of a large following, and, as was often said, of an inspiration from above. Whatever opposition to this spirit there may be, it is overawed and cautious in expression. Whatever doubt and criticism of the spirit in Christendom was shown by oriental religionists, was criticism of a spirit formerly and elsewhere manifest, not a doubt of the genuineness of this spirit of brotherhood and helpfulness in the parliament. This new spirit has come to stay. Those who like it may rejoice in it; those who do not may adjust themselves to it, as to the spirit of the age, which is beyond their control.

It seems likely that a second result of these congresses, and one inseparable from the new spirit they have exhibited, will be a change in the method, and perhaps in the message, of Christian missionaries. Intimations have come back recently from the missionaries in many lands that the natives do not so much reject the Christianity of the gospel in the Lord's words and works, as the sectarian dogmas and the attempt to impose sectarian organization and control upon native Christians. With the new spirit of brotherhood for all who are faithful to their best, and recognition of the great value of the non-Christian faiths to those who are loyal to their teachings, the motive of missions must become more helpful, and the methods more accommodated to native ideas and conditions. Some are fearing that the effect of the congresses will be to discourage missions, at least temporarily; that, from an idea that they are not needed, funds will be cut off, and from a false hope of salvation for all the motive of missions will be destroyed. This may be true to some extent with respect to certain missionary methods, and the appeal of certain societies committed to them; but it is more likely that the desire to carry the fuller light of the gospel to those who are doing their best to please God, but are ignorant and in error, will prove in the long run a stronger motive and a richer enthusiasm than the fear of their damnation or the desire of sectarian triumphs have ever furnished.

The gentle Dharmapala was not by any means free from prejudice, but his prejudice was not directed against the gospel of Jesus Christ or the preaching of that gospel in the East. Addressing Americans, he said: "You are free from the bonds of theology and dogma, and I want you seriously to consider that the twentieth century evangelization is in your hands. I warn you that if you want to establish Christianity in the East it can only be done in the principles of Christ's love and meekness. Let the missionaries study all religions, let them be types of meekness and lowliness, and they will find a welcome in all lands." The Rev. George T. Candlin, missionary in China, said, "The meaning of Christianity from a missionary point of view is infinite desire to give and willingness to receive." The Rev. R. E. Hume of India, discussing "How we might do our work better," said, "First of all, we might some of us know the thoughts of non-Christians better. We ought to study their books more deeply, more intelligently, more constantly. We ought to associate with them in order to know their inmost thoughts and feelings and their aspirations better than we do." Again he said, "Where we find truth we should more cordially and more gladly recognize it;" and he warned against the jealousy that sometimes is found where there ought to be only gladness that God through his eternal Word enlighteneth every man that cometh into the world. And finally, he said there are "phases of Christian doctrine which are put before orientals as essential to Christianity which are only Western theology," and which instead of attracting repel the minds of non-Christian people. Such testimony will have an influence, and we may expect missionary boards sooner or later to adjust themselves to the new spirit in Christendom, and to adopt a new motive, and more generous method in the field. When the motive shall be to instruct the willing-hearted in the simple faith of the gospel, and to preach to all repentance for the real remission of sins, that all may grow more worthily as the children of God, we may expect to see methods adopted which will look to the training of Christians rather than the making of Presbyterians, Congregationalists, Methodists, and so forth. The movement has begun, and Mr. Candlin's conundrum is likely to be meditated: "Given a Christendom of religious sects wrangling about minor points of doctrine, to produce a universal harmony from their united action."

This leads to the suggestion of another result likely to follow these congresses, namely, the recognition of the need in Christendom of a sound basis of faith, simple, self-attesting, and witnessing its divine origin. In the papers read before the parliament, with a few exceptions, there is wanting that apostolic assurance which rests in the confidence of divine authority. It is manifest that the authority of tradition and of councils is a thing of the past, and that the authority of self-evident truth has not been found, except, it may be, in such general propositions as that God is, and that righteousness alone is profitable. The aspiration of reason, in its new sense of freedom, is to know who God is, and how he operates in the universe which he transcends, and such a conception of righteousness as will reconcile the providence of God with the recognized laws of cause and effect. The reliance of progressive thought is just now upon the revelation of God in consciousness and to the reason. It is sure, sooner or later, to discover the weakness of its own methods. The aspiration of the human soul is ever for an ultimate authority, for the voice of God. And when the hope that is centered in the person of Jesus Christ, and the thought that is beginning to see in him the larger meaning of divine providence, seeks to define itself to the oriental religions, and to speak with the authority of a divine commission to wealth and poverty, to sinners high and low, it is sure to feel the need of a more definite, rational, and convincing doctrine than it is yet able to utter. The more it tries to find it, the more it will see it can not make it, but must find it in the Word that is written, in the Scripture that calls itself the Word of God; and in that as the vesture of him who is so named in apocalyptic vision. When God is seen in Christ, and Christ is seen in the written Word "opening in all the Scriptures things concerning himself," men will search in the Scriptures, and not in the processes of their own thought alone, for the faith of God — universal, self-attesting, divine. The world's religious congresses reveal the need of such assured, universal truths, coming down to man from above, meeting all needs, applicable to all conditions; the need, in short, of a gospel which is the gift of God, and not a troublesome tradition of the elders, nor yet an immature speculation of the newly enfranchised reason. The recognition of the need, if it becomes general, will lead to the prayer that goes before reception. All history witnesses that the providence of God is beforehand with his people's need; and that before they ask he provides the answer, to be revealed when they shall be ready to ask.

> Our human needs are prophecies of gifts.
> They were not planted else. We crave, we have;
> We yearn for and obtain; the soul's deep want
> Prepares the soul, thus thirsting, to receive
> The good it wants.

Even now the answer is within reach. From deliverances before the parliament quoted in this brief review, we could construct a series of statements ecumenical to the practical religious needs of all men, if they could separate their attention to them from the thought of traditions and from their prepossessions. Brought together from different addresses, and from those too which had throughout the clearest tone of authority grounded in a divine conviction, they would read something like this:

That the glorified Lord, Jesus Christ, is God with us, from whose presence comes the Holy Spirit to protect and empower and save. That the Bible is the Lord's Word, containing within the history and symbol and parable of its letter an infinite wisdom capable of unfolding itself in the minds of those who will live as it teaches. That there is a spiritual world where we shall live forever, and that our state there, in heaven or hell, will be the inevitable result of the motives which we make our own by choice and life in this world. That the Lord saves those who love him and keep his commandments, imparting wisdom and power in so far as they shun evil and do good in acknowledgment of him; and that in very truth God is no respecter of persons.

DR. BARROWS' GREAT HISTORY
OF THE
Parliament of Religions.

15,000 SETS (30,000 Volumes)
Sold and being delivered.
10,000 SETS (20,000 Volumes)
To be delivered January 1, 1894.

IF YOU GET DR. BARROWS' BOOK YOU WILL GET YOUR MONEY'S WORTH, HEAPED UP AND RUNNING OVER.

All the World is Buying Dr. Barrows' Great History of the World's Parliament of Religions

1. Because it is Dr. Barrows' book; because it bears throughout the impress of the man to whose wonderful ability is due more than to any other the success of the Parliament.

All the World is Buying Dr. Barrows' Book

2. Because while it does not profess to give in full all the addresses given at the Parliament and the Congresses, it does give unchanged and complete those in which the world is especially interested. It gives the oriental papers almost without exception in full. It gives sixty pages of Pung Kwang Yu's great address on Confucianism, whereas its imitators give but six. It gives all of Professor Drummond's powerful paper; its imitators give one-third. It gives Canon Freemantle's splendid address on the "Reunion of Christendom" and W. T. Stead's unrivaled paper on the "Civic Church," not one word of which appears or can appear in the cheap imitations. It gives in its 1624 pages just that which the world desires to preserve.

All the World is Buying Dr. Barrows' Great History

3. Because in its editing, its scholarship, its typesetting, its printing, its illustrating, its paper, its binding, its convenience of handling it is as thorough and creditable a piece of book-work as was ever sent from the press. We have not saved money by making it a cheap scrapbook of newspaper reports, or by jamming into one unwieldy, insecurely bound volume a mass of matter which can be made serviceable only when divided into books of smaller bulk.

All the World is Buying Dr. Barrows' Book

4. Because its superb illustrations of quaint and curious religious buildings, scenes, customs, and its lifelike portraits of the great men and women of the religious world, gathered at great expense from every corner of the globe, render it worth its price as a religious album alone.

All the World is Buying Dr. Barrows' Book

5. Because it seems that all the rest of the world and the provinces are after it; because everybody knows that we are running two great printing houses night and day to provide the 15,000 sets (30,000 volumes) which have been already purchased, and the 10,000 sets (20,000 volumes) which we must deliver before January 1st.

PARLIAMENT PUBLISHING COMPANY,
CHICAGO.

Board of Reference
- A. C. Bartlett.
- M. D. Wells.
- Byron L. Smith.
- O. S. A. Sprague.
- Henry L. Turner.

HENRY L. TURNER, President and Treasurer.
SCHILLER HOSFORD, Vice-President.
DWIGHT B. HEARD, Secretary.

SIR EDWIN ARNOLD'S GREAT POEM,

THE
LIGHT OF ASIA

WITH FULL AND COMPLETE EXPLANATORY NOTES BY
MRS. I. L. HAUSER.

Cloth, $1.50.   Half Morocco, $2.50.

PRESS NOTICES.

"A task which, when one thinks of it, one must wonder was not undertaken before, has been successfully performed by Mrs. I. L. Hauser."—*Literary World, Boston.*

"These notes will be a real help to most readers."—*Chronicle, San Francisco.*

"That there will be a wide demand for it, goes without saying."—*Tidings, Buffalo.*

"Mrs. Hauser has done a great deal to make Arnold's Poem duly impressive and understandable."—*Interior, Chicago.*

"'The Light of Asia' has just been published by Rand, McNally & Co., Chicago, in a luxurious form, with notes. This poem of Sir Edwin Arnold, which made its author's reputation, will be widely read in this edition. The typographical make-up is superb."—*News, Philadelphia.*

"These notes, which explain the meaning of terms not otherwise intelligible, add much to the interest of the reader. Mrs. Hauser's long residence in India has enabled her to illuminate many of those half hidden suggestions and local allusions the effect of which would otherwise be lost."—*Advance, Chicago.*

For Sale at all Booksellers' and News Stands.

Send for complete catalogue.

RAND, McNALLY & CO.,
CHICAGO AND NEW YORK.

LOOP

Ask for a Picture of Chicago showing the Elevated System.

All trains of all the Elevated Systems in the city now run around the

New Union Elevated Loop

AND ALL STOP AT THE

GREAT ROCK ISLAND ROUTE STATION

The only one on the Loop.

JOHN SEBASTIAN,
GENERAL PASSENGER AGENT,
CHICAGO.

When answering this advertisement please mention Globe Library.

THE LATEST
ACKNOWLEDGED
STANDARD MANUAL

FOR

Presidents, Secretaries,

DIRECTORS, CHAIRMEN,
PRESIDING OFFICERS,

And everyone in anyway connected
with public life or corporate bodies

IS

Reed's Rules

BY

THE HON. THOMAS B. REED,

Speaker of the
House of Representatives,

"I commend the book most highly."
    WILLIAM McKINLEY,
     President of the United States.

"Reasonable, right, and rigid."
    J. STERLING MORTON,
     Ex-Secretary of Agriculture.

CLOTH, 75 CENTS,
LEATHER, $1.25.

RAND, McNALLY & CO., Publishers,
CHICAGO.

www.ingramcontent.com/pod-product-compliance
Lightning Source LLC
Chambersburg PA
CBHW020320240426

43673CB00039B/869